£4.50

1107

No Guts, No Glory

NO GUTS, NO GLORY

Conversations with
Bette Davis

by

Whitney Stine

VIRGIN

First published in Great Britain in 1990 by
Virgin Books
A division of W. H. Allen & Co Plc
26 Grand Union Centre
338 Ladbroke Grove
London W10 5AH

First published in 1990 by Pocket Books, a division of
Simon & Schuster Inc., New York

British Library Cataloguing in Publication Data

Stine, Whitney
    No guts, no glory: conversations with Bette Davis.
    1. Cinema films. American acting. Davis, Bette 1908–
    I. Title   II. Davis, Bette 1908–
    791.43028092

ISBN 1–85227–343–7

Printed and bound in Great Britain by
Butler & Tanner Ltd, Frome and London

Acknowledgements

The publisher expresses grateful acknowledgement for the use of the following quotations:

Quotation on pages 28–30, by James Powers, review of *Hush . . . Hush, Sweet Charlotte* in *The Hollywood Reporter*, c. 17 December 1964.

Quotation on page 53, by David Shuft, review of *The Little Foxes,* in the *Los Angeles Herald Examiner*, January 1982.

Quotation on page 63, by Frank S. Nugent, review of *Dark Victory*, in *The New York Times*, 21 April 1939. Copyright © 1939 by the New York Times Company. Reprinted by permission.

Quotation on page 65, by Thomas Middleton, review of *Beyond the Forest*, in the *Los Angeles Times*, 10 September 1985.

Quotation on page 83, by Mordaunt Hall, review of *Of Human Bondage*, in *The New York Times*, 29 June 1934. Copyright © 1934 by The New York Times Company. Reprinted by permission.

Quotation on page 97, by James Powers, review of *Dead Ringer*, in *The Hollywood Reporter*, c. 23 January 1964.

Quotation on page 126, by Andrew Sarris, review of *The Letter*, in *The Village Voice*, 21 March 1977. Reprinted by permission of the author and *The Village Voice*.

Introduction

Whitney Stine became a Bette Davis fan in 1938, at the age of eight, when he began watching her films and collecting Davis memorabilia. But he didn't meet her until July 1972, when she summoned him to her home to discuss his manuscript, entitled *Mother Goddam*, about her film career. Whitney was astonished that Bette liked his book, and even more astonished when she agreed to write a running commentary for it. Published in 1974, *Mother Goddam* became an instant best-seller, notorious as much for its format—Bette's comments were printed in red ink—as for its subject matter.

Whitney and Bette became close while working on *Mother Goddam* and remained so until her death in 1989, nearly twenty years later. *No Guts, No Glory* is Whitney Stine's book about his years of friendship with Bette Davis. But most of all it contains Bette herself: her own opinions, voiced in complete candor to one of her most intimate companions, about her costars, her lovers, her four husbands, and her career—all in her own distinctive voice.

Chapter 1

I *do* have a bone to pick with you," Bette Davis went on somewhat testily. "You mentioned in your manuscript that I have a 'low bust'! You're right, of course, I do. You weren't afraid of tackling certain subjects. You've got guts." Her mood changed. She giggled and said, "When I first came to Hollywood, there was no Howard Hughes to build a wired bra for me like he did for Jane Russell!"

I looked at this woman sitting opposite me, not really realizing that I had at last reached my goal. It was the middle of the afternoon on Thursday, July 24, 1972. The place: Twin Bridges, One Crooked Mile, Westport, Connecticut. I had just met Bette Davis for the first time, and I could not quite believe that we were discussing her bosom.

"I matured in the 1920s when girls with big breasts wrapped their bosoms to look flat under those straight dresses," she was saying, "but I never, ever flaunted what Jack Warner used to call my 'bulbs.' And Orry-Kelly, who did my screen clothes, always put me in the right foundations for the period I was working in. But, frankly, I'd just as soon that you left out the 'low bust' business. Okay?"

"Of course."

On the 12:15 train from Manhattan, I had prepared myself not to expect the Bette Davis of *Dark Victory, Now, Voyager,* or *Mr.*

"I never, ever flaunted what Jack Warner used to call my 'bulbs.'" WHITNEY STINE COLLECTION

Skeffington, but I had not anticipated such forceful energy to emanate from her. Arriving at the station fifteen minutes late, I had rushed to a pay telephone. "Yes?" The voice was unmistakable. I discovered that she always answered in that no-nonsense way that precluded long conversations. I introduced myself and explained my tardiness.

"Oh, hi," she said. The voice, that I had expected to be on edge, nervous, a trifle impatient, but somehow not benign or genial, and certainly not casual, was warm and friendly. "I thought you were coming up by car, otherwise I would've met you. Hell, catch a cab. Just tell the driver to take you to Bette Davis's. They all know where I live."

Her cordial laugh was unsettling, because it was not the laugh of any of her famous women. "See you in five minutes," she announced abruptly and hung up.

I knew, then, what Damocles must have felt like with that sword hanging from a single hair over his head.

I had almost as much at stake as Damocles. While it was true I had been summoned to court, I did not know what role to play; I only knew that I was ill suited as a jester to the queen. There had been ample opportunity for insulting her in that 338-page manuscript my agent had sent her nine weeks earlier. I must have had a bad lapse of reason to write about a world-famous woman whom I did not know personally.

I was well aware that Miss D. was regarded, in some studio quarters, as a cross between an N.T.—National Treasure—and a T.B.—Total Bitch. In earning two Oscars and a busload of national and international awards, she had somehow antagonized half her profession. She had more enemies in Hollywood than Napoleon at Waterloo.

My first impression of Bette Davis had been a silhouette in back of a front screen door. Twin Bridges was a two-story New England clapboard, located on the west branch of the Saugatuck River with wide, spacious lawns and surrounded partially by a hedge. While by Eastern standards the house was certainly elegant and commodious, it was not the upscale dwelling one associated with a Hollywood star.

She opened the door wide. I was conscious of a slash of fire-engine-red lipstick; huge, pale, aquamarine eyes with cobalt-blue lids, and a face composed of finely etched lines.

Dressed in a pink silk dress, she had thrust a billed, pink-and-blue plaid hat straight on her head; an attached pink scarf gathered her hair into a snood. Headgear, I was to learn, was a Davis passion. She was the only person I ever knew who wore hats indoors more often than outdoors. The antique hallway tree sported an assortment of headgear that would have done a milliner proud.

Bette had thrust out her hand. "Hello, author," she said, with a wide, welcoming smile. She gave the impression of being an ingenue or at least a diminutive coquette.

"Hello, Miss D.," I replied, looking straight into her eyes, and shaking her hand.

There was at once a curious fascination with each other as if we were squaring off, testing one another.

"I bet you haven't had lunch!" she exclaimed. "Let me fix you a cheese sandwich."

She moved about the kitchen like a young girl, talking all the while, but not looking at me. This was a technique, I discovered later, that she always employed when meeting new people; a tactic to dissipate any awe that might be felt about her. I found myself relaxing at the barrage of small talk about her adopted son, Mike, who was away at college; her adopted daughter, Margot, brain-damaged at birth, who lived in a special school; and Barbara Davis (B.D.), her blood daughter, who lived a few miles away with her husband, Jeremy, and son, Ashley.

Twin Bridges was furnished in well-used antiques, with only a smattering of Hollywood memorabilia. This homey type of atmosphere seemed more suited to a retired New England schoolteacher than a legendary actress whose eighty-four films, if spliced together, would take five days and eight hours to view.

And there had been something so incongruous about Bette Davis making me a cheese sandwich that it dissipated any wonderment that I had of her. Early in her career, Miss D. had been terrified at meeting such great stars as Eva LeGallienne, Laura Hope Crews, George Arliss, and Ruth Chatterton; and she was determined to place newcomers at ease if she ever became an important star. When fifteen-year-old Betty Perske, an ardent fan who later became Lauren Bacall, first met Miss D., she was so nervous her teacup rattled so hard it almost broke the saucer. "I damn near fainted," recalled Bacall in August of 1986.

"What would you like to drink?" Miss D. asked, in a tone of voice that at once suggested she could produce anything from a *pousse-café* to a glass of milk.

"Coffee, if I may."

She pursed her lips expressively. "Mr. Stine, I must say that you've got courage," she went on forcefully, "to write this book about me without my by-your-leave."

"If I had asked you," I replied seriously, "you probably would have said no."

She grinned impishly. "You're damned right! I've turned down all the others." Her eyes lighted up. "But you've done a smashing job," she said warmly. "What intrigued me most about your book is the fact that it's not only *my* story, it's the entire history of the era in which I made pictures."

"You used past tense, just then."

She shrugged her shoulders and pulled her mouth down at the corners. "Let's face it," she said sadly, "my Hollywood is long gone. They don't want me anymore out there. All that is left is television and that's death."

She had set the sandwich plate before me on a large pine table, the middle of which was a huge built-in lazy Susan that almost covered its circumference.

Miss D. was a fine example of a split personality. This homebody, puttering in the kitchen, was a crucial side of her that I was to know as well as the actress in full war paint who strode across a motion picture set.

In her autobiography, *The Lonely Life*, Miss D. had given her two selves separate identities: Ruth Elizabeth—her real name—for the housewife and mother, and Bette Davis for the actress and public person. Both were as different in operation as a Honda and a Lamborghini, yet the energy, the source of power, was the same. Early on, actress-writer Ilka Chase (Lisa Vale in *Now, Voyager*) referred to the Davis persona as nuclear—what fission was—an accurate description.

Miss D. went on reflectively, "There are certain times that I wish now that I'd taken a breather, but in those days when I was building a career, I couldn't, or I'd have got lost in the shuffle. The way you made the public notice you then was to make three or four pictures a year—each totally different. Studios understood that, even before actors did. Oh, we bitched and moaned, but the result showed in the top ten at the box office. Look at Greer Garson at Metro; she eventually played everything, and she was limited. Or among the men, Spencer

Tracy and Fredric March. We women had full sway for about ten years, from the midthirties to the midforties. We had it big then. You caught a lot of that activity."

"Miss D., sometimes I'd wake up in the middle of the night and say to myself: What if you have this woman wrong? What if those were not her reactions at the time?"

She chuckled. "Let me say that you were right more than wrong. How long did it take you to write the book?"

"Two years."

"With no assurance that I would even read it, much less cooperate with you?"

"Yes."

"Jesus!" Then she went on with more compliments.

I flushed. I had expected criticism, intricate probings of how I had reached certain conclusions, sharp questions about who had told me what . . . Yet, even with our initial conversational ease, I could not call her Bette and she could not call me Whitney.

She moved to the arm of my chair. "It's amazing the way that you described my career. You're beautiful, too!" She laughed, then explained, "When I was making *Madame Sin* with Robert Wagner, we had a scene where I say, 'You're beautiful.' Well, we laughed so much about the line, it became a catchphrase for us. When we totally agreed—or totally disagreed—we'd say, 'You're beautiful' and laugh like mad!"

Miss D. glanced at me with a smile and went on with glee, "Robert Wagner is something else! I told Natalie Wood that she was lucky to have him. If I were thirty years younger, she'd have to watch out! Seriously, though, he's a stunning guy—a better actor than people think."

"What about that Jim Beam bourbon advertisement that you did together?"

She leaned forward. "It was fun to do. The ultimate generation gap promotion. The ad was shot at the Plaza Hotel in New York. We ended up on billboards all over the country—and cases of free bourbon in our cellars."

"But everyone knows you drink scotch!"

"Apparently not everybody!" There was a pause. "Robert has only one flaw to my way of thinking. He's money-oriented. He's absolutely got to make it. I told him once that he should slow down and enjoy his life and kids more.

"Well, you're a smashing guy," she continued graciously, "and you've written a smashing book." She got up, cleaned my ashtray, and glanced in a mirror. "How old are you?"

"Forty-two."

"Too damn young! Oh, Christ, I wish I was your age. I'm sixty-three, as you know. I'd really like to be thirty-five forever. That's the best age for a woman. By that time you don't make a fool of yourself as much as you did when younger, and you're old enough to call the shots."

[I always saw beyond to the girl inside, which Miss D. essentially was. I am not saying that she was immature—only that some of her reactions could be childlike and petulant. It was a trait, along with a basic insecurity, that she shared with all of her profession. Beneath the facade of people in show business is an overwhelming desire to be liked, to shock, and to enlighten. Part of the celebrity charm is that they never grow up. I used to refer to Miss D. as "My Lady of Whims."]

"Now, how can I help you?" she went on kindly. "Do you want me to write a foreword, a backword, or . . ."

"Surely, Miss D.," I mused, "when you were reading the manuscript, you would run across pages where you thought: 'Yes, that's right, but he couldn't have known thus and so,' or 'That wasn't really what happened at all.'"

She looked startled. "Yes, to a degree, that's true."

"I want the book to be very special, not just names and dates. We Aries people like to be first in everything."

I paused and thought, *now comes the big question.* The warmth between us seemed so extraordinary that I plunged on quickly: "Would you add a running commentary to what I've written? That way we will have two points of view; my straight reportage and your reactions. Just the same sorts of things that you've been talking about this afternoon. It's never been done."

She frowned. "I'll have to think about that. I'm not a writer." She visibly shook away the thought, and brightened. "You're seated on a potty chair, you know," she said whimsically before going into the kitchen.

"Beg pardon?"

"Robert has only one flaw to my way of thinking. He's money-oriented." Bette and
Robert Wagner in *Madame Sin*. LESTER GLASSNER COLLECTION

The smell of fresh coffee wafted into the room. She lounged casually against the doorway, relaxed and friendly. "All my dining chairs are pressed backs with cushions over the holes. My mother, Ruthie Favor Davis, and I scoured antique shops all over New England one summer to find them."

She lowered her voice to a stage whisper. "When I entertain someone who's very stuffy at a dinner party, I remove their cushion before I seat them!" She paused expectantly. "Get the picture?" She threw back her head and roared with laughter.

I got the picture and grinned, still trying to place her personality within the constraints of the dozens of characters that she had played on the screen. But so far, the only resemblance I could detect was an infectious gaiety. It was much the same feeling I had experienced while watching her movies: impossible to imagine what emotion she was going to project next.

"I know you've just returned from Italy," I said. "What was the film like?"

"Well, its English name is *The Game*. It was fun working with Joseph Cotten, although he's very bitter about Hollywood," she went on with a sigh. "I play a rich American bitch in a wheelchair who visits this little Italian town once each year to play a card game. The townspeople pool their money and select a person to play with me. Every year, they get fleeced. It's the high stakes that intrigue them."

"It sounds unusual to say the least."

She shrugged. "You really have to be Italian to have the film make much sense. Joe and I are the only ones speaking English in the film. But a white wig and beautiful clothes do not a performance make. I'm afraid it turned out badly."

[*Lo Scopone Scientifico, The Scientific Cardplayer,* was not released in the United States, but was shown at the Bing Theatre at the Los Angeles County Art Museum in 1986, and I was surprised that the film contained such excellent performances. The contrast between the poverty of the villagers and the grandiose villa on the hill of the American millionairess was wonderfully realized. Miss D. was authoritative and gracious. *The Game* was a film of which she should not have been ashamed.]

"But today, you have to go where the work is," Miss D. was saying. "I would go to Timbuktu if the script was good!" She gave her Baby

Jane cackle, then quieted down, leaned forward, and lighted an unfiltered Philip Morris cigarette by striking a kitchen match under the table. While she puffed energetically, she proceeded to clean every ashtray in the room. "What sign did you say you were?" she asked with a twinkle in her eye.

"Aries."

"Yes," she said seriously, in a complete switch of mood, "you would be." She glanced at me surreptitiously. "We're not easy to get along with sometimes, we Aries. We can be exhausting to others who don't have our terrific energy. We can also be hard to take. Do you believe in the stars?"

"I learned astrology from a woman when I was nineteen," I answered, "and it's come in handy. In fact, I ghost books for a famous astrologer." I gave the name.

She raised her eyebrows. "I've read some of them." She looked at me with renewed interest. "I do believe in the stars to a certain degree. Knowing what signs people are born under can be very helpful. Ruthie was a Virgo; my sister, Bobby, a Scorpio; B.D., a Taurus—all typical of their signs. I'm glad we're Aries. We can take on the world!

"You're something else, Mr. Stine!" she continued, snuffing out the cigarette in a porcelain foot ashtray and patting my fat manuscript on the table. "How did you arrive at the title of *Mother Goddam* for your book?"

"I thought it would be interesting to name the book after a character that you wanted to play very badly in *The Shanghai Gesture,* but didn't. An unattainable goal."

"As you know, I ended up naming my book *The Lonely Life,* but I almost called it *Mother Goddam.* Isn't that a coincidence? I always felt that I was a little like her."

"Why wouldn't Warner Bros. buy *The Shanghai Gesture?* They bought so many other Broadway plays for you."

She rolled her eyes. "Because she was the madam of a whorehouse and was also Eurasian. Remember, this was 1941 and my boss, Jack Warner, didn't mind me playing a bitch once in a while, but after *In This Our Life* he was trying to steer me back into playing heroines. To him, Mother GD was totally evil, didn't have one redeeming feature. He was wrong, of course, because she had many sides to her character. She wasn't a one-note woman. In fact, she had a lot in common with Regina Giddens in *Foxes.*

"I put up a fight about it, I can tell you, but my producer, Hal Wallis, said I was sure'n hell not going to play an Oriental, and that was that! But I did get to play a similar character last year in *Madame Sin*. Was *The Shanghai Gesture* ever made?"

We were playing off each other's energy as if improvising a scene on a movie set—involved creatively, feeding each other cues, but uncertain of the replies. We were establishing the pattern for all future encounters; there would always be a running spark of excitement. She was a monologuist of the first water.

"Yes," I replied, answering her question, "Josef von Sternberg filmed it for United Artists in 1941, but because of the production code, Mother Goddam became Mother Gin Sling! Ona Munson played her rather well, very artificial looking with elaborate wigs and slinky kimonos."

"I always wanted to meet von Sternberg," she exclaimed suddenly. "What would have happened to Dietrich without him? She was his Trilby. He built the sets, and put her into them like a rag doll. Then he forgot everything else but her—and so did the audience. Willie Wyler was different. He created the atmosphere of a movie, and placed the characters into it."

She grinned suddenly, mysteriously, and her eyes widened. "I had wonderful cameramen, but I wouldn't have minded being photographed like Dietrich once in a while!" She lighted another Philip Morris. "I had the shock of my life when I finally met her during the first year of World War II. I expected feathers, bugle beads, Chanel Number Five."

"And what did you get?"

"A blue and white striped apron, hair in a net, short eyelashes, a peeling manicure. I went into the kitchen at the Hollywood Canteen and there she was—washing dishes! I almost flipped. Of course, when she was a hostess on the dance floor, then she was all glamour. One time, she almost caused a riot; she came to the Canteen straight from the set of *Kismet*, her body completely covered with gold paint and as few beads as censorship would allow. The boys were enthralled. They had never seen anything like that, I can tell you! And neither had I."

I placed my napkin on the table. "Thank you for the sandwich."

"Come in the living room." She waved me to a comfortable overstuffed chair, set my coffee on a table beside me, brought an ashtray and a footstool. This routine never changed over the years. She always made certain that visitors felt at home, and men were always treated as if they were the 'man of the house.' She enjoyed waiting on guests; that was the hausfrau side of her personality.

There was a knock on the back door, and B.D., Jeremy, and Ashley came into the living room. Barbara Davis (B.D.) was twenty-five, tall, blond, and somewhat overweight. Jeremy, her husband, was a nice-looking man—a few years older than she—who wore cowboy boots and hat. Ashley was very self-composed for a three-year-old.

Her family, I noted, was as unpretentious as she was; quite ordinary people. After a bit of small talk, Miss D. turned to B.D. "Mr. Stine took two years out of his life to write *Mother Goddam.*"

"Really?" B.D. said, looking unimpressed.

"He's asked me to add personal comments throughout the book. What do you think?"

"Well, Mother," she replied quickly, "I think it's a good idea. I'm sure you'll have lots to say."

[I didn't think anything about it at the time, but when B.D.'s scurrilous book about her mother was released in 1985, I wondered if her remark had not been tinged with sarcasm. Perhaps she thought that this little exercise would keep her mother out of her hair for a bit. And, I suppose, it did . . . at least for a while.]

When the Hymans left, I turned to Miss D. "They're a very nice family—very put together."

She nodded. "Isn't B.D. something else? It's very strange, this role reversal."

"What do you mean?"

"Well, for years I had her as a daughter, then somewhere along the line, she became my mother. B.D. says that I'm about fourteen years old, and of course, she's right! I suppose this happens very often. As we age, power swings to the young. She's so much in command of her house—which she runs beautifully. She decorates for the seasons, and at Christmas there's holly and mistletoe, well—it's just the nuts. I love her terribly. She's one good reason for living at this stage of the game."

Miss D. beamed. "Do you know what happened on *Payment on Demand?* As you know, B.D. was three years old then, and played my screen daughter. Well, it was a short scene, but Curt Bernhardt, the director, told her, 'B.D., I know you've done this four times, but we have to do it again.' She looked at him in a very straightforward way, and he said, 'I have seen that exact look from your mother. You are going to do it one more time.' And she did—perfectly.

"Then I wanted her to be in *Baby Jane*—another memento—and there was a line that had to do with the 'fat sister next door,' which was me. B.D. said, 'I can't say *that*.' And I said, 'You must, it's in the script.' Well, she went to the studio the next day to do her scene, and about three o'clock the first assistant director called, 'Come on in, you have to go to work.' I said, 'You don't mean my daughter is finished already?' And he said, 'Yes,' and I said, 'She's really worse than I am!' "

I glanced at my watch. When Harold Schiff, her lawyer, had set up my appointment with Miss D., he'd advised me to come up to Westport for a *couple* of hours. It was already four o'clock. "Miss D., I should be going."

"Do you have a hot date in New York tonight, Mr. Stine?" she asked with a wide grin.

"No."

"Then stay for dinner. I won't cook, because we've got so much to talk about. We'll send you back on the last train at eleven o'clock. Do you like Chinese food?"

"Yes."

"Then we'll send out." She made a telephone call and came back into the living room.

I looked up and smiled. "Miss D., when you came in just now, with the light in back of you, it was like when you came in from the porch in *Jezebel*."

"My god!" she cried, then laughed self-consciously. "Where have the years gone? That was, let me see, thirty-four years ago!"

"But Wyler is a great director. You and he were very special together."

Her eyes widened. "Willie brought me the script of *Wuthering Heights* right after we finished *Jezebel*. I would have loved to play Cathy opposite Olivier, but there was no way that Warners would loan me, and, of course, Merle Oberon played her. Willie was hysterical because Sam Goldwyn always called the film *WITHERing Heights!* She pursed her lips. "Hah! The parts that slip away in the night."

"Wyler must have loved you very much." The sentence rushed out before I caught myself.

She snubbed out her cigarette, rose, and paced back and forth, then stopped in front of me, cleaned my ashtray, and squinted her eyes. "How did you guess that Willie and I were lovers?"

"I assumed so."

She frowned and examined my face intently. "Just like that—you assumed so!" Her voice softened. "I *adored* him. *Jezebel* was on television a couple of nights ago," she said, lighting another cigarette from a lighter instead of a kitchen match. "It had been a long time since I'd seen it. It was strange watching it alone."

"The Olympus ball sequence has a certain tension that is remarkable," I said.

"That was all Wyler's doing!" Miss D. exclaimed. "The script had one line describing the ball, and the assistant director had allotted half a day to shoot it. With all the camera setups, Willie took five days! That long scene has a complete beginning, middle, and end. It's terrific.

"But then, we had everything going for us. We had a great script that John Huston worked on. Hal Wallis was our production chief, Jack Warner, our boss, and Henry Blanke, our producer. My usual crew was on the picture. Hank Fonda and George Brent were my leading men. Fay Bainter was wonderful casting for Aunt Belle, plus Ernie Haller, my favorite cameraman, to make me pretty. Only Margaret Lindsay as the Northerner Fonda marries was wrong, but it was a namby-pamby part anyway. She was under contract to the studio, and we were stuck with her."

"I suppose," I ventured, "when you watch the movie, you see Wyler behind the camera, telling you what to do . . ."

She nodded, a faraway expression in her eyes. "I'd met him in 1931, during my first year at Universal Studios. I was up for *A House Divided*, a sea story, but the part eventually went to Helen Chandler. I showed up to test in the only dress that wardrobe could find in size eight in a hurry. It was so low cut it showed the separation of my breasts. I was embarrassed; girls in New England didn't dress that way—even for fun.

"Wyler was having a bad day, and when he saw me he shouted so everyone on the soundstage could hear: 'What do you think of these dames who show their tits and think they can get jobs?' I was so humiliated, I could have fallen through the floor! Of course, in Willie's defense, he had no way of knowing that I wasn't one of those 'starlet

"Willie brought me the script of *Wuthering Heights* right after we finished *Jezebel*. . . . How did you guess that Willie and I were lovers?"
Top: Bette and Fonda, with Wyler looking on, on the set of *Jezebel*. Bottom: Bette and Wyler on the set of *Foxes*. Both photos: LESTER GLASSNER COLLECTION

types.' Coincidentally, I didn't get the role. He told me years later that I was lucky he didn't cast me, as he was an awful director in those days."

She grinned wryly and shook her head. "There was no way then that I'd know, of course, that we'd have so much to do with each other's careers a few years later." She paused, and then went on seriously, "When I had my first meeting with Willie before the start of *Jezebel*, I was steamed up, remembering that earlier encounter, and I prepared to do battle. Hell, he didn't even remember the incident! But he did apologize, saying that those early years at Universal were a terrible strain on him. He was a cousin of Carl Laemmle, the owner of the studio, who had so many worthless relatives on the payroll that everyone thought that Willie was another loser."

"Ogden Nash wrote a great couplet." I quoted: *"Uncle Carl Laemmle/Had a very large faemmle."*

Miss D. laughed. "Indeed. Well, Wyler worked very hard and proved himself. No detail, however minor, ever escaped him. He would probe like a fiend, then turn sarcastic; or he'd be aloof and drive you crazy. He had a disarming, gape-toothed grin that could melt a dragon, but sometimes he had an evil eye. But I had an evil eye too! After a while, we knew each other so well that he'd look at me, and I'd know what he wanted in the scene. He'd remain silent, take after take after take, then when I was exhausted, he'd give a suggestion that turned the whole scene around and made it live. When I wasn't hating him, I was loving him."

She went on hurriedly, "But if Willie's stars were important, every other detail was just as important. He created what I guess you'd call the mood of the picture in his mind on the first day of shooting. Then he regulated everyone's performances to that mood. He had the most expressive eyes I've ever seen. He could be blunt, too. When he'd say, 'Don't wiggle your ass so much,' I wasn't offended. If Mike Curtiz, who directed me several times, and with whom I had a mutual loathing, had said that, I'd have screamed bloody murder.

"Willie corrected a lot of my bad habits. I just wished to hell later on that I'd had him on a few pictures, when I felt I needed special attention and the directors didn't know—or were afraid—to give me the kind of direction I needed.

"He forced me to go to the first rushes on *Jezebel* when I was very tired one night and didn't want to go," Miss D. continued. "We had done a simple scene—about thirty times. I had to come down a staircase, and the first and the last take seemed identical to me, and I was boiling. But he picked a shot that captured a fleeting devil-may-care expression on my face that made the scene suddenly come alive."

[*The National Board of Review* magazine wrote of *Jezebel:*

> At the center of it is Bette Davis, growing into an artistic maturity that is one of the wonders of Hollywood. The erratic and tempestuous career of this actress has saved her from playing sweet heroines and glamour girls and given her chances at parts that most players out for popularity would balk at—the result is an experience that has made her unique, in a field of character creation that is practically empty. Her Julie is the peak of her accomplishments so far.]

"After that, I never questioned anything he asked me to do." She grinned. "I was at a party after *Jezebel* came out and Hedda Hopper was there. She came up to me and whispered, 'I've just seen the picture and you were marvelous, but I know one thing for sure.' I asked, 'And what's that?' She answered, 'You had to be in love with Henry Fonda. Oh, the way you looked at him!' She could be bitchy.

"I just smiled. I couldn't tell her that all those close-ups of me showing my love for Hank had been shot after he had finished all of his scenes for the picture and had left the lot. It was Willie—off camera—I was looking at! Hedda knew that I had a crush on Hank when we were in summer stock years before."

She snubbed out her cigarette. "Wyler also was a genius at blocking. He never asked you to make a move that wasn't logical. If he told you to go to a window, there was a reason for it. I've had directors who wanted me to do this or that and couldn't tell me why. But Willie wasn't my Svengali—except in a very broad sense. Some actors hated to work for him; he could be nasty and he always had one scapegoat on every picture."

I laughed and added, "Charlton Heston once said that doing a picture with Wyler was like getting the works at a Turkish bath. You might damn near drown, but you come out smelling like a rose."

"Hedda Hopper said, 'I've just seen the picture and you were marvelous, but I know one thing for sure. You had to be in love with Henry Fonda. . . .' I had a crush on Hank when we were in summer stock years before." C 1937 WARNER BROS. PICTURES, INC. REN. 1964 UNITED ARTISTS TELEVISION, INC.

Miss D. giggled. "He's right."

"Why didn't you marry Wyler?"

She gave me a quick look and waved her hand. "What a question!" She leaned forward. "Willie was enormously attractive, and the sexual sparks were there from the beginning." Miss D. went on with a sigh, "But, he never let me get away with a thing; he was always on my back about one thing and another. But when he picked away at me, I knew he was right. I'd done too many pictures with directors who didn't give a damn about performances, just so they finished on time.

"Willie knew how to blow down your ego like no one else I ever worked with. He'd do fifty takes, and I'd scream at him, 'Why? Why?' And, if he chose to answer at all, he'd say, 'Let's just do it again. It's not quite right.' After a bit, I began to realize that he was hoping for something that he couldn't identify—some distinctive quality that would add to your performance."

Her face softened. In the reflection from the window she looked much younger, more delicate. I was to discover that the way the light took to her face could change its structure and her expression. There would be moments during this day when she looked thirty; other times, seventy.

"I had always thought," Miss D. continued quietly, "up until *Jezebel*, that I always gave the same performance each time in a scene. Directors always complimented me on this because, if we had to do a lot of takes for different reasons—say, the sound was off or someone in the scene didn't hit his marks—they had a lot of material for the cutter to work with, and a lot of salvaging could be done. But Willie showed me that there *was* a difference between takes, little nuances that make the scene better and add to the character."

[She was thirty and Wyler was thirty-six when they first met for preproduction talks on *Jezebel*. Both were in the right frame of mind for a love affair: he was divorced from Margaret Sullavan and she was on the outs with Harmon Nelson.]

"Well, our romance was doubly difficult because we could not be seen in public. When I think of today, I could cry, when the papers are filled with stories about the affairs of the stars, and no one thinks anything about it! But *then*, my god!"

Miss D. got up and went to the fireplace. "It ended badly. We had fought and made up and fought and made up, and we were both miserable. One day a letter from Willie came in the mail. I was feeling touchy and I put it aside. I would show him!"

She made an empty gesture. "A few days later, I opened the envelope. It said that if he didn't hear from me, he was going to marry someone else. That damned letter! A letter had undone Leslie Crosbie in *The Letter,* and a letter almost undid me personally. The irony was not lost. It could have been only a few minutes later that a news broadcast announced that Willie had married the gorgeous Margaret Tallichet, who'd tried out for *Gone with the Wind.* I was beside myself!" She looked at me savagely. "Why, oh why, am I telling you all of this?" Miss D. gave me a sheepish look, gauging my reaction to her confession.

"It's because you know I understand, and that's not a cliché, Miss D!"

She smiled and nodded. "I know."

I think one of the building blocks of our friendship was the fact that Miss D. could never throw me with an emotional transformation. She could be irritable, kind, angry, warm, explosive, affectionate, outrageous. She could be gowned to the nines for a public appearance, wearing an apron making chili in the kitchen, or dressed in blue jeans poking around in the flower beds, and it was all the same to me.

Miss D. picked up a tube of lipstick, and, without looking in the mirror, made two, quick passes over her lips. "How long did it take you to do the research for *Mother Goddam?*"

"Thirty-four years!"

"What?"

"I started collecting the material when I was eight years old. If you'll forgive me, Miss D., at the time when you were making *It's Love I'm After.*"

"My god!" she exclaimed, and then grinned in a deprecatory way. "You probably would have been better off playing baseball!"

I laughed. "I wasn't playing shortstop," I explained, "because I had all those childhood diseases one after the other, whooping cough, three kinds of measles—and I was driving my family up the wall. Finally, my sister, Maxine, came into my bedroom and tossed a stack of fan magazines on my bed (she collected Jean Harlow), along with a pair of shears, scrapbook leaves, and a pot of paste. 'Now, get busy, you little worm,' she said.

"I cut out, rearranged, and repasted all of the articles as well as the advertisements. When I got well, I found that I had assembled more pictures of you than of any other star. I threw all the others away and that started my collection—which I've kept up to this day. The sixteen-by-eighteen-inch scrapbook is five feet, six inches tall."

"Why, that's four inches taller than I am!" Miss D. exclaimed.

"Finally, Maxine marched me to the Blue Moon Theater in Garber, Oklahoma, the town where I was born. 'You like this lady so much, you might as well see her act,' she exclaimed. The picture, of course, was *Jezebel.*"

"Mr. Stine, it took me all those early years, through all those turkeys, but finally the people out there could accept me in a costume role, such as Julie in *Jezebel,* or Carlotta in *Juarez,* or Charlotte in *The Old Maid,* or Queen Elizabeth—or Regina in *Foxes,* or much later in *Baby Jane.* Those were all character parts." She looked up at me squarely. "I must apologize. I've been going like a hurricane today, Mr. Stine, talking up a storm about very personal things. It's not fair to you. We've only just met."

"I first saw you in a theater thirty-four years ago, remember? Am I objecting?"

She shook her head. "No. You just sit there with that coffee cup in your hand and let me roll on and on." She sighed gently, "I don't know, it's as if I've known you for years . . ."

"Do you believe in reincarnation?"

She shrugged. "I was reared Episcopalian, but I know that people are born with old souls or with new souls. So, if that's reincarnation, then I guess I believe in it. Do you?"

"It explains a great many oddities. *Talent* for one thing. Where do we get it? What about Mozart composing his first symphony practically as a babe. What about you? You went to dramatic school and appeared in plays before your Hollywood career, yet you had the talent from the day that you were born."

"Yes, that's always bothered my sister, Bobby. Why wasn't she like me? We had the same genes, the same upbringing. Why did I have it and she didn't? I think that may have been one of the things that brought on her mental problems later on.

"Ruthie, as you know, was psychic, there's no question about that.

When we were young, she was always telling Bobby and me things that were going to happen, and they always did. And I have met people— like you—whom I feel as though I've had a long association with. It's a deep subject."

The evening had scarcely begun, yet quite without realizing it, we had formed a firm bond.

Chapter 2

*C*omfortable with Bette Davis now, I asked a question that had intrigued me for a very long time. "How did you get along with Joan Crawford on *What Ever Happened to Baby Jane?*"

Miss D. threw back her head and screamed with laughter. "I was wondering how long it would be before you asked! In all of my years in Hollywood, that question is the one most asked of me."

She puffed for a long moment. "Joan's peculiar. You know, on *Jane* she wouldn't even shake hands with anyone. She always carried disinfectants with her and she'd scrub the john on her hands and knees. I think it was because she had a venereal disease when she was a kid, and as she got older it preyed on her mind. Her apartment in New York has plastic sprayed on the walls and the furniture is covered with the stuff.

"We were polite to each other—all the social amenities, 'Good morning, Joan,' and 'Good morning, Bette' crap, and thank god we weren't playing roles where we had to like each other! But people forget that our big scenes were alone—just the camera was on me or her. No actresses on earth are as different as we are all the way down the line. Yet what we do works. It's so strange, this acting business. It comes from inside.

"She was always so damn proper. She sent thank you notes for

"Joan's peculiar. On *Jane* she wouldn't even shake hands with anyone. She always carried disinfectants with her and she'd scrub the john on her hands and knees. I think it was because she had a venereal disease when she was a kid." Bette and Joan on the set of *Jane*. LESTER GLASSNER COLLECTION

thank you notes! I screamed when I found out she signed autographs: 'Bless you, Joan Crawford!'

"But sometimes during the midthirties when I was being cast in crap like *The Golden Arrow* and *The Man in the Black Hat* . . ."

[The latter was the original title for the film, *Satan Met a Lady,* the 1936 version of *The Maltese Falcon,* which John Huston made classic in his 1941 remake with Bogart. Miss D. was so horrified with the sixty-six-minute film that she developed a block and could never remember the release title, and promptly took off for England to sue Warner Bros. over her 'slave contract.' She lost the case, which Olivia De Havilland won later, but she won better parts.]

Miss D. continued: "I would have liked to have some of the roles Crawford got at Metro in the 1930s. I was given little secretaries and gun molls, while she was doing some really interesting parts."

"Yes," I said, "but in the forties, you were getting all the great roles, and she was cast in junk."

Miss D. nodded. "You're right, and most of her pictures don't stand up today." She paused. "She always wanted to work with me. At Warners she found a script once, called *Women Behind Bars,* that had two equal female characters—but I didn't want to do a prison drama."

"Crawford's an Aries too," I reminded her. "Aren't you and she somewhat alike?"

Miss D. stood up, and I thought she would take my head off. "Alike? Alike?" she exclaimed. "How can you say that? We are totally opposite."

I held up my hand. "Hear me out, Miss D.," I said as calmly as I could. "Think about it."

Miss D. snuffed out her cigarette, lighted another and puffed. "Damn you!" she said humorously, plopping down on the sofa. "We work entirely differently, of course." She reflected quietly. "She is such the great star. Little Miss Perfection!" Her voice quieted. "But yes, I suppose we have the same drive. She's a survivor, and so am I. And, I suppose I do infuriate people the same way that she does."

Miss D. frowned. "You know, when she's doing a scene, she can't start and stop. She's got to work into it and out of it. But on *Jane* she was under pretty good control—because I suppose, she wanted to be as professional as I was. And I've got to give her credit. Since it was she who brought the script to Robert Aldrich's attention, she knew damn well that my role was better than hers."

[Sam Lesner wrote about *Jane* in the *Chicago Daily News,* November 7, 1962:

> The screen hasn't had such acting and face-making since D.W. Griffith and Sergei Eisenstein dominated the directorial field. This film is a field day for Bette Davis, Joan Crawford, and director Robert Aldrich, who saw in Henry Farrell's novel of the same title the outlines of a modern Greek tragedy. Yet it is great fun, too, because this is pure cinema drama set in a real house of horrors. No Frankenstein tricks were needed here.]

"Before *Jane,* Joan and I had long conversations about our characters, so by the time we started shooting—and remember we shot the whole damn thing in a month—we knew the relationship between the sisters pretty well. The script was marvelous, very tight, and we had fairly long scenes. Bob really cut the picture in the camera. He had to, because we didn't have time for many setups, and he wanted to show the picture for a week in the Los Angeles area to qualify for Academy consideration.

"When I showed up for tests in that dead-white Jane makeup that showed every line in my face, I saw a look of repulsion in Aldrich's eyes. 'You can't appear like that, Bette,' he said. 'Oh, yes I can,' I replied. And, I did.

"When Crawford saw me the first time as Jane, she looked at me with envy. 'It's right,' she said, and that was the only time during the shooting of the entire movie that she gave me a compliment, and it was a compliment for her. Perc Westmore had a hell of a time concocting that white makeup. It kept blowing up in his oven. It had to be chalky without any grease.

"Crawford wanted to look prettier. She had given up the Crawford mouth makeup, and the long polished fingernails, and the false eyelashes, and the shoulder pads, but she wouldn't give up the boobs. They kept getting bigger and bigger and bigger. That last scene on the beach—which was shot in the studio—would have been ridiculous if Aldrich hadn't stepped in. She's dying, lying on the sand. It's her big scene, where she tells Jane it was she who caused the car accident that paralyzed her—that I, as Jane, was too drunk to know what happened. When a woman lies down, her breasts flatten out, but there they were,

"When I showed up for tests in that dead-white *Jane* makeup that showed every line in my face, I saw a look of repulsion in Aldrich's eyes."

sticking up like twin Matterhorns!" She grinned wryly. "But Crawford's boobs or not, it was a hell of a picture.

"Ernie Haller, who was also Joan's favorite cameraman after she came to Warners, didn't have to worry about making us beautiful. I was fifty-four, and Joan was fifty-nine—although she said she was the same age as I was!"

She giggled. "I think Ernie had secretly always wanted to photograph us like a couple of witches. And thank god it's not like today, when he would have to use color. *Jane* would have been awful in color. Some pictures are meant to be in black and white. *Hush . . . Hush, Sweet Charlotte* was the same way. It would have looked like *Gone with the Wind* in color. *Hush* was like one big graveyard. It was made up of ghosts.

"But, like Wyler, I trusted Aldrich. I wanted to please him. Sometimes I'd be apprehensive about a scene and ask, 'Wasn't that maybe a little too much?' Only twice, I think, he told me to 'cool it a little.' I had confidence in his judgment.

"The scene in *Jane* where I'm singing 'I've Written a Letter to Daddy' is the one people always remember. The old Jane gazing in the mirror from about twelve feet away looks pretty good. Then she walks forward. Ernie had a high light, straight down, which is always bad for a woman. Especially me. When Jane finally gets up to the mirror, she sees herself as this decrepit, old hag, when in her mind, she's still young. I covered my face with my hands. He had wanted a loud scream, but what came out was a hoarse cry—I'd been having laryngitis. It was right and we both knew it. Bob had tears in his eyes. 'You just won yourself an Oscar,' he whispered. I went home that night singing 'And the Angels Sing.'

"*Hush,*" Miss D. said quietly, "on the other hand, was devilishly hard to do, because Charlotte was a sort of fantasy character, plus, she kept slipping back into the past. But while *Jane* was made for peanuts, *Hush* cost a lot of money, and thank god, it paid off!"

[James Powers in *The Hollywood Reporter,* December 17, 1964, wrote:

Bette Davis plays Charlotte and, given a baroque character to play, gives a bravura performance. The hardest thing about these characters is to keep them human. Miss Davis plays with an antic manner but reins her madness with pathos. She tries a new voice

"There they were—sticking up like twin Matterhorns." Joan and Bette in the final beach scene of *Baby Jane*. LESTER GLASSNER COLLECTION

level, a muted quality, speaking with a fine Southern accent. Even in her shrieks and hysterical facial contortions, she is a recognizable human being, not an uprooted mind, beyond reaching or beyond interest . . .]

"We had a similar situation to Jane's looking in the mirror, in *Hush*," Miss D. explained. "The scene at the bottom of the stairs, after Joseph Cotten's head has rolled down, when Charlotte's finally gone over the edge, and I sort of whimper. It's the kind of thing that can get an unwanted laugh—but we kept the faith.

"Later, I sometimes wished to god that some of the directors of my television films had that same kind of moxie. Most of the kids took the easy way out—and it showed. Sometimes, I just gave up and said, 'What the hell, if this bastard pulls in his horns and we do it the easy way, can't he see that the scene won't work the way it's supposed to?'

"You know, Bob asked me if I wanted to see the rushes. Sometimes on a picture, I do, especially lately on these television things. If I have to look presentable, I want to know how I'm being photographed. But I was scared to death to go in that projection room. I heard that Joan crept in once, and swore under her breath. Whether she was displeased at how she looked, or jealous of my performance, who knows, but she didn't stay long.

"I didn't see *Jane* until we went to Cannes for the festival. We're in this theater crammed with people all around, and I'm wearing a white evening dress and I must say, looking good, and there I am on the screen in that awful makeup. I couldn't keep from crying and my mascara ran all over hell. Bob had the sense to hold my hand. He knew what I was going through. He knew that it wasn't the star thing, it was me looking a thousand times worse than I'd ever looked before. I thought to myself, 'You sure as hell better get a good-looking part for your next picture or people will think you really look like Jane!'

"My press agent, Rupert Allen, felt the same way, and when I was offered *Dead Ringer,* he said, "Bette, you've got to use straps. I didn't know what he was talking about. He introduced me to Gene Hibbs, who used to work for Perc Westmore in the old days at Warners. Gene did makeup tests and used 'lifts' on my face and neck for the first time."

[Gene Hibbs was an innovator in the use of tiny pieces of strong, transparent adhesive tape placed on the back of the neck, in front of the ear, and on the temples. These pieces, strung with rubber bands or "straps," as Miss D. called them, circled the head and could be tightened to a proper tautness, drawing back the skin so that a face looked about ten years younger. Makeup was applied, then a wig with strands of hair combed over the pieces of tape.]

"Straps," Miss D. expounded, "are very uncomfortable; you're always aware of them. And, about three o'clock in the afternoon, you start to perspire under the lights and your makeup begins to run and the damn things can come undone. If they have a long shooting schedule, your skin gets raw, because the straps have to be glued in the same spots every day. That's why I've decided to have a face-lift. Ashley in Beverly Hills is going to do it in October. I'm going into a hospital, none of those office visits for me!"

"But why?"

"Now, just why do you suppose?" she asked coyly, and batted her eyelashes. "I've always said I'd never have one, because I've always wanted my body to match my face, but I'm at the point where I'm tired of photographing like someone's grandmother. What do you think?"

I was in an untenable situation. If I urged her not to have the lift, which she felt she needed, she might take my suggestion to heart. If I agreed with her that she needed a lift, she might think that I did not approve of her the way she was. "The decision is up to you, Miss D. It's a major operation."

She took my arm. "Well, I've made up my mind to have it done."

"May I come and see you?" I asked.

"Of course, after the black-and-blue has gone. When I come to the coast I'm going to sue American International Pictures over *Bunny O'Hare*. The finished product is not the script I accepted. I thought the idea of Bette Davis, a grandmother dressed as a hippie on a motorcycle robbing banks, might be fun and different. And I'd worked with Ernie Borgnine before. Also it said something about older people. But they changed it all around, shot extra scenes after we finished the picture. Did you see it?"

"Yes."

"And?"

"Well . . ." I hedged. "It was not one of my favorite pictures."

"That bad, eh?" She gave me a long look. "I haven't seen it."

"You sued them without ever seeing it?"

"I've been given a blow-by-blow account of what they did to it."

"Frankly, you were photographed badly, I thought."

"I'll take your word for it, but I wasn't playing Margo Channing! Loyal Griggs, the cameraman, is pretty good, but I didn't see the rushes. New Mexico is vile, weatherwise. I hate location shooting. Everyone waits for the damn clouds—and sometimes you have to hole up for days if it's raining. They shoot the scenery, and if the actors are in the right places, fine; if they're not—then what the hell! All those years at Warners, we almost never went outside the studio gates. They built the whole desert on a soundstage for *Petrified Forest,* for Christ's sake."

"And," I added, "the entire Welsh village for *The Corn Is Green.*"

She smiled. "Why do I talk to you? I keep forgetting that you know all about me."

"Correction: your *career.*"

Suddenly, she was not the housewife but the actress. "Ah, yes," she said with an elongated sigh, "my *career.*" She paused. "I'm proud of *Corn.* Barrymore played it differently than I did on the stage, but she was a lot older. I wish I could do it over now at my present age. Thank god I was able to do Elizabeth again in *Virgin Queen.* What in the hell did I know about life in 1939, at age thirty-one, when I did *Elizabeth and Essex?* But one thing for sure, Elizabeth wasn't a virgin, but whether she went to bed with Essex or Bacon or Raleigh or any of the others is problematical. But being surrounded by handsome young guardsmen, well, I don't think she could have resisted them all!"

She shook her head. "But I was stuck with that beautiful ass, Errol Flynn. He walked through the picture. He always liked to put his tongue in your mouth during kissing scenes, and if he'd been out all night drinking, which was frequently the case, it was very unpleasant. During *Elizabeth* I kept my mouth closed during our love scenes— which you can see, if you watch the picture! Poor Errol burned himself out inside before it showed on his face. Besides, I'm always suspicious of beautiful men."

"Miss D., I saw *The Private Lives of Elizabeth and Essex* recently, and I know you'll disagree, but I didn't think he was all that bad. Essex was not a brain, but an opportunist who took advantage of the old queen. Flynn was callow, but so was Essex."

"I never thought of it that way." She frowned. "When we were shooting the picture, all I could think of was all of Maxwell Anderson's blank verse going down the drain. I wanted Laurence Olivier."

"Then you were attracted to Olivier?"

"I was stuck with that beautiful ass Errol Flynn. He walked through the picture. He always liked to put his tongue in your mouth during kissing scenes." Bette and Flynn in *The Private Lives of Elizabeth and Essex*. LESTER GLASSNER COLLECTION

She shook her head violently. "No, not personally. I only met him once. But I always wanted to work with him. In the late thirties he was the most handsome thing on earth, and it was the image of his sexiness that I dreamed about. It's the same thing that men saw in Marilyn Monroe. They thought about her when they were making love to their wives—but they wouldn't necessarily like to go to bed with her in real life. Too threatening."

"It's true," I nodded and continued, "that Olivier would have spoken the lines the way they were written, Miss D., but he would have also given the role so much stature that Essex would have gone to the guillotine as a hero. The audience would have had less sympathy for Elizabeth. As it was, Flynn did it as a sort of noblesse oblige."

She looked at me shrewdly. "You have a way of putting things that's very different. But what you don't realize is that I would have played Elizabeth differently with Olivier. We would have found more common ground."

She giggled. "You know, Flynn wanted to have an affair with me about the time that we did *The Sisters*. I turned him down flat. I wasn't going to become a number in his little black book. I didn't want him confiding to his pals that he had 'slept with Davis.' That's what those Hollywood types did then, when they had bedded a star, and probably still do. They'd say, 'Last night, I had Crawford or Lombard or Bergman,' and everyone would snicker. I've certainly had affairs in my day, but they weren't that kind."

She paused and looked at me with wonder. "Why am I telling you all this? It's peculiar. Maybe there is something in this reincarnation business. Wouldn't it have been fun if we had been lovers?" She laughed self-consciously, arose, and stretched her back. "The thought of adding those comments to your book scares the hell out of me," she said.

"It will just be like talking."

She nodded. "Oh, yes, that's the only way I could do it. I'm not a writer."

"Why don't you try the first chapter and see how it goes."

She looked at me intently. "I want you to be pleased."

"If you disagree with me here and there, it will only add spice to the material."

"God, you *are* Aries!"

A car drove up in the driveway. "That's Vik Greenfield, my man Friday," she explained. "He lives in an apartment over the garage. It's his day off, but he hung around because he wanted to meet you. He's picked up the food."

Vik was in his early thirties, a little taller than his employer and, like her, small-boned. He had worked for her for five years and from association had picked up certain elements of her enunciation in his speech, which was slightly clipped, almost British.

Before she went into the kitchen with the food, she turned to Vik. "Tell Mr. Stine about the manuscript of *Mother Goddam*."

Vik launched into the story with relish. "We had just gotten back from Rome, and there was a mountain of mail to be answered. At the very bottom of this huge pile of scripts and letters was your book. I read it on my day off and that evening I came in to Bette's bedroom and said, 'If you never read anything else in your life, you must read this.' She looked at me rather peculiarly."

"How about a drink?" Miss D. asked, coming in from the kitchen. "The sun has gone over the yardarm." (I was to learn this was one of her favorite expressions.)

I wanted a clear head. "May I have more coffee, Miss D.?"

"Of course." She made another pot of coffee and poured herself scotch over ice.

"Yes," Miss D. answered, "I finished it at four o'clock in the morning. At nine o'clock I called Harold Schiff and said, 'Get me Stine. *Mother Goddam* is extraordinary. It's got to be published.'" She turned to me. "Where you found out all of that information, I'll never know."

She disappeared for a moment and then returned with plates of egg rolls, fried shrimp, lobster Cantonese, and chicken chow mein.

"Well," I replied, as we sat down at the pine table and Miss D. whirled our plates to us via the lazy Susan, "in 1961, I was living in New York, when I heard that you were going to write your autobiography. I called my agent and said, 'I must do that book.' He called right back and said, 'Sorry, she's already hired a ghost, Sandford Doty.' So I thought to myself, 'I've waited this long, I can wait a little longer.' When your book came out, it was all personal material, very little about Hollywood. So I knew there was room for a book on your career. I waited eight years."

"I wish you had come to see me then," Miss D. said warmly, picking up an egg roll. "Sandy was a capable writer and was good at making me remember certain things, but his knowledge of Hollywood was nil—plus he wasn't all that familiar with my pictures. I also had an editor at Putnam's who wanted a lot of dirt, which wasn't my style. Sandy had a good beginning, but from there on, it was disappointing."

"But," I interjected, "if you had concentrated on the professional side of your life, there would have never been a *Mother Goddam.*"

She stared at me. "Of course, you're right." She handed me a serving of fried shrimp. "You've come into my life at exactly the right time, Mr. Stine. I've very little to do now, picturewise. I'll work very hard on my comments . . ."

Five hours earlier we were strangers, and now, suddenly we were collaborators. It seemed all too pat, too convenient. This book had been in the back of my mind for twenty-five years, and now my dream was coming true—quickly, easily, without fighting. If this was to be the case, I owed something to Bette Davis; and she obviously felt that she owed something to me.

"You know," Miss D. was saying, "in this business, you start out doing junk and end up doing junk. The last really good thing I did was *Charlotte* and that was an eternity ago."

I knew the signs; she was starting a monologue, wound up like an old-fashioned Victrola. I was fascinated.

She cleared the table and brought in fresh blueberries and cream. "No actor would do television if picture work was available. I've been trying to get a TV series, if only for the financial security. It would be murder, with the long hours, but hell, we made films fast in the old days. *Victory* was shot in a month, *Jezebel* in six weeks.

"I think Loretta Young had the right approach with her anthology series. She got to play all the parts they wouldn't let her do when she was making movies. When she swept out of that door in a new gown each week, well, that was glamour. But anthologies are dead now. The networks want continuing characters.

"I made a pilot about an interior decorator, called *Paula,* in 1964. When that didn't sell, Universal thought a Western might work. I played a dance-hall hostess with girls under her wing on *Wagon Train,* with the hope of spinning it off as a series—but that didn't work either.

"Robert Wagner thought *Madame Sin* would make a good series, so he had himself killed off at the end of the pilot film so that I would be the continuing character. She paused. "I didn't want to play Madame with those eye pieces that make an actor look oriental, so we accomplished the results with eye shadow and false eyelashes, but can you picture me in oriental makeup for ten months a year? Neither can I!" She grinned. "So, in a way, I got to play a kind of *Mother Goddam,* after all."

"What about *Paula?*" I asked.

"It was the story of an interior decorator who always lived with the family she was working for. She was like Margo in *All About Eve:* helpful, rude, honest, very human, and she had never been married because she was too bright for any man to put up with! She lived in a chic house at Malibu. If we had filmed more than the half-hour pilot, there would have been men in her life. Paula was very like me. She had the sort of life that I might have had if I hadn't married. The only way that you can do a continuing series on television is playing yourself or a character like yourself, otherwise you'd go mad. The producer was Aaron Spelling, who is so bright. He's got a big future in the business, and one day I'd like to work with him again."

[Spelling was to figure importantly in Miss D.'s future. Twelve years later, he produced the pilot for the weekly one-hour series, *Hotel,* but she could not proceed as star of the series because of a serious illness.]

She lighted a cigarette, striking the match under the table again, then went on earnestly, without a trace of bitterness. "For all I know, Hollywood has written me off, and with *Bunny O'Hare* such a flop, my career may be over."

"A career is never over for an Aries," I said, "something will turn up. It always does."

"Platitudes!" she exclaimed fiercely. "Platitudes!" Her voice softened. "But I can always be a homebody. I never understood until lately about Dietrich, with all that glamour and beauty, being a hausfrau at heart."

She got up from the table. "How did you get started in the business?" she called from the kitchen, where she was brewing another pot of coffee.

"I wasn't published for a long time. I was a greenhorn from Oklahoma when I started out as a dish-up man in the Italian Kitchen in Hollywood, when I was seventeen. I was out on my own, having finished my junior year at Cathedral High School in Wichita, Kansas."

"You're Catholic? I assumed you were Jewish."

I shook my head. "No. Many people think so because of my name. But the original S-t-i-n-e-s were from Alsace-Lorraine. I attended a parochial school in Wichita during World War II, only because that was the best place to learn. I was the first non–Catholic they'd ever admitted.

"My senior year was spent at the Hollywood Professional School, four hours a day, so I could work at night. Then after the service, I was a chef for ten years before I finally got published at twenty-eight. My last job was working breakfast at Dupar's restaurant in the Farmers Market."

She shook her head. "Jesus, you've paid your dues! I waited on tables when I was at Cushing Academy, and I adore cooking," she added, replacing my ashtray with a clean one.

"Miss D., if I may say so, you are driving me crazy emptying trays. I snuff out one cigarette and it's gone!"

She raised her hands in a sweeping gesture. "Excuse me! I'm more hyper than usual. It's not that you make me nervous, it's just that you're bringing my life back—things I hadn't thought of in years." She paused. "Can all of this really interest you? The directors and the clothes and the makeup and the fights?"

"All those things are involved in a career, right?" I answered quickly. "I am a writer first and a man second."

"Yes, like I've always been an actress first and a woman second." She gave me a direct look. "Complicated, eh?"

"I really owe my writing career to you, Miss D., because, while I was collecting material for my scrapbook, naturally, I read a great deal about motion-picture history. When I first began to write, my agent obtained ghost jobs for me from writers who had overcommitted themselves or celebrities who needed help with their autobiographies. I did about twenty. One of the first books I ghosted, a job that I got mainly because I knew so much about you, was Orry-Kelly's *Women I've Undressed*. Unfortunately, he died, and it was never published."

"Pity. If he had told about all the stars' defects bodywise, it would have been a best-seller! Kelly made me look taller for the camera. I'm only five-feet-two, but looked about five-feet-seven on film."

I finished my coffee. "Only the last half of Kelly's book was about Hollywood. The early part was his early years in Australia. He knew all the pickpockets and pimps and whores—the half-guinea girls called 'Sheilas.' Many of the clothes that he designed for Rosalind Russell in *Auntie Mame* were based on what the expensive prostitutes wore in Sydney in the 1920s. They stood under the streetlights with belladonna in their eyes so that light would reflect in their pupils and catch the attention of would-be customers passing by."

She guffawed. "Brother! Wouldn't Russell love that? Well, Kelly was a very special guy. He created some wonderful wardrobes for me. His only flaw was that he drank too much, but I suppose that's understandable when you figure that he had to supervise all Warner pictures. He even had to select what the beggars wore in costume films. It was years before he did only the stars' clothes. Edith Head went through the same thing at Paramount—but, of course, she wasn't a drinker.

"Kelly never let his personal taste intrude on his work—like Adrian did at Metro. Jesus, some of the clothes Adrian designed for Crawford are hysterical today—bows and drapes and huge collars. Kelly's work always had a classic quality. His clothes for *Victory* and *Voyager* are still in style today—outside of the hemlines. And his work on *Elizabeth and Essex* was absolutely authentic. The costumes weighed so much that I lost fifteen pounds while doing the picture!

"But *Skeffington* had his best all-around designs. Not only were they gorgeous, but they helped characterize both the old and the young Fanny. With Perc Westmore's makeup and Maggie Donovan's hairdos, I really *felt* beautiful—and old, too, when Fanny lost her beauty. The makeup people took four hours to glue those rubber pieces to my face. Today, a complete facial mask would be used and just fitted over the head, which is not really uncomfortable, but they didn't have the technique to do that in those days. Think what poor Karloff had to go through on the Frankenstein pictures and what Lon Chaney, Jr., must have endured when they turned him into the wolfman! Torture."

"Miss D., Kelly always felt that you looked better in period costumes."

"Yes," she agreed, "I was always at home in long dresses. Never had any problem with hoop skirts, either. By the way, how did you like working with him?"

"It isn't a pleasant memory," I replied. "He was very temperamental, but cold sober, but only because his liver was shot. He'd call me at ten o'clock at night and call me a son of a bitch for something I'd written, and we'd have a hell of an argument; then the phone would ring at 6:00 A.M., and it would be Kelly apologizing. It went on like that for months. I only got three thousand for the job."

"Ghosting can't be easy."

"*Skeffington* had Orry-Kelly's best all-around designs. Not only were they gorgeous, but they helped characterize both the old and the young Fanny." Bette in *Mr. Skeffington.* AP/WIDE WORLD PHOTOS

"It's not, especially when you're dealing with picture people. If you'll forgive me, Miss D., actors are the most self-centered of any profession."

"We have to be, Mr. Stine," she announced flatly. "We were brought up that the sun rises and sets with us. You couldn't even get a pimple on your face without all hell breaking loose. Today, so much on television disgusts me. The women mostly look terrible, makeup is bad, hair usually a mess. Men's faces sag, and they often look unshaven even if they aren't."

She looked at me through her lashes. "Do you know where the best makeup is today on television? The daytime soap operas! Boy, those people look great! They just layer on the pancake!"

I laughed. "Maybe it's because the shows are taped so quickly."

"I've nothing against fast shooting, but those nighttime series are usually filmed in bad light and one rehearsal, and it looks it. It's not fair to the actors. The situation comedies filmed in a studio are not much better, and what does the statement 'filmed before a live audience' mean? What it comes down to, is that you rehearse the damn show and then play it before all those people—usually fans—who react to every expression and every gesture until you don't know whether you're any good or not! And you've got to do it twice, and they pick the best one or mix the two!

"It's the same thing that actors had to endure on radio, when we did adaptations of our films. I never liked live audiences like we used to have on the Lux show and so many others. We were trying to concentrate on voices, and particularly if it was a comedy, the reactions of those people out there could throw your timing to the winds. Give me a closed studio with just the cast and microphones any day! But radio was important, not only to publicize your work, but the money was terrific. I used to say that I had to live on my radio earnings, because almost all of the rest went to Uncle Sam—ninety percent during World War II!"

"I watch very little TV," I put in.

"So do I," she replied. "The news mostly. The actors and actresses who're all ego and little talent are sad. I can't stand that breed. But we who *do* care—and I'm afraid we're in the minority now—it's all on our shoulders. A film either hits or misses because of us. The director may be lousy, the cameraman bad, the script a piece of crap, but it's us that the public takes to or rejects. You don't see the director or the cameraman or the script writer up there, so we get blamed for all their incompetence." She gave me a long look. "On the other hand, if it all works, we get all the credit and they don't.

"You're only as good as those you work with. I've heard it said that Dietrich—why am I thinking of her today?—had romances with all of her leading men, so that they'd be so emotionally attached that they'd throw the picture to her. Maybe that's why the audience only saw her; they never really saw the guy she was playing the scene with."

Then, since it was a warm night, she took me to a porch at the back of the house, three sides of which had been screened in by Jeremy. The sounds of rushing water from the nearby Saugatuck River and the croaking of frogs made a strange accompaniment to our conversation.

Over another scotch Miss D. lit another Philip Morris. Her mood had changed. She fiddled with the cigarette. "I'm smoking too much. Right now I remind myself of Susan Grieve in *Winter Meeting*." She looked heavenward. "What a lousy movie that was!"

[*Winter Meeting* was an unfortunate attempt to portray a love affair between a war hero, James Davis, no relation, who wants to be a priest, and a frigid New England poetess, played by Miss D. The film was a drawing-room drama, with dialogue that sounded very twenties, with fourth-rate Noël Cowardish overtones.]

Miss D. was obviously going into another monologue, and I mixed her another drink. "*Winter Meeting* has been on my mind lately. Looking back, I should have stopped that picture in the middle and said, 'Boys, it's just not working,' and gone to Jack Warner and asked him to shelve it. The biggest problem was that censorship was so strict. The second problem was Jim Davis. Burt Lancaster would have been marvelous, but he was busy. I wanted Joel McCrea, but he was busy, too."

She looked at me carefully. "I've always wondered, would a man find a woman in her early thirties a challenge if she was a virgin?"

I shrugged, and managed a weak grin. "I don't know. Today, it would be almost impossible to find an older virgin. There would have to be a good reason for her being chaste, and I would think it would be very difficult for the man."

She sighed. "One thing I know from personal experience: A woman who has not been with a man for a long time *is* almost a virgin again!"

She paused. "But censorship wouldn't allow Jim and me to be

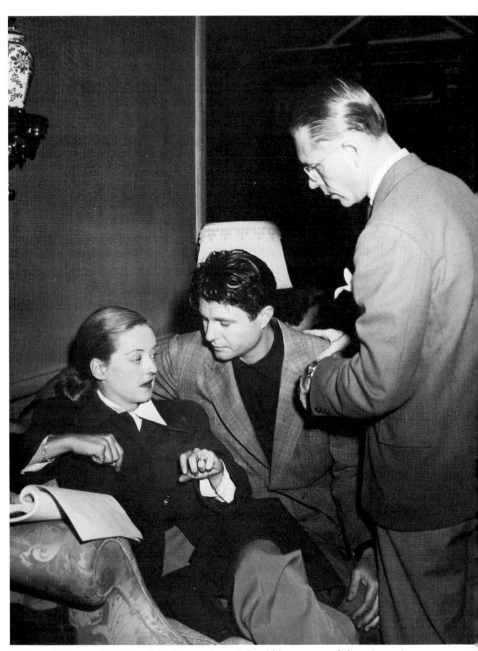

"What a lousy movie *Winter Meeting* was! . . . I should have stopped that picture in the middle. . . . The biggest problem was that censorship was so strict. The second problem was Jim Davis." Bette with Davis and director Bretaigne Windust. C 1948 WARNER BROS. PICTURES, INC. REN. 1975 UNITED ARTISTS TELEVISION, INC.

shown in the bedroom, let alone in bed! It would be a big hit now, because with no Hays office, you could show how difficult it was for Susan to have sex for the first time—with a man who really wanted to be a priest! Think of all those meaningful conversations in the dark over cigarettes after making love! The film bombed because we couldn't do it honestly.

"And poor Jim couldn't find a job for a long time after the film was over—had to go back to carpentry. I was married to Sherry at the time, and he didn't understand my frustrations with the movie. I wore a lighter makeup than usual, and Sherry was convinced that I looked just perfect. None of my husbands, except Gary, had an inkling of what a movie takes out of you, personally. It dries you up, and yet when things *do* go right occasionally, it's the greatest business in the world!"

Miss D. took a sip of scotch. "*Winter Meeting* was bad on several counts. I was thirty-nine and had just had B.D. and had lost too much weight. I was skinny. When I showed up on the set, I knew I was really looking my age. Ernie Haller had set up enormous banks of lights behind huge silk screens just outside of camera range. As a young actress I had seen these same screens on the sets of Ruth Chatterton and Kay Francis, when they were nearing forty, and I knew what they meant. I went back to my dressing room and cried my eyes out.

"Sherry couldn't understand what I was so upset about. 'You've just had a baby,' he said, 'and you look great!' I was furious. My face on the screen looked pinched even with all of Ernie's painstaking work.

"Naturally, Sherry didn't have the slightest understanding that a career can hang on such things as looks. It was the same thing with Gary Merrill when I was going through 'the change.' I put on weight—I was a hundred and thirty pounds! I went from a size twelve to size sixteen. He thought I looked just fine. I was a psychotic eater. Finally, I had enough. After seeing myself in *Virgin Queen* and *Catered Affair*, I went on a diet."

She busied herself cleaning ashtrays again, flitting about the room as restlessly as a young girl.

Vik came out on the porch. "Mr. Stine, I must get you to the station if you're going to catch the last train."

Miss D. followed us out to the driveway and extended her hand. "What can I say? Tonight has been a revelation. You don't know what you've meant to me. It's been glorious."

She smiled warmly, looking a bit like Charlotte Vale in *Now,*

Voyager. "I'm going to go up to a friend's place in Skowhegan, Maine. It's called Red Farm, and I try to get up there once a year to recharge my batteries. I'm going to walk in the country; I'll add my comments to the first chapter of your book, and we'll see how it goes."

We shook hands and waved good-bye. My last impression of her was a tiny figure silhouetted by the light pouring through the open door behind her. She was standing behind the screen, just as when I had first glimpsed her that afternoon.

Driving me to the station, Vik was quiet, leaving me to my thoughts. The ten hours that I had spent with Bette Davis, which seemed like days because we had covered so much ground, took on a fresh perspective now that I had left the house. She had entrusted so many confidences to me. I turned to Vik. "It's like she and I have picked up where we left off a long, long time ago."

"Pardon?"

"It's too hard to explain."

"She's a very complex original," Vik said, then went on perfunctorily, "but you've got two important things going for you: You're Aries and you're a writer."

We were drawing up to the station. "Thank you, Vik, for driving me." I said.

"It's my job, Mr. Stine. Do you have a full staff?"

"My god, no, Vik! I don't have a man Friday, either, but I do have a business manager. I don't drive, you know. He keeps my accounts straight and carts me around. A gardener and a maid come once a week, and that's it."

As we shook hands, he said, "Bette likes you enormously. When I read your book, I knew she would, and she doesn't take to many people. She's been disappointed so often."

I should have asked Vik Greenfield what he meant, but I didn't.

Hal Madison, my business manager, met me at the airport in Los Angeles. A big bear of a guy, he clasped my hand tightly, and asked, "How was the She Dragon?"

"She talks like a stevedore." I grinned and continued, "But wouldn't you know that she turned out to be Bo Peep?"

Chapter 3

O ne morning I was adding to a chapter that had me puzzled, because I couldn't understand why Miss D. disliked certain pictures like *The Little Foxes* and *The Private Lives of Elizabeth and Essex.* I called her in Westport. "Don't you think that you don't care for certain pictures because something tragic happened in your personal life during the filming?"

"Probably," she replied thoughtfully. "My second husband, Farney, died just before I started *Skeffington,* which I never thought I'd get through. It's not that I don't like that picture, but my memories are sad. And each camera setup took hours when I was supposed to be beautiful. I was thirty-seven. Ernie Haller lighted me like a Madonna. He was a genius. He was a quiet, very low-key individual, personalitywise, but god, he knew what he was doing!"

She sighed. "And as much as I loved my husband, I realized that he had problems he hid from me. Maybe I caused some of them, I don't know. He wasn't used to the Hollywood scene. I tried to have a quiet home life for him, away from Hollywood. That's why we lived at Riverbottom in Glendale when I was working, and at Butternut, my home in the White Mountains of New Hampshire, when I was free. He drank secretly. I couldn't understand that. If you drink, then drink! He certainly didn't have to hide it from me. Men! Men!"

"Miss D., something quite interesting happened when I was

"My second husband, Farney, died just before I started *Skeffington*, which I never thought I'd get through." Bette accompanied by her mother, Ruth Davis, leaving Arthur Farnsworth's funeral, August 28, 1943. AP/WIDE WORLD PHOTOS

writing in the book about Farney's death," I said. "It was late at night, and I had just pulled that page out of my typewriter and glanced up at the calendar. It was August 25, 1971, the twenty-eighth anniversary of his death. The hair on the back of my head stood up."

"Imagine! Spooky things like that have happened to me, too," she confided. "Ruthie always visited the set at least once on all of my pictures. She was not feeling well when I did *Pocketful of Miracles,* and died before the picture was finished. But I was doing a scene as Apple Annie in that hag makeup with Glenn Ford—damned difficult because I had to do a kind of Irish jig. I looked up and I thought I saw her, standing off to one side. Her presence filled the whole soundstage. Even now, every once in a while I feel her around, and I think, 'My god, Ruthie, you can see me, but I can't see you!'

"I still miss her," Miss D. continued wistfully. "She was full of fun and gaiety. I inherited her enthusiasm, and I'm afraid, her foolhardiness, too. There was a bitchy streak in all of the Favor girls. Grandma had it, Ruthie had it, Bobby has it, and I have it. Maybe B.D. has it too, somewhere." She paused. "How did we get on that subject. Oh, yes, about personal problems affecting performances. Yes! Yes!"

"When are you coming to the coast for the face-lift operation?" I asked.

There was a long pause. "I've cancelled it. Chickened out. I'm really a physical coward, you know."

On August 21, 1972, the mailman delivered an air-mail, special-delivery envelope from Red Farm, Maine, to my house on Oakshire Drive, which was located on the valley side of Hollywood, very near Universal Studios.

Along with the manuscript, Miss D. had enclosed an eight-page letter, in which she said that she hoped I liked the few pages on which she had written comments, and that she would be back in West-port on the twenty-eighth and would appreciate a note, saying yea or nay about the work done so far and yea or nay about continuing. She indicated that she enjoyed the work but that it was also quite a job.

Her comments on the first chapter were handwritten on the back of my typewritten pages with numbered notations where each squib should be inserted into the script. Her observations were right on the mark; some were quite serious, others fey, humorous, bitchy . . . But all were the work of a caring, intense, intelligent woman. They were absorbing, wonderful, and revealing. I wrote back, thanking her for that "wild" day in Westport and congratulating her on the job.

A fresh copy of the first chapter, including Miss D.'s comments, in capital letters enclosed in parentheses so that our work could be individually identified, was sent to New York. The immediate reaction was not hopeful. I was an unknown writer and Miss D.'s career was in the doldrums. Publishers, I have discovered over the years, are not imaginative when it comes to using different formats, and the fact that they were confronted with two points of view, the author's and the subject's, in one book, confused them further.

Even the editors who liked the material had qualms about the title, which was generally thought blasphemous. An editor from another company exclaimed, "Man, you can't even say *Goddam* on television, and the Baptist bookstores in the South won't carry the title!" The editorial director exploded: "Half the time you don't know who the hell is talking: Stine or Davis!"

On January 4, 1973, Miss D. called from the Bel Air Hotel. The eleven-acre compound, a Mission-style, pink stucco hostelry, located on Stone Canyon Road in West Los Angeles, was a haven for celebrities. Only a stone's throw from Miss D.'s former house, she loved the understated elegance of the place. The entrance brook, the great food, and the fact that guests were not required to go through the lobby, but could proceed via various paths to their rooms, appealed to her sense of privacy.

[The rates were expensive, but even so, brows were raised in May 1989, when a Japanese firm purchased the hotel for more than $100 million--approximately $1.2 million per room!]

"I'm in town to do a television pilot, *Hello, Mother, Good-bye*," she said with her usual enthusiasm. "The funniest thing was when I showed up yesterday at Metro, Jimmy Stewart was on the lot making a *Hawkshaw* segment. Stretched across from soundstage to soundstage was a banner that read: 'Welcome Bette and Jimmy.' Well, as you know, the studio is up for sale, so when I leave the lot, I'm going to have another banner put up that says: 'I've had a ball, MGM TV. Please, NBC, buy it.' I think television is the nuts."

[Miss D. expounded on her views of the small tube to Morton Moss, *Los Angeles Herald Examiner*, January 25, 1983:

The movie studios would have been smart to go along with television sooner. . . . The studios could have bought into the networks when television began. Oh, the fools! the idiots! Warner, Metro, Fox—they were all offered that opportunity. But, no, they didn't want to have anything to do with television. They were telling each other this little monster wouldn't last. . . . They talk about the terrible TV schedule . . . it's hard work. But movie work was always hard. To me, television is much the same. TV is on film. It's an extension of the movies. I was trained this way. . . . I don't think the young are helped today by the freedom they have to choose or reject scripts. They have complete choice of what to do and that means they do the thing they like and comes easiest to them. But is that the best way to learn? I learned from pictures that were not ideal, that weren't easiest for me. The young shouldn't have absolute freedom of choice. That makes more sense later when you really know more about what you are.]

"The publicists put us together for lunch," Miss D. was saying. "It was the first time that we had met."

"Not really, Miss D., you did a Lux radio show of *June Bride* together in 1946."

"Oh god," she laughed, "there you go again! Anyway, he didn't remember it either! But he was far better in the part, I'm sure, than Robert Montgomery! I told Jimmy that I had waited all these years to have a date with him. He was Hollywood's most eligible bachelor, and didn't marry until he was forty. I asked him why he never called me for a date. He laughed, and said, 'I thought about it, Bette, but you were at Warners and I was at Metro, and I'm a plain sort of guy. I didn't think you'd give me a tumble!' I told him that off screen, I was a sort of plain dame. But he has a very nurturing wife, Gloria. I don't know if I was a good nurturer or not."

"Do you know you used the past tense, just now?"

"I did? Well, there may never be another man in my life."

Miss D. took along the manuscript of *Mother Goddam* to the La Costa health resort after finishing her pilot. She worked diligently for two days, then called me, quite perturbed. "Dammit, you've got it all wrong about my walking out on *Foxes*."

"My sources quoted Dr. Dickerson. . . ." I put in gently.

There was a long pause. "Oh, god, then you are right. I had forgotten his name! I must have blocked all of that episode out of my mind. It was so painful."

[There were so many battles on that film that had Wyler not truly loved her, he would have closed down the picture. Samuel Goldwyn, the producer, could have sued her for walking off the set for three weeks, and cast someone else in the role of Regina Giddens. Wyler wanted her to be softer. She played her like a coiled snake, saying that Lillian Hellman had written the part to be delineated that way. Eventually, Miss D. garnered an Academy Award Nomination for her performance.]

"But with Wyler," Miss D. went on spiritedly, "it was all character. And even when we fought, he watched for those nuances, even though he hated the way that I looked, spoke, moved, delivered my lines, my false eyelashes—everything else about my performance. Nothing escaped his scathing tongue. I wasn't pleasing him, but he'd grit his teeth and let me play it my way—or Lillian's way, as I insisted. I must say that the cast kept their mouths shut. I was playing it like Tallulah Bankhead on Broadway, so they were getting the same reactions with their performances.

"Lillian Hellman was so brilliant. Nothing wishy-washy about that woman! We were a good bit alike I always thought, which I told her when we first met. She didn't answer right away, and then she only said, very mysteriously, 'Maybe,' which amused the hell out of me. If I could have been a writer, I would have liked to have her talent. She made it very clear-cut how the character should be played.

"The friction on the set between Willie and me on *Foxes* got to be too much. I was newly married to Farney. I'm afraid he saw a woman that he hadn't married during that period. I was miserable.

"But *Foxes*—that cast was something else. Carl Benton Reid, Dan Duryea, Charles Dingle, and the wonderful Patricia Collinge as Birdie. They had all been playing with Bankhead. I had to find a way to be real that would not detract from the way that they had been playing their roles. These people, with hundreds of performances behind them, had already tried everything and had honed and simplified their work. You don't have time to do that. It's wonderful and it's scary."

[In January 1982, *The Little Foxes* was re-released to theaters. Wrote David Shuft:

"The friction on the set between Willie and me on *Foxes* got to be too much." Bette and director William Wyler on the set of *The Little Foxes*. LESTER GLASSNER COLLECTION

If it's high-style, high-powered melodrama you're after, with a full panoply of hissing human monsters reveling in their own insidious appetites, William Wyler's glossy film version . . . could scarcely be improved upon. This 1941 movie, which features a legendary, all-stops-out performance by Bette Davis, has been pulled from the mothballs in hopes of cashing in on the success of the recent stage revival starring Elizabeth Taylor as the sticky-fingered Southern dragon lady, Regina Giddens. . . . This forty-year-old rouser is still one of the most satisfying entertainments around.]

"Even with all the problems with Wyler that I was having at the time," Miss D. continued, "I'd come on the set when the cast was working, just to watch and learn. Wyler made as many takes as usual, but they didn't mind. I've never thought the stage was different from movies, except, of course, you have to be more subtle.

"Anyway, here I am down here at La Costa spending all this money for exercising and Jacuzzis and working on the book. I'm going to finish it when I go to visit my cousin, John Favor, and his wife, Sally, in Laguna."

"If you get stuck, give me a buzz," I said.

"I will."

[Miss D. always intimated that it took her almost a year to finish her commentary on the book, but the truth is it took only three weeks.] "You've given me a lot of ammunition to play with," she said, "and I finally get the chance to answer all those ghastly rumors that have crept up over the years.

"When I used to get furious about what was written about me, Ruthie always said, 'It's only the best fruit the birds pick at,' but that didn't help much when someone like Sheila Graham took pot shots at me. She's really nasty. And her only claim to fame is the fact that F. Scott Fitzgerald slept with her and died at her apartment. Of the gossip columnists, I rather liked Hedda Hopper. At least she had been an actress and knew the business inside out.

"Louella Parsons I could do without any day of the week. But you had to play ball with those dames or they'd cut you down. We're still sitting ducks for every reporter who thinks they've been snubbed and every picky-picky film reviewer. Now that I can answer some of those bastards back, I'm having a ball!"

Back at the Bel Air Hotel, Miss D. called. "Oh, god, I just did an interview with some college kid, who asked me if I thought William Wyler had created an art form. I gave it some thought and I replied that yes, Willie, along with the great directors—both silent and sound— had created an art form.

"The trouble was that the audience never thought about film as an art form. Movies were something you went to when you wanted to. This kid was so young, he didn't know anything about the double bills of the thirties and forties. He didn't know that films were run continuously in theaters and that people would go in at any time and then leave when the story had reached the place where they had come in."

"Well," I said, "it was only after the 'B' films were no longer made, and 'A' films began to be shown at advertised times, that movies were ever seriously considered."

"Exactly. Now, as a matter of course, people look up show times and, like the theater, wouldn't dream of coming in late. I can tell you, it sure as hell helps our performances to be seen all the way through. Now, with television, we're back to the old way, with the damned commercials. But even with all those interruptions, people will watch our old pictures over and over again—something we never thought about when we were making them. After a film had been played out and retired to the studio vaults, that was it. People like me wouldn't be working now if it wasn't for television showing our pictures. The kids today wouldn't know who the hell we were!"

"Yes," I replied, "think of the stars in silent movies, when theaters were wired for sound; they were forgotten overnight. There was no place to play their pictures."

"How about coming over for drinks at four tomorrow?" Her voice was warm. "It's Sunday. Monday is an easy filming day for me; all I have to do is drive around in a car and make faces, nothing big."

Miss D. was staying in the Kennedy suite, surrounded by lush flower gardens. She was more attractive than I had ever seen her. She wore a red pantsuit with a tailored white silk blouse and her blond, pageboy wig. She had applied a full makeup, including mascara, false eyelashes, and a careful Bette Davis mouth that ignored the natural upper cleft of her lips. Usually, around home, she put on lipstick without looking in the mirror.

There was a knock on the door and she whooped when she saw a perspiring bellhop pushing a cart that contained my huge, ninety-pound Bette Davis scrapbook, which he laboriously placed on the floor.

"I've been thinking about my comments," Miss D. said languidly. "Wouldn't it be fun to have them printed in red?"

"Great idea," I replied, "but it would cost a lot of money. The paper stock would have to be run through the presses twice." Miss D. mixed a scotch for herself and a bourbon and 7up for me, then, delighted as a child, settled down on the floor to look at the scrapbook, exclaiming again and again at the wealth of material. "Don't I look young in that photograph from *Dangerous?* Christ, I was always bitching how I hated my face in those days. Compared to what I look like now, I was an absolute, living doll!

"And there's George Brent and me in *Dark Victory*, photographed by another George—Hurrell. Charles Boyer was supposed to be in it with me, you know. Hal Wallis thought it might be a good idea to change the doctor from a New England type to French—have him over here working on a microbe research grant or some such thing. Thank god, Boyer had another commitment. A French Dr. Steele would have thrown the whole picture off balance. Boyer, you know, wasn't very attractive in person. He was short, bald, had a pot belly, but on the screen he was something else!"

"Miss D., I don't see how he would have fit into the picture as made," I said.

She shrugged. "It's still one of my favorite movies," she said lightly, "even though Ronald Reagan was in it!" [Reagan became a thorn in her side when he was governor of California. She was fond of telling interviewers that he was called "Lit-tle Ronnie Reagan" when under contract to Warner Bros. When he became president she was really miffed, but after his economic reforms began to work early in his reign, she grudgingly gave him credit.]

"I'm really furious," Miss D. went on with equanimity. "I hate to autograph stills of our scenes together." [Reagan was not pleased with the part of Alec, her society boyfriend. The role was not only unrewarding, but he disappeared about halfway through the film. He was quite perplexed because Edmund Goulding, the director, wanted him to be more blasé—a kind of gossipy, buddy-confidant type, very foreign to Reagan's masculine nature.]

"Alec, as written, was a wimp," Miss D. continued. "I told Goulding: Have Casey Robinson write a strong love scene for Ronnie

"There's George Brent and me in *Dark Victory*. Charles Boyer was supposed to be in it with me. . . . Thank god, he had another commitment." LESTER GLASSNER COLLECTION

and me, then when I meet the doctor, who is such a different type, so sober, it will really mean something. The scene, then, where Alec comes by with too much to drink and says he is giving her up, will have more punch. As it stands, he's a ninny.

"Later, when I learned of Reagan's problem on the film," she exclaimed, "I wondered why he didn't come to me. Dammit! But I was a mess emotionally at that time, shaken up by personal reasons, and trying not to make Judy a sentimental fool—which she could not be if the picture was to work. I had my hands full. But really, I should have insisted on a rewrite—an example of one time when I did not follow up on one of my suggestions."

Troubled, Miss D. stood up and went to the window. "What's wrong?" I asked.

She turned around slowly, and gave me a piercing look. "You tell in the book about me being upset before the start of *Dark Victory*, but of course, you didn't know why. We've got to work on a paragraph that will satisfy the reader, without going into the whys and wherefores. Okay?"

"Of course, but . . ."

"The truth is . . . I was having an affair with Howard Hughes, and my husband found out about it, and placed a recorder under the bed where we made love. I was terrified that Ham would go to the press with the recording, which he threatened to do. He wanted seventy thousand dollars. I borrowed the money from the studio to pay him off and he destroyed the disc."

"But, my god, Miss D., Hughes was a multimillionaire, why didn't *he* put up the money?"

She twisted her mouth into an ironic, downward turn. "He could be very strange about anything to do with *cash*. For years, to commemorate our 'anniversary,' he sent me one red rose. Romantic, eh?"

"Incidentally, how did you two meet?" I asked.

She raised her eyebrows. "In the most respectable way possible—at a formal ball. As you know, I was president of the Tailwaggers, and we gave a big party in 1939 at the Beverly Hills Hotel to raise money for the dogs. People were there that I usually didn't socialize with—Norma Shearer, Mary Pickford, and even that bitch, Miriam Hopkins. It was a fabulous evening.

"I was wearing a low-cut, pink-lace gown and when Howard was

"When I learned of Reagan's problem on the film, I wondered why he didn't come to me." Reagan and Bette in *Dark Victory*. LESTER GLASSNER COLLECTION

introduced to me, he looked right into my eyes, not my bosom." She laughed. "I won't say there was magic, but there was warmth. He bought scads of raffle tickets from me and asked for a date. He was so debonair and handsome that I was flattered. Ham and I hadn't been getting along for quite a while, and I was bored.

"Hughes and I had to be very careful about our rendezvous, which usually took place at odd hours, when I wasn't working. Hughes was a night owl, when I tried to be in bed by nine-thirty if I had an early call. When we were alone, some of his shyness left, but he was still a very quiet man. He brought out something in me that no man ever had before. As I look back, it was kind of—well, not quite but almost, a *maternal* instinct.

"He was such a quiet, shy man; endearing in his way. I think part of his gradual withdrawal from society was the fact that he was slightly deaf. He was very vain about this—didn't want anyone to know. Then, after that air crash, when he almost died, I was told that he had a personality change. He was never the same again. His deafness increased after that.

"We never talked much about work. He wasn't the type of man that you could bring your problems to. I used to cook for him at a house he'd rented in Malibu, and we'd sit by the fire and he'd stroke my hair—it was long and very thick then. I don't think any of his girlfriends had been domestic.

"He liked Ruthie and she liked him. She didn't like many men—especially the ones her daughters picked. Ruthie always thought that Bobby and I always married beneath us.

"But Hughes did help me out in August of 1943, when I was desperate to get to Farney. He was ill with pneumonia in Minneapolis, Honeywell's home office, where he'd gone for a company meeting. I thought he might die. In those days, during the war, it was difficult to get flights anywhere.

"I had always been scared to death of flying, and booking a seat on a commercial airline with all of the stops and starts was too much. Also, I didn't want publicity men from the studio to go with me. At that time, Hughes was the single most powerful man in the airline business. I called his office and explained my problem to an aide. He contacted Hughes—who placed a TWA plane at my disposal. Thank god, Farney recovered.

"Funnily enough, after I married Gary Merrill in 1950, he rented a

"Hughes and I had to be very careful about our rendezvous, which usually took place at odd hours." LESTER GLASSNER COLLECTION

house at Malibu. I almost fainted. It was the same place where Hughes and I had had our rendezvous! I never told Gary. He could be mean sometimes, and I didn't think it was any of his business. And my affair with Hughes had been over for ten years. But Gary would have brought it up in a quarrel. He loved to throw things up to me."

Miss D. mixed another drink, then sighed deeply. "God, when I go back over those days, it's a wonder that I wasn't tarred and feathered by the press. One or two of the Hollywood gossips had to have known about Hughes and me, even as careful as we were, but since I had always cooperated with them and treated them fair and square, they stood behind me. Not even an allusion to the mess was ever printed. Brother, was I lucky!

"But *Victory* was my most important film since *Jezebel*, even with the Hughes business eating at me inside. It was a big flop on Broadway with Tallulah Bankhead," Miss D. said with a wink, "and she was beside herself when I got an Oscar nomination for the movie. I'm told she positively glowed when Vivien Leigh got the award for *Gone with the Wind* instead of me!

"Then, when I got *Foxes*—which was her best performance in the theater—she almost had apoplexy. She naturally assumed that she'd get it since Samuel Goldwyn was going to do the film. It never occurred to her that Warners would loan me out. It surprised the hell out of me too! In fact I told Sam Goldwyn he was a fool for not hiring Bankhead."

Miss D. giggled. "She wasn't through with me yet, however. She was furious when the critics said that I looked and acted like her in *All About Eve*—which just wasn't true. We did sort of resemble each other and we had the same hairstyle for years, but I had laryngitis on the picture and my voice was somewhat hoarse, so that heightened the resemblance, I guess."

"What was George Brent like?" I asked. "I always liked him."

Her eyes narrowed. "His hair was snow white even then." She giggled. "He used to stain my pillow cases with hair dye! Actually, he was a charming, caring, and affectionate man, with a wonderful sense of humor. I never could understand why those qualities didn't come over on the screen more often. He could project sincerity and that was about it. He could be so stodgy on film, but he was good in *Victory*, though, and we had fun when we did *Woman of the Year* on radio a few years ago.

"He's one of my few lovers whom I've remained friends with. I haven't seen him in ages; he lives on an avocado ranch somewhere near San Diego." She paused thoughtfully. "All that seems just like yesterday," she went on pensively. "He must be about seventy now. But, one thing with George, he had no illusions about his talent. He knew he was no Errol Flynn or Clark Gable—whom he somewhat resembled—and he played leading men to everyone—from Garbo to Loy to Fontaine to Stanwyck, Colbert, and Oberon."

Miss D. threw back her head and laughed. "He used to say that the only thing he had to be careful about was his haircut, to be sure his head was trimmed well in back, because so often that was the only part of him that was photographed!

"But when George became infatuated with me, I was delirious. After Ham, I needed a strong man like George. I suppose some of the doctor's strength affected him during the playing, because eventually he turned out to be sort of weak. Along with Cary Grant, Clark Gable, and Kirk Douglas, he was one of the tightest men with money in Hollywood. He once gave me a bracelet, B-E-T-T-E spelled out in diamonds, and casually mentioned he was glad I had such a short name. I laughed and said, 'Well, it's really E-L-I-Z-A-B-E-T-H, you know!' He didn't think it was funny.

"The one good thing about our affair was that it could be public. We were both single. We went to a lot of Hollywood places together, even the racetrack, which, in those days, was about the most public place you could go. With my other affairs, for various reasons, I couldn't be seen with the men, or they with me.

"Hal Wallis, who of course knew everything that was going on at the studio, was delighted with our affair. He would come out of the projection room after seeing the rushes, grinning from ear to ear, because he had a gut feeling that the picture would be the huge success it turned out to be. Not so, Jack Warner, who, even after the rave reviews started to pour in, thought we had a flop, and that it would lose box office after a few days. He was wrong, and even grudgingly admitted it to me later. He never, ever, liked to face up to the fact that he could be wrong."

[Miss D. said that in 1978, when she was doing her one-woman show, *Bette Davis: In Person and on Film*, in San Diego: "George sent a note backstage asking me if I could see him before I went on. He didn't want to become involved in the crowd afterward. I, of course, said yes. I told Gene Hibbs to really make me look good that night, and he pulled the straps a little tighter. There was a timid knock on the door and this old, old man sort of hobbled in. I stared at him for a minute and then he giggled. That was the only way I would have recognized him! He was portly and bald with white hair around the edges. He had his own teeth, but the gums had receded. I almost cried. I hugged him and we chatted a bit. I was so shook up, I don't know what I said to him. After he left, I thought to myself, *Thank god I didn't marry him!* I would have ended up taking care of him in his old age. When we were going together he was thirty-five, and I was thirty-one. Those four years didn't mean a damn then, but they sure would have later!"]

I mentioned that Brent had just finished a picture, his first professional job since 1956. "It's called *Born Again*," I said. "He plays a judge. Irving Rapper, who directed, brought him up from his ranch in Fallbrook. He was paid seventy-five thousand dollars for one day's work. At the end of the day, Rapper asked Brent if he would come back the next day and do some publicity, and he answered, 'Sure I will—if you pay for the second day's work!'"

Miss D. laughed and remarked, "See what I mean? But," she continued, "it was very difficult for me the morning after the New York papers reviewed the film."

[Said Frank S. Nugent of *Dark Victory*, in *The New York Times*, April 21, 1939:

> Miss Davis is superb. More than that, she is enchanted and enchanting. Admittedly it is a great role—rangy, full-bodied, designed for a virtuosa, almost sure to invite the faint damning of "tour de force." But that must not detract from the eloquence, the tenderness, the heartbreaking sincerity with which she has played it. We do not belittle an actress to remark upon her great opportunity; what matters is that she has made the most of it.]

Miss D. continued with a soft smile, "I had luncheon in the Green Room at Warners; the New York reviews were spinning in my head. With every eye on me, it took every bit of strength I had to walk nonchalantly to my usual table and casually order a salad. When one contract player after another came by, I cheerfully accepted their congratulations. What I wanted to do was to throw restraint to the winds and run into the middle of the room and shout: 'By damn I was right! Everyone in America wants to see a story where the heroine dies in the end! I've won my battle, and I just may win my third Oscar.'

"Of course, my New England upbringing wouldn't allow me to play that scene. Much too extravagant. And, as far as the Oscar went, I got the nomination all right, but Vivien Leigh rightfully won, and I meant it when I told her that Scarlett was one of the great performances of all time. I'm not sure that she believed I was sincere, but Laurence Olivier did. Of course, he and I are the same kind of actor. But if *Victory* had been released any other year, I think unquestionably I would have won."

Her mood changed as she sat down on the floor and pointed to several *Photoplay* pages. "And look at 'Little Miss Clothes Horse' here in all those fashion shots! Pure drudgery posing, but I got to wear some smashing outfits. Ruthie was always after me to wear designer clothes off screen, but I was more at home in slacks and cottons. Oh, I dressed up when I went out on the town or had to appear at industry affairs, but it was too much trouble otherwise. I wanted to be comfortable then, and I want to be comfortable now. And, besides, I didn't have the time."

She took a sip of her scotch. "Kids in the business today bitch about how hard they have to work. The only ones who have a right to that statement are the soap opera stars; they *work*. Being at Warners was just like a regular job. We showed up every day. When we weren't shooting, we had to go to the picture gallery to be photographed for the fan magazines, or have wardrobe or makeup tests, or put up with a luncheon with some interviewer."

She pointed at a still from *All This and Heaven Too*. "Boyer was so great as the Duc. You know, I've been very lucky to work with so many really wonderful actors. I had admired Charles for years. He had a face that was made for films, and even if he had a heavy French accent, his diction was superb. Sometimes accents get in the way of a performance, and the audience has to listen very closely or they miss dialogue—when that happens, the scene falls to pieces."

"One thing about you, Miss D.," I said, "your diction is wonderful. You can hear every word loud and clear."

She stood up and gave a mock bow. "Thank you, sir! I can thank my stage training for that. My mentor, John Murray Anderson, was a stickler for proper pronunciation. At his school, we were taught how to speak properly and project. There were no 'body mikes' then! My voice was very thin and kind of squeaky, and I worked very hard. When I toured with Blanche Yurka in *The Wild Duck* and *The Lady from the Sea,* we had to be understood with all of that Ibsen dialogue. Yurka had a voice that was an instrument in the true meaning of the word—I've never really felt I had one. She could give you a scowl that hurt worse than a beating! We watched our p's and q's—and our diction, I can tell you!

[Thomas Middleton, *Los Angeles Times,* September 10, 1985, wrote:

> Steve Allen, who probably has as good an ear for sounds, sense, and nonsense of words as anyone, wrote to say, 'Applause, applause for your defense of the good old letter T, which many Americans have a tendency to swallow when it appears at the end of words. In discussing the problem with assorted actors on my TV shows over the years, I have asked them to give me what I call 'the Bette Davis T.' Ms. Davis still holds the American T-pronouncing championship, and long may she wave. Her famous line, 'What a dump!' would not have seemed nearly as arresting had its first word been pronounced with a *wha . . .*"]

Miss D. let out a war whoop, pointing to a page of the scrapbook. "And there is Paul Lukas and me in *Watch on the Rhine.* He was wonderful to work with. His eyes bored into you and burned inside.

"This was Herman Shumlin's first film as a director. Part of the deal was that they would use him since he had directed the play and was famous in New York. He was sort of thrown for a loop; he kept thinking in stage terms. He got a lot of help from Hal Mohr, the cinematographer. Some exterior scenes were written by Lillian Hellman, the playwright, to enlarge the play. But it was a fine touch that the set of the house in Washington, where most of the action was played, was kind of claustrophobic. These people might be in a free country, but the house itself was isolated, almost as if it was in Germany."

"What was working with Lukas like?"

Miss D. looked at me skeptically, as if she didn't want to answer, then reconsidered. "Frankly, I was scared. He had performed the play on Broadway for years. Several members of the original cast were brought from New York—which was a plus, because you've got ensemble playing right from the start. Also, when you perform with

"Paul Lukas was wonderful to work with. His eyes bored into you and burned inside." Bette and Lukas in *Watch on the Rhine*. C 1943 WARNER BROS. PICTURES, INC. REN. 1971 UNITED ARTISTS TELEVISION, INC.

someone for so long, you establish a special relationship, and we were shooting rather quickly, and it was a small role for me.

"Since most of my scenes were with Paul, I had to strike the right note or I'd throw his performance off, and let's face it, it was *his* movie, not mine! At this point he had won all sorts of awards for his role, and it was wonderful when he got the Oscar, too. He'd been around since the silents and played everything from romantic roles to villains. He'd paid his dues."

Miss D. went to the window and looked out over the expanse of lawn that the gardeners at the Bel Air Hotel were manicuring as carefully as the beauticians who work on stars on a movie set. "Paul deserved his Oscar, but I've always felt it basically unfair that New York stage actors who recreate their roles in Hollywood win awards."

"Like Anne Bancroft in *The Miracle Worker?*" I queried.

She shot me a quick glance and frowned. I could see she was contemplating whether to answer sharply or not. Instead, she grinned. "I wasn't thinking about that incident, but she did deprive me of winning for *Baby Jane.* But she was at home in her role after all those performances, while I was creating out of whole cloth. There is a difference!"

For the third time that day, she emptied my ashtray. "Miss Davis," I laughed, "you're driving me up the wall and onto the ceiling with your neatness."

She grinned self-consciously. "I am? Jesus! It's just automatic, I guess. Ruthie used to say I drove her crazy with things like that! Sorry.

"Now," she went on brusquely, "getting back to Paul. He was in his midfifties; I was thirty-five. Another thing I liked was the love scenes." She giggled. "And I don't mean *kissing* Paul! It was the fact that the film showed a long-married, midlife couple—who were still in love—and our good-bye had to have tenderness and *familiarity* right along with the kisses. We made them *intense*, not *passionate*, because they knew that it was their last meeting. With the condition of his health, and what he had to go through getting back to Germany, he would surely die there, maybe not even finishing his mission."

She paused. "I made Sara look tired; they were immigrants and had been through so much. I knew I had to play her very simply, underplay, actually, to Paul. Hellman's words were so beautiful. How can you go wrong with a writer like that? The film was important; it had something to say about fascism, which was rampant all over the world.

She wrote the play just before World War II. That's why I did it. Warners was afraid that the picture wouldn't get an audience with just the Broadway cast."

"Then you did it for patriotism?"

Miss D. got up quickly and lighted a cigarette. "No, not exactly. I've always believed that a star should take smaller roles now and then, roles that are different from the usual thing you're known for. It lets you stretch a little. Remember, *Watch on the Rhine* followed *Now, Voyager* and my musical number in *Thank Your Lucky Stars,* so it was kind of a coup for me. Sara was the best change of pace I could have had at that time. Also, I had *three* children in the film, so I was housewifely and domestic."

She raised her brows. "Willie Wyler told me that Greer Garson, who is my age, didn't want to do *Mrs. Miniver,* because she played a mother with a grown son, played by Richard Ney. I thought that was rather vain. The boy fell in love with Teresa Wright in the movie. I almost wrote her a note, saying: 'I just played her mother in *Foxes,* and she's a damned good actress!'

"But the hysterical part of the story is that when the movie was over, Garson married Ney!" She mixed me another drink. "Here you are, Whitney," she said casually.

"Thank you, Bette," I replied smoothly.

At last, we were now on a first-name basis.

As I left, Bette said, "You can kiss me on the cheek. That's very Hollywoodish, but we do it in New England, too."

I kissed her on the cheek. My probation was over.

Chapter 4

Since I had a business meeting in New York, I was invited to Twin Bridges for dinner. In a way, it was as if I were meeting Bette for the first time. This feeling of newness at each meeting never diminished. It was the same for her, I learned later. Aside from our extraordinary rapport, we had not only admiration for each other but great respect. Perhaps this was the secret of the close friendship that was forming.

We never grew tired of each other's company. I have often speculated that this feeling on both of our parts might have been due to the fact that we were never thrown together for more than three or four days. I doubt that two Aries temperaments would survive very long under the same roof.

For once Bette was not wearing a hat, but a blond, pageboy wig that was most becoming. She wore blue eye shadow that accentuated her eyes.

"You look fetching, Bette," I said, kissing her on the cheek.

"Thank you kindly, suh," she replied, in the highly expert Southern drawl that she had used first in *Cabin in the Cotton*, and dipped into a mock curtsy, then took my arm. "I even crimped my eyelashes for you!"

She was so tiny beside me; suddenly I felt protective. "Don't you miss having a man around?" I asked.

She threw me a sidelong glance. "Yes, of course. And no, of course. I have Michael now—for a while—and he's good and strong and has a fine head on his shoulders. When he leaves, there'll be a big vacancy in my life. As far as a husband goes, yes, but so often the men I'm attracted to are not attracted to me—in that way. If I could find a man, different from my past husbands, who wasn't dependent on me as the breadwinner, I might give it a try again. But to marry for sex is ridiculous!"

"Don't you get lonely?" I asked.

She threw me a quick look. "Sometimes. For instance, you're the first outside person I've seen in five weeks. One thing that people like me—who spend so much time traveling to locations to work and are in the public eye—have to guard against is becoming a recluse. I'm content to hole up for months, but," she said as she tapped her head, "the brain gets petrified. I was so worried when I married Gary Merrill, who was seven years younger than I, that he would get bored staying at home so much, so we went out more than I do usually."

Michael was home from college. At twenty-two, he was a tall, handsome boy whom Bette had always called her "blond bomber." She had fixed one of her specialties, lamb curry. Mike confided as we sat around the lazy-Susan table that he had only seen a few of his mother's films. "Some of my friends have seen more of them on television than I have," he said with a smile.

"Fine with me," Bette broke in, "that's why I brought you kids up in the East. I didn't want you to be a party to all that Hollywood crap that children of stars have to go through. You can't raise kids out there with any kind of real values."

"Then, Mike," I said, "you don't know what kind of a career your mother had."

He gazed at me levelly. "To me, she's always just been 'Mom,'" he said, before bolting down his dish of fresh blueberries and bounding off for a date with his girlfriend, Chou Chou Rains, who lived nearby.

"That," Bette said with a wave toward the door, "is what the younger generation is all about! He's a normal, upright guy, and that's the way it should be! He's capable of fighting his own battles," she went on. "He wants to become a lawyer, so he'll be fighting other people's battles, too—just like I've done over the years."

"I don't understand," I said.

She raised her eyebrows. "At the height of my career, after I'd appeared in so much junk for so long," she said earnestly, "and I was finally getting good parts with good directors and good cameramen, I wanted everything to be right—I wouldn't settle for second best in anything. I had influence and I used it! Once I had box-office clout, I never let Warner forget it.

"I fought battles for little people who weren't in a position to stand up for themselves. I got a reputation for being difficult—a reputation that still plagues me today. But I wasn't and I'm not. All I ever wanted—or want now—is professionalism. Today, producers and directors are aware of how I operate. If they hire me, they know I won't keep silent, that I'll plague them with suggestions, but that I will perform with all I've got. And if I have a great leading man, it's easier."

"Why?"

"Because." She lighted another Philip Morris. "The stronger your leading man is, the more you have to work with and the better you are. Sometimes there's good chemistry and sometimes not. Edward G. Robinson, for instance—whom I used to think of as 'liver lips'—was just awful to kiss; ugh. But we played love scenes in *Kid Galahad,* and no one could tell I wasn't enjoying it."

"What was your secret?"

"Clark Gable came to my rescue. I pretended he was kissing me!"

"But if you didn't like Robinson, why did you do the film?" I asked.

She held up her hands, palms out. "No, no, you don't understand," she said good-naturedly. "I didn't object to working with him, just kissing him. He was a very gentle man, very erudite and cultured, which was a contrast to all those gangsters he played. His wife, Gladys, was a good hostess, too—almost as good as Ouida Rathbone was. But I did the picture—which I think was one of the best prizefight pictures ever made—for two reasons. One, it was a completely different part than I'd ever played: a nightclub singer who was also a moll." She paused, and her eyes lighted up. "Do gangsters have molls today? With so many unmarried couples living together, I guess it doesn't matter! But *Galahad* was a man's movie. That meant a new audience would see me."

[Bette was always conscious of appearing before a public that would not normally be attracted to her films. In 1978 she made a Disney film, *Return to Witch Mountain,* primarily because it was a children's film, and therefore a new audience.]

"Edward G. Robinson—whom I used to think of as 'liver lips'—was just awful to kiss; ugh! But we played love scenes in *Kid Galahad* and no one could tell I wasn't enjoying it." C 1937 WARNER BROS. PICTURES, INC. REN. 1964 UNITED ARTISTS TELEVISION, INC.

"Number Two, Hal Wallis promised that I could actually sing 'The Moon Is in Tears Tonight.'" She frowned. "Let's say, we had words over it. Hal totally disagreed with me when I wanted to talk/sing it. He didn't want the song to be dramatic, just an ordinary ballad, because my character wasn't all that talented as a singer. Well, as it turned out, I had to dub the song, which was miserable to do. I kept lousing up. Michael Curtiz thought it was out of spite, because I hated him so much, but things just kept going wrong."

She raised her eyebrows slowly for a comical effect. "After I'd finally got it right, Wayne Morris, who played the bellboy fighter guy, turned to me and said, 'Well you really fluffed it!' We all screamed with laughter, because my name in the picture was Fluff Phillips!" She rolled her eyes.

"When I saw how perfectly Deborah Kerr, who couldn't even talk/sing, lip-synched all those songs in *The King and I,* I was filled with admiration. Incidentally, I wanted very much to do the part of Anna, which Irene Dunne played opposite Rex Harrison in *Anna and the King of Siam*—the original black-and-white movie made at Fox.

"Also, much later, I wanted to do *Who's Afraid of Virginia Woolf?* I was the right age, but Warners thought I wasn't box-office enough, and Taylor and Burton got it! Albee could have written it for me."

She lighted another cigarette from the one she was smoking, and blew the smoke out of her nose and then inhaled again, a trick she sometimes used in movies. "But I could have done *The Time of the Cuckoo,* Arthur Laurent's beautiful play, on a national tour with Rossano Brazzi, but I decided against it. For one thing, Shirley Booth had done it on Broadway and Katharine Hepburn in Hollywood, and I didn't want to follow them. Comparisons can be odious, and let's face it, the money wasn't all that great, but Brazzi was very beautiful then."

She giggled. "I did finally get to do a torch song that was actually quite funny, called 'Just Like a Man,' in my Broadway show, *Two's Company*." And she sang: "Just like a man/the only thing that Del Monte cannot can . . ."

"But, Bette, what about 'They're Either Too Young or Too Old,' from *Thank Your Lucky Stars?*"

"Well, Mark Hellinger produced that picture, and all of us at Warners pretty much got to do what we wanted to do, which was to show us to the public in a new light. My personal favorite was Hattie McDaniel singing 'Ice Cold Katy.' She was known as a dramatic actress on the screen and was wonderful in *The Great Lie* and *In This Our Life,* but she had started out as a singer and she was great. They wouldn't put her in a full-scale musical, I guess, because of her size — or maybe because she was black. Anyway, by that time, Wallis had left the studio."

"I never understood why," I expounded. "His touch was on all those Warner Bros. films of the thirties and early forties."

"Let me tell you about Hal Wallis," she said. "The same care that he devoted to his job at Warners, he gave to his private life. I adored his first wife, Louise Fazenda, who died. She was a great humanitarian, a fantastic comedienne. But she also had taste and was rather attractive in person.

"Hal's second wife, Martha Hyer, was also an actress, and together they built a fantastic impressionist art collection — a great way to invest money and hedge inflation. He has Degas's *Sur la Scene,* ballet girls, and Monet's *Asters,* to name two."

[Wallis had purchased the Degas in 1959 for $180,000 and the Monet in 1971 for $215,000.]

"Now, what I'm going to say about Wallis has nothing to do with his artistic integrity or his genius at producing," Bette continued, "but he never personally liked the type of pictures I made. He bought the best properties he could find for me, and they were done with great care, but he really preferred the hard, cynical pictures of Robinson — also a great art collector — and Bogie and Cagney. I respected Hal and he respected me and we got along fine — usually. Most of my beefs were with Jack L. Warner."

[Many years later, Bette presented Wallis with an award, and then took his arm to lead him offstage, remembered herself, came back to the microphone and told the audience that this sort of thing was what Wallis had had to put up with all those years at Warners! Quite carefully, she stood out of the limelight while he gave his acceptance speech.]

"But finally, Wallis was screwed in the worst way by Warner, who thought that he, himself, was the best producer who ever walked the earth. He wasn't by a long shot. He was a financial genius, and he was tops at running the studio, but he wasn't one quarter the producer that Hal Wallis or Henry Blanke was, and he knew it! Jack could be so damned petty. He had always been jealous of Wallis, who had put up

"Most of my beefs were with Jack Warner. . . . He could be so damned petty." Janet Leigh, Jack Warner, and Bette at a Hollywood gala. WHITNEY STINE COLLECTION

with his bullshit for twenty years. Wallis finally got fed up with it and gave up his Head of Production duties to make pictures as a sort of independent, with the studio releasing them.

"Anyway, it all came to a head the night that *Casablanca* won as Best Picture of the Year. Wallis was on his way up the aisle to receive the Oscar for his picture, when Warner was already on the stage. He took the honors that night that rightfully belonged to Wallis. He was still burned because Wallis had won the Irving B. Thalberg Award in 1939. Jack L. had peed his pants. Wallis later went over to Paramount where he had complete autonomy." She paused. "Why am I getting into all this, Whitney? Telling secrets out of school! You have a strange effect on me."

"I only saw Jack Warner once," I said, "when he accepted a posthumous award for his brother, Sam, from the Society of Motion Pictures and Television Engineers. Sam was responsible for bringing sound to films, but Jack was very ungracious and rambled on and on about how *he* was just as deserving of the award as Sam."

"That just goes to show you what kind of a man he was: mean-spirited." She rose. "Let me show you the garden. The moon is really special tonight."

The backyard at Twin Bridges meandered down to the Saugatuck River, and I took Bette's arm as we sauntered outside. The crickets were chirping, and the moon was so bright that the leaves on the trees glowed. "This is like the mise-en-scène in Warners' *A Midsummer Night's Dream*," I said.

She sighed. "Isn't it? I wanted to do Titania, you know, but Anita Louise got the part. I'd just done *Bordertown*, and I thought it was time I did Shakespeare. It would have been a great change of pace for me." She gripped my arm. "Instead, I got *Front Page Woman*, playing a screwy reporter!"

"By the way, any new projects in the works?" I asked.

"I've just finished a television movie, *The Judge and Jake Wyler*—written for Rex Harrison, can you believe? Some of the kid actors showed up not even knowing their lines! I bit my tongue. The movie or the role wasn't worth fighting about. I needed the money and just went through my paces. But we're getting far afield! I always end up telling you all the things that can't go in the book! After I'm gone, you've got to do a book about all these things we talk about all the time. You're always so calm. Don't you ever raise hell?"

"I'm not going to take the Fifth Amendment," I laughed, "but sure, I raise hell sometimes. I learned years ago to curb my temper."

"Well, obviously I haven't." She placed her hands on her hips and laughed. "I've never met anyone like you."

"Well, Tennessee Williams and I have the same birthday, but not the same year, of course. Are we anything alike?"

"My god, *no!* He's bitter inside, and kind of namby-pamby on the outside. Gregory Peck was born on my birthday too, but we're not at all alike. God, he can be ponderous. But he was born to play Lincoln. I wanted to do Mary Lincoln for years as a feature film. I should have filmed your *16th First Lady*, but that's water under the bridge."

[I had written *The 16th First Lady* in 1958, with Mary Lincoln as the central figure and Abe only seen in long shots; and Edd Henry, her agent at MCA, had sent it to her.]

"I probably couldn't have found the financing, anyway. But I did get to play Mary on television, but it wasn't the same—a glorified monologue . . ." She shivered. "Let's go inside."

We strolled back by the river, arm in arm; all that could be heard was the rushing water. It was the first time that there was no conversation between us.

We went into the house the back way and she mixed us a drink, then lay on the chaise longue while I took the big chair.

"Speaking of Williams . . ." She paused dramatically. "He offered me the stage play of *A Streetcar Named Desire*. I was living at Laguna with Sherry, but we were visiting Sarasota, Florida, at the time, where Sherry was painting canvases of the winter quarters of the Barnum and Bailey circus, and it was a period when we were getting along well. Williams came up from Key West, and Sherry read the play and said he didn't think I should do it. I had just had B.D., and I wanted to spend a lot of time with her. Looking back, I guess I was just lazy. I pondered over the script a long while and finally turned it down.

"Blanche DuBois, to me, was a fantasy character, and I really didn't think I could be that fey. Then Jessica Tandy did it and she had never done anything fey before, either, and she was terrific. It was then that I knew I could have done it. One of the greatest mistakes that I ever made, careerwise."

I leaned forward. "Isn't it a strange coincidence that Williams also offered you *The Night of the Iguana* while you were in Florida?"

"I had forgotten about that! Gary and I were touring with *The*

World of Carl Sandburg then. Well, thank god I had sense enough to say yes. The funny thing was that Tennessee wanted me to do Hannah—the heroine—but I preferred the bitch, Maxine, although it was the third part." She paused. "Let me say something about these smaller roles in big productions, either on the stage or in pictures: The big roles may have more 'sides,' but if the smaller role is perfectly conceived—as was Maxine—audiences keep waiting for you to come back on scene."

"I saw the play in Chicago and thought you were sensational."

She beamed. "I'm so pleased! The Broadway audiences loved the play, too, but one aspect scared the hell out of me. The moment I came onstage—fully in character, naturally—there was this fantastic ovation. Now, you usually get a polite hand of acknowledgment; that I was prepared for. But the applause went on such a long time that I was forced to step out of character and bow. It was very unnerving, and threw the start of the play off.

"It wasn't fair to the rest of the cast. We finally worked it out so that my first line was offstage. I shouted the name of the reverend, played by Patrick O'Neal: 'Shannon! Shannon!' Then I made my entrance, acknowledged the applause, and went on with the show.

"As you know, I dyed my hair bright red for the part, and that helped my characterization. Maxine was the first—and last—Earth Mother I ever played; gutsy, vulgar, very sexual. I wore an unbuttoned man's shirt, open to the navel, and a special bra so that the audience wouldn't see everything.

"What was disheartening was that my contract did not specify that I would be cast in the movie version. Because O'Neal wasn't box-office, Richard Burton—who was in his midthirties then—got the part, so the die was cast. Deborah Kerr played Hannah, and Ava Gardner played Maxine—both in the same age group. At that point I knew exactly how Merman must have felt when Rosalind Russell was cast in *Gypsy*, or Julie Andrews felt when Audrey Hepburn got *My Fair Lady*.

"But Tennessee promised me that if I did Blanche, he would see that I had it in my contract to do the film, also. I was thirty-nine then, just the right age. Jessica Tandy did it brilliantly, but I thought Vivien Leigh wasn't good casting for the movie version, and she got an Oscar for it. And I could have played with Brando! God, what an actor he is! Ah, the lost causes! But I don't dwell on them. It was simply not to be!"

"How about your Warners' contract?" I asked speculatively.

"Oh, we would have worked something out. Warners was having a hell of a time finding scripts for me at that point. They ended up doing *Streetcar,* anyway.

"The other big mistake I made," Bette went on sadly, "was not doing the film version of *Come Back, Little Sheba.* Hal Wallis, by this time, had left Warners and gone over to Paramount. I should have listened to him. He had never steered me wrong on a part. He begged me to do it, but I had seen Shirley Booth on Broadway, and I couldn't see anyone else in the role."

"Do you suppose, Bette, it had something to do with ego?"

She threw me a penetrating glance. I was about to explain what I meant, but her eyes flashed and I knew she got my meaning.

"Maybe. The character was a slattern, no clothes, no hairdo, but oh, those wonderful words. Booth got an Oscar. Oh, god, hindsight.

"Another regret is not being offered the Lynn Fontanne part of the rich bitch in *The Visit,* with Anthony Quinn in the Lunt role. Bergman got it and was too beautiful. The film wasn't ten percent what the stage play was." She smiled ruefully. "I was in Rome making *Empty Canvas* when Ingrid was shooting one soundstage over. She sent word that she wished I was in her shoes doing the part, so she must have known that she was miscast."

"I've always believed that you could do anything that you set your mind on," I said. "Look what you did with *Of Human Bondage.*"

[In 1936, Graham Greene, the British critic, wrote:

Her performance in *Of Human Bondage* was wickedly good . . . and even the most inconsiderable films . . . seemed temporarily better than they were because of that precise nervy voice, the pale ash-blond hair, the popping neurotic eyes, a kind of corrupt and phosphorescent prettiness.]

Bette pursed her lips. "Mildred's accent nearly drove me up a tree. I had a cockney woman live with me so that I could pick it up, and I drove my family wild because I used it around the house while I was doing the picture. I had learned the proper cockney pronunciation all right, but I had to tone it down so I could be understood. The same when I've used Southern accents. You can't be *too much* or you get a laugh.

"My family was scared to death, because it was such a departure.

Ham was very upset and thought it might hurt my career. My mother, Ruthie, was aghast that I knew how to play Mildred. She had reared my sister, Bobby, and me so carefully. We were what you'd call protected." She grinned. "Hell, I shocked myself.

"*Bondage* was supposedly based on W. Somerset Maugham's youth, when he was a medical student. Of course, he didn't have a clubfoot, like his hero Philip had, but he stuttered, which I suppose was just as bad.

"Much later, Maugham visited the set of *Foxes,* and it was difficult for me to realize that this mild-mannered man who had such difficulty speaking had written all those great books. He had a very dry wit, and I was got up as Regina in a corset so cinched up that I could hardly laugh, but laugh we did. He was an amusing man. I told him that *Bondage* paved the way for me to play all those disturbed women later on.

"But when I came to the big scenes, visitors on the set just *looked* at me in disbelief, and when I finished the takes and went to my dressing room, they followed me as if I wasn't Bette Davis the actress, but still as if I was Mildred.

"Walter Plunkett, the clothes designer, was a great boon. His waitress uniform and cap were typical of the type used in English tearooms. Since I've always been round-shouldered, I stooped just a little more as Mildred standing there taking orders, as if she was bored out of her mind. She was just marking time to get off work and go out with one of her beaux.

"But, anyway, Leslie Howard was something else. He was as cold as ice on the set, and I resented it. I had admired him for years; I wanted him not only to like me as a person but to approve of me as an actress. That was too much to hope for, I guess. He went into the picture with the idea that it was *his* film; after all, he was the star and I was supporting him. My name was under the title. When I was doing my close-ups he would sit off to the side, reading a book, and give me my cues.

"Because Mildred had to be so indifferent to Philip—she didn't look at him directly very much—Howard had to give more of himself than he was used to giving. But, after a week or so, I began to feel a difference in our scenes, a difference I knew well. He was giving a much better performance, because of the sluttish way I was playing Mildred. It was a masculine feeling.

Of her part in *Of Human Bondage*: "My family was scared to death because it was such a departure. Ham was very upset and thought it might hurt my career. My mother, Ruthie, was aghast that I knew how to play Mildred." Top: LESTER GLASSNER COLLECTION. Bottom: C 1946 WARNER BROS. PICTURES, INC. REN. 1973 UNITED ARTISTS TELEVISION, INC.

It was the same thing with Paul Muni when we did *Bordertown.* I was being very feminine, very seductive—he reacted as Muni, the man. In the scenes when I was domineering, there was a certain look in his eye that said, 'If you don't behave, I'm going to slap you silly.' But Leslie had to look at me adoringly, no matter what I did.

"I went to Pandro S. Berman, the producer, and said: 'We've got a perfectly good makeup man on the picture, but his job is to make me look dreamy. He'll put a couple of lines under my eyes when I'm supposed to be sick—and that will be the end of that. I've always felt that Mildred died of a social disease, although they called it 'locomotor ataxia.' I want the audience to know that Mildred is *dying.* Let me show you how I think she should look in that last scene.'

"He stared at me as if I had lost my mind, but he also realized that I was trained on the stage and knew something about makeup. He picked up the book of *Of Human Bondage,* which was on his desk. 'Maugham said Mildred looked *green,*' he said. 'Miss Davis, we've gone this far. Show me!'

"My bleached-blond hair—which I wanted to look strawlike, because illness takes away body from hair—contrasted with the makeup that I used to show Mildred's deterioration. When I showed Berman and Cromwell the result, they absolutely *recoiled.* I was thrilled. He exchanged glances with Berman. 'Miss Davis,' he said, 'if you are willing to look like that on the screen, we're behind you one hundred percent.'

"When we came to do the scene, Leslie took one look at me, smiled slowly, and said, *'Damn!'*

"That one word was worth thousands. He had his clubfoot, and I had my locomotor ataxia! It was an even match and he knew it. After that it wasn't too difficult for him to interact with me in our scenes together. I made him love me and loathe me at the same time. If he was going for pathos, I was going for the jugular.

"Mildred was a complete shock to Hollywood, because they really hadn't seen me act before. Neither had anyone at Warners. After the picture came out, certain directors at the studio, with whom I'd worked, avoided me; others like William Dieterle, who had directed me in *Fog over Frisco,* treated me differently." She grinned suddenly. "Not as an equal, mind you—directors never treat actors as equals—but more respectfully."

[Mordaunt Hall, in *The New York Times,* June 29, 1934, wrote:

At the first showing yesterday of this picture, the audience was so wrought up over the conduct of this vixen that when Carey finally expressed his contempt for Mildred's behavior, applause was heard from all sides. There was further outburst of applause when the film came to an end.]

"If Mildred was a bitch," I said, "how about Rosa Moline in *Beyond the Forest?*"

Bette shrugged indifferently. "Edith Head made me look blowsy in that one. I didn't even wear a bra, but in 1949 I was too old to look sexy."

"Although the critics hated it," I said, "I liked the ending, where Rosa, dying of lockjaw, crawls out of her sickbed and, in delirium, smears on makeup and lurches down to the railroad station to catch the train to Chicago."

"You *liked* that?" She was incredulous. "One review said that I was a 'truck driver's dream,' whatever that meant! That last scene was hellish to do. That was the worst I'd ever looked on the screen up to that time—since the ending of *Bondage* when Mildred died."

She paused and took a sip of scotch. *"Forest* came along at a bad period of my life. My career was going downhill. I hated Warners at that point, but I was nuts to do the role anyway, looking back. Initially, I thought Rosa Moline would be a challenge. I hadn't played a bitch in years. Also, I was fighting with Sherry, whom I was married to at the time, and that didn't help my disposition on the picture. But, if they had cast the role of the husband with someone like Eugene Pallette—who played my big, fat slob-of-a-husband in *Bordertown*—it might have been logical for me to run away to Chicago to get away from him. I was forty; Eugene was sixty—about the right age.

"But Warners felt it had to use people in my own age group, so they borrowed Joe Cotten for my husband. David Brian was already under contract for the rich guy. This thing about age can throw an entire picture off. Many times a story has been ruined because, if they sign a star over forty when the plot deals with someone who's thirty, then everyone else in the picture has to be cast with fortyish actors, too. It throws the whole thing off.

"Rosa Moline certainly wouldn't have stayed with her husband all those years if she was dying to get to Chicago—that would have been a younger woman's dream. The picture would have worked beautifully if they had cast Virginia Mayo and Steve Cochran in the roles. They were young enough to pull it off.

"I thought that King Vidor would help the picture; he'd just directed *The Fountainhead*. But we didn't get along too well. Maybe it was because I was so unhappy and raised so much hell; I don't know. He had one magnificent touch—which for once I think Max Steiner overdid, musicwise—and that was using the symbol of the train as my lover. That, and those belching smokestacks in the background, showing my unhappiness was good.

"But dear Max, he knew how to compose for me. He certainly helped me get an Oscar nomination for *Voyager*. For years every time I went into a nightclub, the orchestra leader would play the theme song, 'It Can't Be Wrong,' from that picture. It was fun at first, and then it got to be too much." She laughed at the memory.

Then, since I had an early flight, Vik took me to the station in time for me to catch the ten-o'clock plane back to Los Angeles.

I left Bette in the front yard, waving a white silk handkerchief, then as I looked back, she walked into the shadows of the driveway—just as she had disappeared down the dark street in the ending shot of *Deception*.

Chapter 5

*I*t was cold and windy two weeks later, when I got off the plane at Kennedy Airport. I was twelfth in line to register at the Plaza Hotel, when the manager brought me a telephone with a long cord. "Bette Davis!" he said, in the loudest stage whisper that I'd ever heard. In order not to miss a word, my neighbors leaned forward en masse, and the queue became as cockeyed as the Leaning Tower of Pisa.

"Hi love, how long are you going to be in town?" Bette asked.

Conscious that ten pairs of ears were listening to every word, I replied carefully, "I've got to go over some photographs for the book with Neyland."

"That young man is really our midwife, isn't he?"

I laughed, but the term stuck. "I had planned to go back on Saturday."

"What time is your flight?"

"One-thirty in the afternoon."

"Why don't you come up Friday for dinner and stay all night? There's good limousine service from Westport to the airport. I need company." She expostulated, "I haven't seen a soul, except Vik, since I got back from Hollywood. It's snowing and the streets are like glass."

"In that case, let me take a cab."

*   *   *

Unbelievably, the manuscript of *Mother Goddam* had been rejected by twelve publishing houses before we found the right editor at Hawthorn Books. A thirty-two-year-old Texan, James Neyland had a solid background in editing both fiction and nonfiction, but he was especially fond of Hollywood books. His mammoth editing job on Frank Capra's *The Name Above the Title,* published by Macmillan, had scooted it onto the best-seller lists.

When our book was first brought up in conference, all the editors glanced away, except Jim. "Look," he said, "let this be my 'hunch book' for 1974." Editors in those days were allowed one book each year that particularly appealed to them. "And as far as differentiating who is speaking, we'll use black ink for Mr. Stine and another red ink for Miss Davis."

"That's what Bette has wanted all along," I chortled when he gave me the news. "You know that a reviewer somewhere along the line will make a comment like: 'Jesus Christ and Bette Davis use the same red ink.'"

The Westport station was cheerless even in the height of summer foliage, but in winter was bleak, forlorn, and snowy enough to suit Charles Dickens. And, thinking about the analogy, I just might be visiting Little Nell.

When the cab turned into the driveway, Bette rushed out to meet me. She had thrown a navy-blue cape over her shoulders, circa 1945 Hollywood Canteen, decorated with hundreds of shoulder patches from her beloved World War II GIs. She wore a blond wig, lipstick, and blue eye shadow. I kissed her cheek and she beamed, then gestured at the white-covered trees. "Isn't this just like a Currier and Ives print? God, I love New England and I hate Hollywood!"

Inside the house, she gaily swirled off the cape in a burlesque of a mannequin in a fashion show, to reveal a deep-red dress with sparkling buttons. "My one and only Valentino!" she exclaimed, then placed a waiting bourbon and 7up in my hand. "The sun has gone over the yardarm." She winked.

"I've seen photographs of you wearing that cape," I said.

A tender expression crossed her face. "All of my memories of the Canteen are wrapped up in it," she said wistfully. "I'm very proud of those war years. When John Garfield and I opened the Canteen on

Cahuenga Boulevard, the town really needed a place for servicemen. The boys never had any money, and they wanted to see movie stars. For some of them it was their last leave before going overseas. They all knew they might be killed the next week."

She sighed. "I have a funny story about the Canteen. Just before it opened, I was sweeping the floor, and a soldier peeked into the room. 'Aren't you Bette Davis?' he asked, and when I smiled and said yes, he said, 'Well, your pictures sure stink, but you're all sweetness and light, now!' It broke me up!"

She chortled. "He called me Bett. I've had to live with that all my life. I used to tell people that it was pronounced *Betty*, but I don't bother anymore."

"I don't know how you did it, Bette," I said, "running the Canteen, and going on war-bond tours, and making pictures, and keeping a marriage going—all at the same time."

"Thank god I had energy and still have," she cried exuberantly. "But I was young and feisty as hell. It was hard work, but rewarding. The look in those servicemen's eyes was all the reward I needed. After Farney died, I'd have gone mad without the Canteen to keep me busy."

"That must have been a low point in your life."

She sipped scotch while waiting for the main course to finish in the oven. She had set a small table before the fire, complete with finger bowls in which tiny, dried winter flowers were floating.

"It would have been if I'd let it. But there was one man who saved my life." She glanced at me quickly. "Hell, I don't mind telling you. I could have met him nowhere else. Johnny Mercer was a couple of years older, and not much taller than I. He was a delightful guy with a wonderful sense of humor, and very different—both physically and mentally—from the other men in my life.

"I loved his songs, especially 'Chattanooga Choo Choo' and 'Blues in the Night'—which I used to sing occasionally with Kay Kyser's band at the Canteen. Johnny was working at Paramount, and of course, I was at Warners. Our affair was passionate and intense, and we kept it very quiet.

"One night he asked me what my greatest fantasy was, and I told him it was being made love to on a blanket of gardenias. We had a good laugh. Some months later we scheduled a meeting in New York. He was performing there, and I was on my way to Butternut. Johnny had engaged a suite at the Waldorf-Astoria, and I came up the back way in the service elevator—like Hepburn used to do in London when visiting Tracy—and what do you know? Johnny had covered the bed with gardenias! It was really the epitome. Never again did I think about that particular fantasy—because we acted it out!"

"Bette, did you quarrel, is that how it ended?"

"No." She shrugged. "These hot affairs always burn themselves out. Plus, we were so busy with our careers we couldn't spend much time together—which also prolonged the relationship, I suppose, because of that wonderful sense of anticipation. Later, we'd see each other at industry affairs, and he'd always smile and wink at me.

"One wonderful thing happened, though; he wrote 'And the Angels Sing' for me. It was on the Hit Parade in 1944 for a long, long time. I still think of him when I see gardenias." She paused and her voice grew husky. "I was watching television one night with friends when it flashed on that he had died, and I had to get up for a moment and be by myself."

Bette went into the kitchen, and I had the feeling I should change the subject when she returned with our plates of food.

[In 1983, when Bette was writing *This 'n That,* the sequel to *The Lonely Life,* she included the Johnny Mercer/gardenia incident, but left out his name. The beautiful Kathryn Sermak, her woman Friday, was so intrigued with the romantic angle of the story, that one night when Bette came in to bathe before going to bed, she found dozens of gardenias floating on top of the water, and a bottle of iced champagne. Bette screamed with laughter, and Kath took a Polaroid snap of her employer, luxuriating among the flowers.]

"The entrée looks magnificent," I said as Bette came in from the kitchen. "An old family recipe?"

"Hah!" she scoffed. "This fish dish I found about twenty years ago in a newspaper. That's where I get all of my 'famous' recipes. It's very simple. You just have good portions of fish for two people which you put into a greased flat casserole. In a bowl you mix one cup of grated cheddar cheese, an undiluted can of cream-of-mushroom soup, and a cup of very good dry sherry. It looks rather messy, but spread the mixture on the fish and place the casserole in a 350-degree oven for about twenty minutes or so until it is brown and bubbly. Always serve it with sourdough toast, so you can sop up the gravy, and a little side dish of peas. A salad and fresh fruit, like we're having tonight, is all that's needed to go with it."

[I have served Bette Davis's fish dish many times. It is simple and elegant, and wholly American. I gave up trying to cook in the Continental style after a painstakingly prepared main course went awry. Film historian Lotte Eisner, of the Cinémathèque Française, was in town researching a book on director Fritz Lang. She was staying with Fritz and his lifelong companion, Lily Latte, on Summitridge Drive above Pickfair in Beverly Hills, and driving them up the wall talking— and sometimes writing—in three languages. I took Lotte, who could be entertaining in small doses, off their hands for an evening and cooked her a meal. She lifted a generous portion of the entrée, dripping in rich sauce, to her mouth. "Theese is so goood," she trilled in her continental accent. "Vat is theese deesh, Vhitney?" I figured that if Lotte Eisner didn't recognize coq au vin, I should give up. "Oh," I went on as casually as I could, "just an old timey Oklahoma recipe!"]

"You're a wonderful cook," I said.

"Thank you!" She beamed. "Actually, I'm a newcomer to the kitchen. I'll give you some recipes if you like."

Bette cleared away the dishes. "A man's place is not in the kitchen, unless," she was fond of saying, "of course, it's his own." We sat before the fire in an introspective mood, which was heightened by the icicles falling off the roof, the result of a warm wind.

Bette looked up suddenly and told me I was a 'smashing guy.'

I was always embarrassed by her compliments. "I can afford to be nice," I replied lightly, "because when I'm writing a novel, I'm able to murder and rape and pillage and express all of the emotions of my characters on paper. When I get up from my typewriter, I'm spent. It's just as if I had participated in an orgy."

She grinned. "I know what you mean. If my husbands thought I was a holy terror at home, what would I have been if I hadn't used my feelings to play all those characters at work? That's why now I feel so unfulfilled. The parts I'm offered don't give me a Chinaman's chance to use a tenth of what's inside.

"The last role outside of *Baby Jane* that took some gumption was *The Catered Affair*. Everyone ignored it, yet it's one of my favorites. They loved it in England.

"Richard Brooks, the director, was absolutely astounded when he saw me made up as Aggie. I was fat then, weighed about a hundred and thirty, and my clothes were off the rack at Sears. He said I looked exactly like his mama!

"When I was young," Bette continued quietly, "and Ruthie and I were living in New York, I used to see women like Agnes Hurley, hanging wash out the windows and pinching vegetables in markets. I knew just how to play her."

Bette poked around in the fireplace, and then presented a bombshell. "Why don't we get married?" she asked matter-of-factly, not looking at me. She went on hurriedly, "I would keep this house here and you could keep your place in California. We could be together when we wanted and apart when we wanted. We're so compatible. This would be a good setup, don't you think?"

At that moment, Vik came in the back door. "Where is that manuscript I was supposed to read?" he asked.

Bette helped him search while I recovered my composure. I loved her very much, but the thought of marriage had never crossed my mind. Mentally I had placed her, as with the wives and lovers of all my friends, safely out of bounds in neutral territory.

It was not only the fact that she was twenty-two years older than I, but my life had been set in a disciplined pattern for years. Now at the age of forty-two, barely on the threshold of a late-blooming career, I either had to achieve my goal of being actively published or go back to ghostwriting.

I understood Bette extremely well and her vicissitudes did not bother me in the least. Her moods, which could swing from the height of gaiety to extreme anger and often left others feeling helpless, were merely amusing to me. I knew when and when not to take her seriously.

It was not so much that I would become "Mr. Bette Davis," a term that had continually bothered her husbands, because her career was at a low ebb. There was the possibility that she might never make another picture. But I had no desire to become the stepfather of B.D. and Mike, nor did I want the publicity that would surround such a relationship. Money matters did not enter the picture, because at this point in time, I had more than she did.

Also, selfishly, I could not envision Bette Davis tiptoeing into my writing room with a cup of coffee at dawn or becoming the sort of nurturing partner that my career demanded. This role, I was certain, she would play to the hilt for a time, a role that she would grow to hate—especially if her own career had faltered to the point where she could not find work. She could not be expected to be content to cater solely to a younger husband. The furies would rage, and our relationship would go up in smoke: Exit Husband Number Five.

Later when Vik learned that Bette and I were going to tour with *Mother Goddam,* he casually mentioned that he would "teach me to pack." I was not overwhelmed. I had no intention of packing for Miss Bette Davis.

After Bette found the manuscript, which Vik took to his apartment over the garage, she freshened our coffee and rejoined me by the fire. I took her hand. "Bette," I said, "if I had met you in 1945 as a published writer and was the age that I am now, and you were the age you were then, we might have had a chance. I do love you very much, but everything in the world is against us now."

She squeezed my hand and sighed, "You're right, of course. It's just that we're so perfect in so many ways." Tears came into her eyes. "What are we going to do?"

"Why can't we go on the same way?"

"All right," she said with finality, and went into the kitchen to make another pot of coffee. When she returned, she was smiling, and I knew that she was not going to dwell on our previous conversation. "One thing about the book which we haven't discussed and ought to," she said evenly, "is our names on the cover . . ."

I broke in quickly. "I think . . ."

She waved a pot holder at me. "There is only one way that our names should appear. You wrote the book. Your name comes first. I won't have it any other way, and no 'and' separating our names, either! After your name could come something like, 'with a running commentary by Bette Davis.'"

I grinned, and flushed. "I can't bitch about that!" I laughed. "It's been a long time since you took second billing to anyone."

As I stood at the end of the driveway the next morning waiting for Vik to bring the car, I looked back. Her form was again silhouetted by the screen door. She waved. "Come back to me," she called.

I waved and promised I would.

When I returned home, I found an autographed picture in the mailbox. Bette had written:

To Whitney, my alter ego.
Love,
Bette

Lord knows, Bette Davis was intelligent; she had the kind of brain that came out to meet you, but she could be curiously closed-minded. Once she had formed an opinion, even a snap judgment, it was very difficult to change her view. Perhaps it was the result of learning all those pages of dialogue for fifty-odd years. She always memorized scripts from first page to last. Once something was set in her mind, it was like stone.

But aside from changes of dialogue on the set, which always upset her, she was most malleable as to the actual playing of scenes. Once she had worked out what she wanted to do, a director's pertinent suggestions on new bits of business were always met with enthusiasm. She'd been around so long, there was not much new territory. She would try anything if she had confidence in the director, but he'd better have a good reason for what he wanted, because she would wear him down, point by point, until he threw up his hands and let her have her way, sometimes to the detriment of the scene. Her favorite question was, "Why?"

She could be overbearing, and in certain instances liked to throw her weight around, especially if she found injustice being done to actor or crew member. For instance: Gordon Hessler, the director of the television movie, *Scream, Pretty Peggy*, which Bette made in the spring of 1973, insisted that the script be filmed in continuity. This proved to be a trial for technicians and crew.

Since the picture was shot all on location at the old Noah Dietrich mansion above Sunset Strip, the heavy cameras, lights, and other equipment had to be continually lugged upstairs and downstairs and into the gardens. "The production is running needlessly behind schedule," Bette complained on the phone. "Why can't Hessler shoot all of our scenes that take place in the same room, and then go on to the next location like we usually do?"

Universal wanted Bette as marquee lure for this poorly written effort, a trifling thing with overtones of *Psycho*, and offered her the paltry sum of fifteen thousand dollars for the small role of the alcoholic mother with a disturbed transvestite son. But Bette had not worked in a year, and no money was coming in, and the studio gave important concessions.

Part of the agreement was that (1) She could only be required to work from ten in the morning to two in the afternoon, (2) She would be picked up and returned home via limousine, (3) A luxurious Winnebago would be placed at her disposal for a dressing room, (4) Peggy Shannon would dress her wigs, and (5) Gene Hibbs would create her makeup, using "lifts" to smooth out her face and neck.

Hibbs was probably the most expensive free-lancer in Hollywood. The studio gave him the usual union pay scale, and paid him an extra hundred dollars a day for his "makeup box." Hibbs was much in demand, doing makeup for aging actresses on television talk shows. It was good money and he only had to work two hours. He told me once: "Whenever you see an actress over forty who has her ears covered on a talk show, you damn well know that she's wearing "lifts," either mine or someone else's."

Peggy was a tall, redheaded woman with a nice sense of humor, who always called Bette "Miss Davis." She had worked with Joan Crawford for years and knew all about the famous Aries temperament. She found an upswept, blond wig for Bette in *Scream, Pretty Peggy*. The wardrobe for the picture was simple. The character only appeared in expensive nightgowns.

Producer Lou Morheim had assembled a cast that included Barbara Allen and Charles Drake, who had played the young Charlotte Vale's unfortunate boyfriend, Lieutenant Trotter in *Now, Voyager*. (Bette did not recognize him at first.) These actors who worked mainly in television were accustomed to fast shooting. The delays made everyone edgy.

Allen, a Universal contract player, was interesting, but not beautiful, with long, stringy black hair. Bette drew her aside one morning and said: "The studio is not treating you right, my dear," and pushed her hair back from her face. "You've got good bone structure and nice eyes, but your makeup doesn't do anything for you, and they should dress your hair differently. You've got to put up a fight for these things. It's too late to do anything on this picture, but on your next one raise a little hell. You've got to be distinctive!"

Bette and Vik were staying in Melrose with antique dealer Chuck Pollock. Bette liked Chuck. He was intelligent, fun to be around, and a fabulous gourmet cook. My Okie/French dishes paled in comparison to his international cuisine.

With the delays, Hessler kept Bette late one night for a bed scene, which for one reason or another had to be shot several times. Bette was tired, hungry, and in need of a drink. Finally she screamed at him: "If I didn't have a son in college and other responsibilities, I wouldn't be appearing in this crap!"

The next day, I was on the set after lunch. Bette had to fire a gun and was scared. "That damned thing makes me nervous," she said to Hessler, "can't we dub in the sound of it going off?" He agreed.

She was laughing and joking, and then just before the start of the scene she looked down a moment. When she looked up there was a kind of life in her eyes. She did the scene in one take. Her last scene took place on the staircase with Allen, and once again she looked down just before the camera turned. I discovered this was the way that Bette always prepared herself for filming, the closest she ever came to Lee Strasberg's "Method."

After a few more takes, Hessler ordered, "Print it." Bette motioned for Peggy, Gene, her stand-in, and me to follow her. We all knew something special was going to take place. The perspiring crew had just brought the camera equipment into the upper hall for the umpteenth time, and we four, led by Bette, marched up the long staircase to Hessler, who was setting up the next scene. As we trooped by, Hessler whistled, then whispered, "What an entourage!"

Bette held out an oblong box to the director. "For you, sir," she said with an icy smile.

Hessler opened the box and pulled out a twelve-foot-long cat-o'-nine-tails.

"Slave driver!" Bette announced quietly before we all withdrew.

Hessler was not amused, but everyone on the set applauded.

I escorted Bette to the Winnebago, where she had a "luncheon" of yogurt. "I never, ever, take a drink on the set," she said, as if reading my mind. "I have memories of Errol Flynn and Ann Sheridan drinking vodka in their dressing rooms at Warners. When I was doing *Two's Company* on Broadway and Sheridan came backstage, I scarcely recognized her. It was all that booze over the years."

[Bette was very upset when B.D., in her 1985 book, related that her son Ashley had said that Bette drank on the set of *Family Reunion*. "It was simply not so!" she said tearfully.]

Before Bette left Chuck's house for Twin Bridges, I asked her advice about the back-cover photograph for the book. "How long has it been since you've seen George Hurrell?"

"About thirty years, but we exchange Christmas cards."

"Wouldn't it be great if he could take the shot of us for the book?"

"Fantastic idea!" she said, and telephoned him at once. An appointment was arranged.

I had admired Hurrell ever since, as a boy, I slipped into the doctor's office in Garber every month to look at *Esquire* magazine. The medic was the only person in our small, rural town who could afford to subscribe to that expensive magazine in the 1930s. I wasn't drawn to the naughty Caliph and his bevy of beauties, but I *was* fascinated by the two-page spreads of Hurrell's movie-star photographs. I became such a connoisseur, I could recognize his work at a glance.

When it came time for the book-jacket photo session, seventy-year-old Hurrell set up his lights in Chuck's kitchen because the living room was not yet finished. I had expected the great man to be a granitelike stone god, but he was relaxed and funny and whistled between his teeth.

Gene Hibbs and Peggy Shannon had performed their jobs flawlessly; Bette looked wonderful. Vik brought a bunch of fresh violets, which I pinned to Bette's black sweater. Vik and Bette were exchanging rather bitter sallies, picking at each other, and I thought to myself, *His days are numbered.*

And in fact, he would shortly leave her employ. He had been with her for seven years and frankly admitted that he missed a private life. Along with all of the obvious perks of his job, it must have been difficult to be constantly in the presence of a supercharged woman who could wax enthusiastic one moment and throw a tantrum the next.

Bette turned on the radio. "We must have music," she said. "Hurrell always works with music."

Fountain pens in hand, with the manuscript spread out before us on the kitchen table, Hurrell took the photographs.

[This was the beginning of a great friendship between myself and Hurrell, and eventually led to the publication of a book, *The Hurrell*

Style. When Bette saw the proofs, she called me. "You're going to do for George what Joe Mankiewicz did for me in *All About Eve.* You're going to raise him from the dead!"

[Within a few years, and perhaps in part because of the book, Hurrell was shooting again: a double spread of Brooke Shields for *Life,* Joan Collins for *Playboy,* and fashion layouts for *Paris-Match.*]

Chapter 6

*B*ette fixed drinks after Hurrell left, and we went outside and
sat in the sun beside the pool. "Aren't you going to take off
your makeup?" I asked.

"Nah," she said, "I'm going to the Henreids' tonight."
She lowered her voice a notch and went on in a thick, Austrian accent.
"Vor dinnair and I mitt hass vell leave von my 'straps.'"

I laughed. "Where did you get that accent?"

"Lisl, Paul's wife; she's an interesting dame. Helped Paul at the
beginning of his career. You know, he always wanted to direct, even
when he studied with Max Reinhardt in Vienna." She paused. "He's
damn good. We had a ball doing *Dead Ringer*, with all of that
split-screen stuff."

"Since you had already played twins in *A Stolen Life*, what was the
difference between them and the twins in *Dead Ringer?*"

Bette threw back her head and laughed. "About twenty years!"

James Powers, in *The Hollywood Reporter*, January 23, 1964,
wrote:

> Miss Davis is careful not to overdo the roles. She is simple
> and credible in both parts without making sharp or superficial
> distinction between the characters.

* * *

"No, seriously, Whitney, the best thing about the picture was that it was shot at Warners. That was the thrill. Jack Warner inviting me back home after being away for fifteen years. Then too, with Paul directing me—and he was coming back to Warners where he had been a star—well, it just worked. Good sets, good costumes, Ernie Haller to photograph me, Gene Hibbs to do my makeup, and an eight-week shooting schedule. Playing the twins was not all that difficult, except when I had to do both roles for the same scene; that was murder."

"I liked the fact that they cast Karl Malden as your boyfriend," I put in.

"And Peter Lawford. I wasn't a kid—fifty-six is not a kid—so it helped to have Karl; he was rugged and right. Peter was the international playboy, so he was right, too. My only beef about the picture was that the twin who killed the other one has to be taken into custody at the end. That was too spelled-out, phony. As it was originally, the audience knows she is going to be caught, but we had to change it. That damn censorship. It spoiled so many films!

"However, one of the things that bothered me was that when the film was released a lot of theaters booked Joan Crawford's *Strait-Jacket* as the companion feature. I thought that was tacky."

"At least you got top billing!" I rejoined. "By the way, Bette, do you realize that *Dead Ringer* was the last film where you had hot love scenes?"

She waved a cigarette. "By god, you're right! I hadn't thought about that." She sighed. "Well, it just goes to show you that I would have been finished years ago if I had only appeared in romances. In a way, I've been blessed. There were many pictures where I never got kissed at all! For instance, in *All This and Heaven Too*, with the great Boyer, and not even a peck on the cheek!"

Bette took me by the hand and pointed out a framed shot on the bedroom wall that Hurrell had taken of her during the *Dark Victory* shooting, one that I had never seen before. An extreme close-up, her face registered pain. "It is the most revealing portrait ever taken of me," Bette whispered. "Look at the eyes! I was in agony that day, scared to death that my career was over. That was the morning Ham had told me he had placed a recording device under the bed where Howard Hughes and I had made love, and he planned to tell the world."

Bette seemed mellow, so I decided to ask a question that had bothered me for years. "Don't you think that one reason RKO offered to put up the money for *Payment on Demand* in 1950, after *Beyond the Forest* was such a bomb, was because of what you once meant to Howard Hughes, who had just bought the studio?"

She squinted at me. "I never thought of that," she replied. "Do you suppose he was paying me back?" She lighted a cigarette. "Bruce Manning and Curt Bernhardt wrote the script, and it was commercial. I've had a block about Hughes for years; maybe he did have a soft spot for me. After we broke up it took a while for me to admit to myself that I was only one of the many Hollywood dames he'd slept with, and that was a blow to my ego. While we were going together I thought I was special, and maybe I was. I don't know.

"I only saw Hughes once after our affair ended, and he was anything but soft then. In fact he was a bastard. He changed the original title of *The Story of a Divorce* to *Payment on Demand*, which was ironic. I wonder if my personal life had anything to do with *that*, because 'payment on demand' was how I finally disposed of Sherry when we divorced.

"The original finish showed the couple back together after their divorce. This bitch, Joyce, is starting the miserable carping again at the breakfast table. She's still the same social-climbing shrew. Women like that never change. In Hughes's ending, Joyce turns the tables on her divorced husband, whom she's taken for every penny. He wants to come back and she indicates she possibly might let him.

"You had this in your book, Whitney. What you didn't know was that I went to Hughes before we shot the new ending to plead my case. He was living in a bungalow at the Beverly Hills Hotel—ironically, where we'd first met in 1940 at the Tailwaggers charity ball.

"He had changed physically so much in that ten years. He looked unkempt. He had a scowl on his face. His eyes shifted around all the time we talked. He didn't look at me directly. I was furious. He was using the same technique I had used on Jack Warner so many times during our confrontations.

"Hughes was flanked by two bodyguards. I couldn't believe that this was the same man I had once loved. While I stated my case he glowered at me and barked: 'A woman will do anything for a lay!' And I almost retorted, 'Is that all I meant to you?' But his henchmen were there, and I kept my silence."

[A strange coincidence occurred when Hughes died at seventy-one on Bette's sixty-eighth birthday; April 5, 1976.]

"It was ironic . . . 'payment on demand' was how I finally disposed of Sherry when we divorced." Left: Bette and William Sherry leaving the church on their wedding day. WHITNEY STINE COLLECTION. Right: Bette with her L.A. and Mexican attorneys after she signed the petition for divorce from Sherry, 1950. AP/WIDE WORLD PHOTOS

She lighted a cigarette and blew the smoke to the ceiling. "If he did give me the chance for a comeback, which you think he did, he was really being perverse, because he had the last word by ruining the true ending to the story!"

Bette was on the telephone, her voice a full octave higher than usual. "I really feel up today," she cried. "I may do the film of *Mame*, if Lucille Ball will have me. I'll play Vera Charles, the actress. The role is short, but I'd get to sing 'Bosom Buddies' with Lucy, which has to be a knockout."

Bette sang a chorus of the song in full, rhythmic voice, then took a deep breath and plunged on. "Also I may do the role of the psychiatrist in *I Never Promised You a Rose Garden*. I'll play her in horn-rimmed spectacles and a short, butch-type wig. Two roles as opposite as you can get."

She paused and then let out a whoop. "Oh, there is something else. Guess who telephoned yesterday? When I answered, there was this whispery voice, and I said, 'Elizabeth Taylor!' She was houseguesting with Edith Head, who now owns Casa Ladera, the house I rented in Coldwater Canyon in the thirties. She wants me to do the part of an old lady in *Driver's Seat*, to be filmed in Europe. When I asked her to send along the script, she said they didn't have one yet, but they were going to start shooting in a few weeks. I said, 'My dear, I must have a script.' I've heard that it's the latest thing to improvise, but I won't."

But Bette was not destined to perform in these films. Beatrice Arthur, who had played Charles on Broadway, made the film with Ball; Mona Washbourne played the old lady with Taylor. Bette flew to Chicago to accept the Sarah Siddons Award on May 14. Ironically, the award had been inspired by the nonexistent "Sarah Siddons Trophy" presented to Anne Baxter by Walter Hampden in *All About Eve*.

When Bette, wearing a white dress, was introduced, the curtains swept back and Anne Baxter appeared to present the award. "I made an absolute fool of myself," Bette told me later. "Anne went on and on about me and I cried. It was the first time that I've ever broken down in public."

Bette's son, Mike, and Chou Chou Rains were married on May 19, 1973, in Westport, and Gary Merrill flew in for the wedding. When I asked Bette about the nuptials, she raised her eyebrows. "Gary and I were on our very best behavior. He was very gallant, and no one, positively no one, can be as gallant as Gary when he wants to be! And I should damn well know!

"Anyone seeing us together would never have guessed that we had been divorced for thirteen years. Whitney, I seem to keep reenacting scenes from my movies. It was very similar to my daughter's wedding in *Payment on Demand* with her divorced parents showing up!

"Mike has always been Gary's pride and joy. And funnily enough, the whole wedding had a déjà vu effect. At times, it even seemed to me that Gary and I were still married. The only thing was that I found there was absolutely no feeling left for him, one way or another. I certainly didn't hate him, but there wasn't any closeness, either. He was like a stranger. During the ceremony I tried to go back over those years and make sense out of it; I couldn't.

"But we were in the prime of life when we married. Plus, while we did have enormous battles, we had good times, too. And until the magic of being together wore off, as it always does, we had it made. Then Gary began to drink too much; whether it was boredom—neither of us worked much—or me, or the fact that he really should have remained single, I don't know.

"I tried to hide his drinking from the children, but it got to be too much. One time when we were having a clambake for friends, Gary staggered up the lawn two hours late to his own party. Michael asked, 'What's wrong with Daddy?' At that point I had had it with Gary's behavior, and I said, 'He's drunk.' Looking back, maybe I shouldn't have said that, but I was near the breaking point. I just hope that Mike and Chou Chou won't fall into the same traps that we did."

After Mike's marriage, Bette planned to lease Twin Bridges. "There is simply no money," she said when I spent the weekend as her houseguest. "My sister, Bobby, has flipped her wig again and is in the hospital in Phoenix. As usual, it will cost me a fortune!"

"Let's hope a good script turns up," I said. "It's a crime that you're not working."

She laughed hollowly. "Yes, but who knows if I'm box-office? If the money men won't cast me in a good picture, how can I prove myself? But I do have time to tour with you on the book; that's important, too."

"Bette, don't think that I'm not appreciative . . ."

She ignored my statement. "It's a collaboration. I don't want to sit

"We were in the prime of life when we married. . . . Until the magic of being together wore off, as it always does, we had it made. Then Gary began to drink too much." Top: Gary and Bette out on the town. LESTER GLASSNER COLLECTION. Bottom: Gary, Margot, Bette, and B.D. in Malibu, 1951. AP/WIDE WORLD PHOTOS

here at home doing nothing and drinking more than is good for me. I'm proud of my career and I'm proud of the book, and I'll do anything I can to promote it."

She turned out the light beside the sofa. "I'm very tired," she said. "You always make me tired, because we talk so god-damned much and it's hell remembering—usually."

"Will you move back to the Coast, Bette?"

She shook her head violently. "All that relentless sunshine! No, a friend of mine has found a rental for me in nearby Weston, on River Road, on another branch of the Saugatuck. I'm getting it for five hundred a month!

"The owner nearly had a heart attack when he found out I was going to live there. If I had rented it myself he would have charged at least another two hundred and fifty a month! It's made of stone and clapboard and it's small and cozy, just what I need at this point in my life. I'm going to call it My Bailiwick."

She shivered. "I've been putting it off—you know how we Aries procrastinate on things we don't like to do—but I must have a meeting with Harold Schiff. I haven't made any money in such a long time that he must be paying my bills out of his own pocket!"

She telephoned on February 12, 1973, her voice filled with awe. She had just given her first talk of what became a lecture series, *Bette Davis: In Person and on Film.* "You should have been with me last night at Town Hall. You'd have to see it to believe it! I'm flying a mile high today. The film clips from my career that John Springer chose are perfect. And that audience! My god, you would have thought it was the second coming of Christ! Goodness knows I'm used to fans, but this scene was incredible—a packed house and those who couldn't get tickets were screaming to get in! And I thought there would be mainly middle-aged types and gay people, who have always supported me. I suppose there were those contingents there, but the majority were young people on dates!

"Whitney, I don't know what came over me. I answered all those questions without a moment's hesitation. It was like I was one step ahead of them. One thing that helps is the fact that you know what the question is going to be after they have the first words out. When I was asked to do this program, I thought it would be hell. It wasn't. It was fun. I had a ball.

"One woman thought it was terrible to be a grandmother. She was a grandmother, and that was all right, but not Bette Davis. The crowd wanted to know all sorts of things, I suppose you'd call them trivia. One little chap, who could have been no more than ten, stood up like a soldier and chirped, 'All my life I've wanted to be Bette Davis.' I almost cried.

"But the whole evening came into focus later when a man stood up and said, 'I want you to know that everything I know about acting and directing, I learned from watching you act.'" She took a deep breath. "I nearly fainted. It was the great director, Jose Quintero. What he and Colleen Dewhurst did with *Moon for the Misbegotten* was absolute magic."

Bette's voice caught. "The show was so successful that we're thinking of taking it on the road!"

"Won't that be rough?"

"Of course it will be rough," she replied impatiently. "But Gary and I got *so* much out of the Carl Sandburg tour, reaching people we never could have otherwise. Of course, that was different, Gary and me reciting Sandburg's great poems and Clark Allen singing folk songs, but the crowds were so appreciative. We could have toured forever, but we were fighting all the time, and after ten years, suddenly the marriage was over."

Her voice had grown husky, as it so often did when she spoke about Merrill. "John hopes to do other shows with Rosalind Russell, Sylvia Sidney, Lana Turner, and maybe even Joan Crawford." She giggled. "I told him if he did get her, I'd sit in the first row and knit while she was doing her question-and-answer bit!"

I laughed. "You wouldn't!"

"Oh, yes I would!" she giggled.

Bette needed this kind of uplift, because she had almost reached the point where she felt her audience had deserted her. Town Hall proved to her the opposite was true.

So was launched a lecture series that Bette grew to love, *Bette Davis: In Person and on Film*, the first successful one-woman show of its type, that would spawn many other similar shows with Hollywood stars. Much later, even Cary Grant, a very private man, took to the circuit, and in fact, collapsed and died while doing a show in Akron.

* * *

Bette was on the phone from Connecticut. "I've decided to go back to the stage," she announced quietly. I recognized the tone; she would start out low key and then build.

"But I thought after *Two's Company* folded, when you had osteomyelitis, that you'd never . . ."

"I believed it then. But," the voice rose, "this is a musical version of *The Corn Is Green*. Hell, I was only thirty-seven when I did the picture, too young. Now that I'm in the same ballpark agewise as *Miss Moffat,* I can do a much better job. You see, when you reach my age, you think about the mistakes you made. I never should have gone to Hollywood so young. I should have stayed in New York. Good parts were coming up, and if I had built a better name, and say, come to the Coast in 1934 or 1935, it would have been easier. I wouldn't have had to go through all those terrible pictures, trying to prove myself. But everyone was going to Hollywood then, Cagney, Blondell, so many others, and I just followed suit.

"What Emlyn Williams has done is miraculous," Bette went on. "Logan co-wrote this new version and he's going to direct. I've admired his work for years. *South Pacific* was terrific, and I loved *Mr. Roberts.* Anything he does is special. Morgan Evans is now a black field hand. It works beautifully."

Bette asked Robert Andrea, a big six-foot-three guy, head of the limousine service that she used in Manhattan, to bring Logan and Lantz to Westport, and they went to the local high school that sported a baby grand piano. Bette did not want to use the upright in her home, because it was slightly out of tune, and she felt a rehearsal hall would be more professional.

Logan remembered that while he and Lantz were attentive, Bette seemed more interested in Robert's reaction to her singing than in theirs! Logan felt that she made up for her tonal deficiencies with sheer showmanship.

"And my songs are sensational!" Bette continued. "The one that ends the show is a knockout. It's a quiet little number called, "I Shall Experience It Again"—the same line from the movie." She paused. "Moffat has sent her prize pupil off to Harvard, and she's alone. It just tears your heart out."

"When do you start rehearsing?" I asked.

"In the fall. Oh god, what a relief to do something good again. A

"Hell, I was only thirty-seven when I did *The Corn Is Green*—too young." Bette with John Dall in *Corn*. C 1945 WARNER BROS. PICTURES, INC. REN. 1972 UNITED ARTISTS TELEVISION, INC.

script came in the mail the other day, where I ended up hanging by my neck in the attic! Those kinds of parts are all that's offered to me for movies. But after the Broadway run of *Moffat*, we film it," she said triumphantly. *"Miss Moffat* rides again!"

"I'm so pleased for you," I said.

"You know, this project is going to take years. If it goes well, and is the hit I think it will be, and the film is a success, I just might retire at seventy."

"I can't see you retiring, Bette."

"Well, you have to look at it like this. Let's face it, I've had a hell of a career. In many ways Garbo was right to retire at thirty-six. She was still gorgeous. Shearer, too, was wise to give it up at forty-two. I lasted a lot longer than they did—the glory years. I don't want to be like Ethel Barrymore, taking small parts till I die. Go out with a triumph. Good night. I love you."

"Good night. I love you."

At a party later that month I met Leonard Spigelgass, who had known Bette since 1942 when he was writing *All Through the Night* for Bogart at Warner Bros. He had seen Bette occasionally through the intervening years at Academy Awards telecasts, which he often helped to write.

When Leonard heard that Bette was going to be directed by Josh Logan, he whistled through his teeth. "Does she know him?"

"No," I answered, "but I assume that she's seen enough of his work to know that he's a great director."

Leonard nodded. "Great, yes, but he's also a manic-depressive! Four years ago he directed a musical play of mine, *Look to the Lilies,* based on the movie *The Lilies of the Field.* Sometimes he *was* marvelous, other times not so marvelous. He takes a drug called lithium, which keeps him under fair control, but if his dosage is off, he can be impossible! Just tell Bette to be very *aware.* She'll have to excuse his behavior sometimes—usually when it really gets tense. She'll need a clearer head around." He raised his eyebrows. "From what I know of Bette, he'll have to excuse her a *great deal.*"

"What do you mean?"

"You're her friend. You know she can be difficult."

"It's all attitude," I replied defensively.

"Attitude? Bette sometimes has to create turmoil. It's my opinion that her energy feeds off it. She's explosive because she *needs* fire around her."

I shook my head. "I know she has this reputation," I countered, "but I think it's because people don't know how to treat her, and they rub her the wrong way. It's a mistake to take her too seriously all the time. It's important to let her know how far she can go."

"Perhaps she's grown mellow in her old age," Leonard conceded, "but when I was at Warners, she could be hell to deal with. She almost drove Irving Rapper crazy on *Now, Voyager* and *Deception,* and he was a fine director."

When I passed on the information about Logan and his lithium to Bette, she said, "Thank Lenny for the tip."

Chapter 7

*B*ette was on the telephone from Connecticut. "Springer is going to take our clip-and-talk show on the road for a few performances. Maybe visiting some of the college towns like Gary and I did with *Sandburg*. Then, if this goes well, we'll take it all over the country. But it's frightening to expect people to pay good money to see old film clips and me answering questions. What if no one shows up, or so few that it's embarrassing?"

I assured her that I did not think that would be the case.

The last of October, when the show was booked into McCarter Hall in Princeton, Bette arrived to find a long line waiting to purchase tickets. After all 1,350 seats were sold, there were still so many fans outside that the film clips were repeatedly drowned out by their clamor. The police had to disperse the crowd.

Hugh Wheeler and John Flaxman, who wanted to film the Stephen Sondheim musical, *Follies,* came backstage to offer the Yvonne de Carlo role to Bette. "I get to sing 'I'm Still Here,' " Bette said later, "the greatest song in the show in my opinion. It's the story of my life. It could have been written for me."

Unfortunately, the musical was never filmed, but Bette learned the lyrics anyway. Her rendition was right on the mark; tough, brazen, and yet filled with pathos. It was a song that she should have recorded.

* * *

I moved into a new house in the Colfax Meadows area of Studio City and invited Bette, who was staying at Chuck Pollock's, for drinks and dinner. Vik lost his way on the country road and they arrived ten minutes late. I was waiting out front and could hear Bette screaming down the block, "No! No! It's not *this* house, that one down there!"

She calmed down when she saw me in the driveway. "Your directions are lousy!" she cried, as I kissed her cheek. "I hope the bar is open!"

I assured her that it was and fixed her scotch over ice. She wore a longish blue-and-white dress, full makeup, and her blond pageboy wig.

"You look fantastic," I said.

She gave me an impish grin. "Thank you, but I can't wait to get back to Connecticut. All you've had is rain out here this trip."

Since this was Bette's first visit to my house, she looked over everything thoroughly. My taste in furniture and decor is modern, and, of course, hers is traditional, but she studied my books and my artifacts, and finally pronounced the house livable, even charming. Before leaving she even picked a couple of lemons from a tree in the backyard.

In her usual extravagant manner, she exclaimed over the Caesar salad, pontificated on the pot roast of beef and homemade noodles, and went into ecstasy over the apple pie.

One of Bette's most endearing qualities was heaping praise on the accomplishments of others. Her friends, in favor, were always the most delightful, the most conversant, the wisest, the most talented, the best cooks . . .

Conversely, her directors were often the lousiest; the producers, the most crass; her costars, the most untalented; the script, the purest crap . . . Everything was always the best or the worst: There were never any halfway measures with Bette. Yet with all of her comments, ridiculous or profound, there was always a sprinkle of wry humor even when she was being scathing. You always knew where you stood with her.

What made B.D.'s book so devastating was the fact that, whether by design or the fact that she was not a writer, even when she was quoting her mother accurately, she failed to impart the mocking tone that pointed the conversation *up* or *down*. Half the time Bette was serious, half the time she was not, and there were all shades of gray in between. One had to gauge her true meaning at any given time.

Bette repaired her lipstick in the living-room mirror and grimaced at her image. "God, I look old!" she exclaimed. "When I was young I played all those old parts, so the public never expected me to be a sexpot. I never had to do cheesecake after about 1933. I wore swimming attire in *Golden Arrow,* because most of it was shot on a yacht, but thank god, no one remembers. It was a terrible movie. But once Warners could sell me alone in a movie, I played all those great roles. Queens and empresses and middle-aged women and crones, and then I'd do a chic part in modern dress, looking as good as I could. The female stars today don't get roles that show the range of their talent, and historical roles are out of fashion."

"What would you like to do now, if you had your choice of roles?"

She gave me a long, patronizing look, then grinned. "I still want to do *Ethan Frome,* playing the part of old Zenobia. When I was going to do it at Warners, I would have played the young girl, Mattie. I'm also the right age for Mother Goddam in *The Shanghai Gesture.* Wouldn't that be a hoot?"

I asked Bette if she would like an after-dinner drink. But before she could answer, Vik broke in, "No thank you, we never have drinks after dinner."

It was then that I knew for certain that Bette had a drinking problem.

In designing the dust jacket of *Mother Goddam,* I assembled a collage of fifteen of Bette's most famous magazine covers, from the beginning of her career in a *Photoplay* (1932) drawing, to *Time* (1938), and *Life* (1940). The color transparency had been turned into a mock jacket and was ready to go to press when Jim Neyland called in a panic.

"*Time* magazine," he complained, "will not permit us to use *their* cover on *our* cover. The people at *Life* required a fee, and *Photoplay* has changed hands so often over the years that we can't trace the ownership of their color shots. Have you any ideas? How about Miss Davis?"

"I don't want to bother her right now, Jim," I said somewhat hesitantly, "there are some things you can't discuss on the telephone with her and this is one of them. She and John Springer are going to open the *Bette Davis: In Person and on Film* tour in Denver in a couple of days, and she's nervous as hell. Vik and she have had a parting of the ways, and she's traveling with Springer, Gene Hibbs, and Peggy

Shannon. But, since I want to see the show anyway, I'll fly in for the performance and discuss the cover."

I thought it might be fun if I just dropped by her dressing room after the show, so I didn't inform Bette I was coming. But, when I checked into the Brown Palace Hotel about one o'clock, I encountered her in the elevator!

"What are you doing here?" she asked.

"Two guesses," I answered, and kissed her cheek.

"Come on up to my digs," she said. She had a large suite on the top floor, and immediately called room service and ordered two whiskey sours for herself and coffee for me. I was surprised that she was drinking so early in the day.

When I explained the dust jacket situation, she fumed. "Those bastards, they are my covers. Where do they get off with this kind of crap?"

"What are we going to do?"

She considered the question for a moment, and her eyes lighted up. "Do you remember the little black-and-white sketch in the small bedroom off the hall at Crooked Mile?"

"The one of you as Charlotte Vale in the ship-docking scene from *Now, Voyager?*"

"Yes. If you look closely, there's one difference. Instead of the diamond brooch I wore at my throat in the film, the artist, Michaele Vollbracht, drew the Warner Bros.' 'WB' shield."

[Six months later, when I was coming out of a television station in San Francisco, a sweet little old lady with blue hair held up the book for an autograph. "Isn't it clever," she chirped, "to have *WB* lettered on that brooch? Imagine, 'Whitney' and 'Bette'!" I nodded mutely and got into my cab.]

"Vollbracht only does female stars," Bette was saying, "and each one has something that identifies her in some special way. Would you believe that for Crawford he wrote 'Pepsi Cola' in the ruffles of her scarf!"

I laughed at the thought. "The drawing would be perfect, but it's too small."

"Oh, that's not the original; it's huge." She was on the telephone at once to Harold Schiff. He gave her Vollbracht's number which I, in turn, gave to Jim Neyland, who called back in five minutes. We had a cover.

Vollbracht burst into tears when told that we wanted to use his drawing on the cover of *Mother Goddam*. This was the twenty-six-year-old artist's first book break. Since our budget was nonexistent for cover art, Jim could only offer three hundred dollars. I had to admit that the drawing was more striking than my color collage.

The night of the opening of Bette's show at the Denver Auditorium, March 11, 1974, was a revelation. I had purposely asked for tickets in the middle of the house where I could observe more easily. I had expected to see a great many older people and a considerable number of androgynous types, but was surprised to find a smattering of age groups. A young man in front of me, about twenty years old, grasped his date's hand. "We're going to see a legend tonight!" he whispered. This was a new generation. They could have only seen Bette's early movies on television.

The lower floor and balconies had been set up with microphones, and James Bronson, who had handled the road tours for Marlene Dietrich in her one-woman shows, was in charge of the arrangements. A co-owner of a Long Island restaurant, he had come out of early show business retirement to act as company manager for Bette.

The forty-five minutes of film clips, trimmed from the original two hours, began with a scene from *All About Eve* and included excerpts from *Of Human Bondage; Cabin in the Cotton; Jezebel; Dark Victory; The Letter; Now, Voyager;* and *Mr. Skeffington*. Bette's song "You're Either Too Young or Too Old," from *Thank Your Lucky Stars,* ended the first half of the program.

After a ten-minute intermission the second half of the bill began with the Elizabeth Taylor/Richard Burton scene from *Who's Afraid of Virginia Woolf* where they discuss in what Davis film the line "What a dump!" occurred. This clip was followed by the scene from *Beyond the Forest,* where Bette uttered the famous line, quietly and without emphasis. Then came clips of *The Catered Affair, What Ever Happened to Baby Jane?* and ended with Margo Channing's famous line from *All About Eve:* "Fasten your seat belts, it's going to be a bumpy night!"

The house lights dimmed, and Springer stepped out of the wings and introduced Bette, who appeared to a standing ovation. She was dressed in a blue-and-gold Chinese–style gown. Gene Hibbs had performed his usual makeup miracle. He used straps and heavy stage makeup that would stand up under the bright lighting. Peggy Shannon had expertly recurled the familiar short, blond pageboy wig.

When the applause diminished Bette came forward, looked up at the imposing architecture of the house, paused a moment, and cried, "What a dump!"

The audience cheered, howled, and whistled. From then on the audience knew that they could ask her anything . . . and they did.

This opening gambit was calculated to set an informal tone to the proceedings and remove any First Ladyish preconceptions the audience might have entertained. Bette had been desperately afraid that she would be treated like a grande dame, hence the evening would be stuffy and shallow, and she would not be able to relax with the audience.

After Springer lighted two cigarettes à la Paul Henreid in *Now, Voyager,* and started a conversation, Bronson relayed the questions from the audience about everything from her experiences appearing with Miriam Hopkins ("She was so difficult to work with, that it finally ruined her career. No one could put up with her. She tried to steal scenes. She was a pig about it. She was eaten with jealousy for others."), to what it was like to be kissed by Charles Boyer ("I wish I could say it was heaven, but if you remember, we never got close enough even to embrace in *All This and Heaven Too*"!), to what she had paid for her "designer" dress ("I got it off the rack for sixty-five dollars!"). At that point, there was a commotion from the men in the audience who were nudging their wives as if to say: "If Bette Davis buys clothes off a rack, why can't *you?*"

The evening was marred only by a slight problem with the microphones. After a rousing forty-five minutes of give-and-take, including a question from actor Richard Erdman who had appeared in *Deception,* Bette begged off and closed the show with: "You've been a wonderful audience." Then she repeated her famous line from *Cabin in the Cotton:* "I'd love to kiss you, but I just washed my hair!"

There was a long, noisy, standing ovation. A dignified, middle-aged man sitting next to me was so taken with the excitement of the moment, that he jumped to his feet and cried: "I love you! I love you!" His gentle, white-haired wife looked at him as if he had gone mad. Suddenly realizing that he was on his feet shouting, he flushed beet-red. It was that kind of evening.

Bette was presented with flowers and left the stage with a wave of her hand.

On what it was like to be kissed by Charles Boyer: "I wish I could say it was heaven, but if you remember, we never got close enough even to embrace in *All This and Heaven Too*"! Bette and Boyer in *Heaven*. LESTER GLASSNER COLLECTION

As I was making my way to her dressing room, a middle-aged man stopped me. "Oh, Mr. Stine," he said breathlessly, "would you please do me a favor? I have brought this scrapbook for Miss Davis. I've been a fan of hers all of my life. Would you please see that she gets it?"

Remembering my own Davis memorabilia, I was touched, but when I opened the leaves, a cold sweat broke out on my back. Instead of the expected photographs and newspaper cuttings, there were hundreds of morbid sympathy and death cards pasted haphazardly on the pages, including obscene comments written in red ink.

This was the first time that I had encountered a disturbed fan. Controlling my face, I looked at this normal-appearing man and answered very gently, "It would be better if you left this at the stage door with Mr. Bronson."

Later, on the way to the hotel, Bronson cautioned me not to mention the incident to Bette. When asked what I thought of the performance, I replied that I felt it was excellent. I had only one suggestion. "Bette does a fabulous job of an impersonator *impersonating* her."

"We'll plant that bit," he said. It became one of the highlights of the show. ("All you have to do is move your arm in a wide circle, puff a cigarette like mad, and say Petah!") Hibbs and Peggy acted as shills. At every performance he asked Bette to do the impersonation, while she inquired about Bette's age. Upon learning that she was sixty-six, the audience always cheered. Outside of these two questions, the shows were always spontaneous.

Over drinks in her suite, the evening was dissected by Bette, Springer, and the two representatives from Columbia Artists Theatricals Corp., the agency presenting the attraction. After they had left, Bette, filled with insecurity, remarked worriedly, "I'm afraid I'm going to cost them money."

"If all of your appearances are as well attended as this one," I remonstrated, "you'll come out in green ink."

"Oh god, I hope so!"

"By the way, Bette, that 'washing hair' line from *Cabin in the Cotton* broke me up."

She gave her Baby Jane cackle. "It does everyone! It's hysterical. What does it mean?" She paused, then went on pensively, "*Cotton* was damn good. It was my fifth film in my first year at Warners. Michael Curtiz, the director, didn't want me to play Madge, the bitch; didn't think I could do it. Darryl Zanuck was boss then, and he cast me in the part over Curtiz's objections."

[This class-A production, essentially a "man's picture," deals with the plight of sharecroppers in the Deep South, trouble at the country store, and an accountant, Richard Barthelmess, who brings management and labor together, but in so doing is compromised by the plantation owner's daughter, Bette.]

"I was third billed after the title," Bette went on earnestly, "after Dorothy Jordan who played the good girl."

"It's one of your films I haven't seen. Was Madge bad?"

Bette shook her head. "Not really, but she was . . . alluring, I guess that's the word—a modern femme fatale. It had a kind of glamour that was new to me. Dick was an old-fashioned actor, and his role was passive."

"Do you mean that you dominated him?" I asked.

Bette threw me a penetrating look. "Yes and no." Her eyes widened. "I had to seduce him, make him fall in love with me. If he had been very strong, I would have had to play it differently. Dick was too old for the part. He was nearing forty, and it would have been better if he was no more than thirty. I was twenty-four."

"How did you surmount the age thing?"

"I didn't!" She hurriedly lighted a cigarette, eager to explain. "You see, when audiences accept an actor, they suspend belief. Gary Cooper, John Wayne, Clark Gable, Cary Grant, and many others, played opposite leading ladies that were sometimes twenty years their junior— and it worked. It has never worked with actresses and younger men.

"Remember in *The Man Who Played God,* my first picture at Warners, I was George Arliss's leading lady and he was sixty-four!" She giggled. "With Dick, I just pretended that he was the same age as myself. I looked at his eyes—he had nice eyes. He realized mine was a helluva part, but I don't think he knew what I could do with Madge.

"In our love scenes I worked hard to get some sort of reaction out of him, he was so subdued. In a strange way I felt I *was* seducing him! Then, too, I got to sing 'Willie, the Weeper,' an old folk song, which Cab Calloway made famous later as 'Minnie, the Moocher.' The song started the seduction in a hammock, which wasn't very easy because Curtiz was such an overbearing ass. He'd make faces at me behind the camera, and actually muttered once, 'No-good, sexless son of a bitch!' But it was a good part, except my next few pictures were perfectly

"*Cotton* was damn good. . . . Michael Curtiz, the director, didn't want me to play Madge, the bitch; didn't think I could do it. Darryl Zanuck was boss then, and he cast me in the part over his objections." Bette with Richard Barthelmess and Dorothy Jordan in *Cabin*. C 1932 FIRST NATIONAL PICTURES, INC. REN. 1959 UNITED ARTISTS ASSOCIATES, INC.

awful. Yet it was Madge who got me *Bondage* later at RKO. She and Mildred were sisters under the skin."

In the midst of the Denver show the following night, there was a brief commotion in the rear of the auditorium. Suddenly a naked young man, wearing only cowboy boots and a knitted ski mask, ran down the aisle, up to the stage, handed Bette a bouquet of purple daisies, which in the confusion she dropped, then rushed into a side entrance.

The audience was delighted, and there was much turmoil. "I think I've been streaked," Bette laughed. "I'm not quite sure what I just saw, but it looked damned beautiful."

The flower card read, *The best of everything,* and it was signed, *The Streaking Flash.*

[The recent Academy Awards show had been "streaked" and the nimble-witted emcee, David Niven, saved the moment for posterity by remarking, "Isn't it fascinating that probably the only laugh this man will ever get in his life is by stripping off his clothes and showing his shortcomings!"]

Bette in reply to a question said that her children had explained that streaking was the latest thing among young persons.

Surely enough, the wire services picked up the incident. Bette's show was "in." It had been "streaked." However, the accounts left out the fact that she had called the boy "damn beautiful."

But there was a coda to the story. The next day a man identifying himself as "the streaker" telephoned the *Denver News.* "Why streak at a hockey game," he burbled, "when you have a classy lady like Bette Davis to streak for? That's what the flowers were all about."

Later, Bette, swearing me to secrecy, confided that the man had been a "plant." "We wanted publicity and we got it!" she said. "However, I wasn't told until after the show. I guess it was the consensus of opinion that I wouldn't have acted surprised enough!"

Between gigs for her film clip and talk show, Bette spent one night as houseguest of Leonard Sillman, who had produced so many of the *New Faces* Broadway shows over the years. She signed the *Miss Moffat* contract seated at a desk that had once been owned by Florenz Ziegfeld.

Bette had always hoped that Sillman would introduce her to Greta Garbo. Sometimes, when Robert was driving her around New York, she would catch sight of a tall, gaunt figure in a coat and slouch hat striding down Third Avenue, and would order him to follow at a safe distance. That was as close as Bette ever got to meeting Garbo.

"It's a great pity," Bette told me once, "that in the old days, stars from different studios didn't meet, let alone become friends. In fact there were lots of players on our home lots that we didn't get to know. It wasn't until the Hollywood Canteen opened that stars from all the studios got to meet and chat, and it was great fun.

"If we did meet at a benefit or a social gathering it was fleeting, and we just shook hands, or maybe nodded across the room. The public has never understood this. They automatically think that if you are in the picture business, then, of course, you know everybody. It just isn't so.

"I would have loved to know Hepburn, for instance, and Gable and Lombard. Also, when I was between husbands, it would have been nice to know Jimmy Stewart or Cary Grant or some of those other eligible bachelors from other studios.

"It's worse now, because no one is under contract to studios anymore and these kids today never get to meet each other!"

One legend that Bette did finally meet was octogenarian Mae West. At their first meeting, Bette was impressed with West's famous pink-and-white complexion. "Sitting next to you, Miss West, I really feel old. Your skin is fabulous."

"Thank you, Miss Da-vis," West replied as she moved her head forward and pushed up her hair to show there were no scars left by a plastic surgeon. "My recipe is very simple. An enema twice a day. Keeps you cleaned out real good."

Bette continued the tour, and was served a giant birthday cake on the stage of Symphony Hall in Boston on April 5, her sixty-sixth birthday. There were so many candles on the cake, her black chiffon and coq-feathered dress almost caught fire. She remembered when Blanche Yurka had permitted her a solo curtain call when they were performing the Ibsen plays in the same city, forty-five years before. Her life had come full circle.

On April 6, I went to Hartford, Connecticut, with Jim Neyland for the last performance of her show. The performance in Hartford was sold out. Bette, bowled over at the reception that her "hometown" had given her the night before, was still elated. During the preceding month she had sharpened and honed her answers, and Peggy had added a new question that always brought a round of applause: "Have you ever had a face lift?" To which Bette replied, "No, isn't it obvious?"

During the tour Bette had agreed to see the fans backstage who had sent flowers and gifts. One by one, Bronson ushered them into the "Green Room," keeping a sharp eye out for "crazies." He was a genius at sizing up people. Anyone who looked the least bit peculiar was left until last, then regretfully informed that Miss Davis had been called away suddenly.

I would have been skeptical of this procedure had I not encountered the disturbed man at the Denver show. There was always the chance that someone had concealed a vial of acid on their person or would create a scene difficult to control. Bette did not employ security guards.

"Look," Bette said, "the public can be a strange lot. I've played so many neurotic women in my career, that some borderline mental case might identify herself with me. *Baby Jane,* for instance. It gives me pause."

I spent the next day and night at My Bailiwick, her new place on River Road.

"Where are all your books?" I asked.

"I shipped them all to Howard Gotlieb at Boston University to go along with my personal papers, which I contributed some time ago. They're in a special collection."

[These Twentieth Century Archives, valued at $15 million, contained collections from nine hundred prominent individuals, including Martin Luther King, Jr., Alistair Cooke, Roddy McDowall, Bernard Shaw, Martha Hemingway, and Libby Holman, whose collection included a pair of Elizabeth Taylor's gloves, left behind when Mike Todd proposed. My Davis memorabilia will also be displayed there.]

"Just how *personal* were the papers?" I queried.

She laughed. "Don't worry! I burned all my love letters, and anything else that I thought was none of anyone's business. I could have given the material to the Academy, but hell, why should they have them, when I'm a Maine girl?"

The night was chilly and we sat before the fire, sipping drinks before dinner.

She spoke enthusiastically about the tour. "One town I will never forget is Toledo, Ohio. The 16mm film projector at the theater was on the blink, and of course, we only found this out about seven-thirty that night. Trying to find a machine after closing hours was impossible, but finally one was located at a porno house."

She rolled her eyes to the ceiling. "That was all good and well, but we had to find someone who could run the damn thing. I was in my dressing room backstage when Bronson came in and said that a priest and a couple of nuns were outside. They had to leave immediately after the performance and asked to see me for a few moments.

"This was the first time that any of the clergy had visited me backstage, and I explained that I wasn't sure that we were going to have a show because there was no one to operate the projector. One of the nuns very gently said that she was familiar with audio-visual equipment in school and volunteered to run the machine! You can imagine my delight and Bronson's relief.

"At the end of the show, I told the audience about how our problem had been solved and asked the nun to take a bow!"

"Bette, you don't think that Providence had something to do with it?"

She grinned. "Well, God was certainly on our side that night! The other thing on the tour was the fact that so many of the little airports had only tiny waiting rooms, but I must say that the public was very nice and left us pretty much alone. But backstage, oh, I got tired of hearing my own voice every night from those same damn clips."

"Bette, I liked Springer's selection, except I would have preferred a different clip of your Leslie Crosbie character from *The Letter*. The sexual tension in that movie underscored every scene."

She laughed. "Leslie Crosbie and her lover's, not Willie's and mine!"

Bette sat down beside me on the sofa. *"The Letter* was very exacting for me. We couldn't use the wonderful original curtain line, where Leslie cries to her husband, 'I still love the man I killed!'—because she had to be murdered in the end to satisfy the Production Code, since everyone in those days had to pay for their crimes. Also, when I said that line I wanted to look away in shame from Bart Marshall, who was playing my husband. I felt that the wife couldn't face him with such a confession, but Willie wanted it straight into the camera. That was our only argument on the picture." She smiled tightly. "We shot it both ways, but Willie won. We still argue about it."

[Andrew Sarris, in *The Village Voice,* March 21, 1977:

"*The Letter* was very exacting for me. We couldn't use the wonderful original curtain line, where Leslie cries to her husband, 'I still love the man I killed!' because she had to be murdered in the end to satisfy the Production Code." Bette with Herbert Marshall in *The Letter*. C 1940 WARNER BROS. PICTURES, INC. REN. 1968 UNITED ARTISTS TELEVISION, INC.

If I were to pick my favorite Bette Davis performance, it would have to be her Leslie Crosbie in William Wyler's *The Letter,* particularly her amazingly quiet, tense, sensitive scenes with James Stephenson's gently probing defense counsel, the scenes in which talk dribbles on and on until it is transmuted into the most ringing truth. There are also the sequences in which she does her needlework with such passionate devotion that we come to understand all the maddeningly quiet moments in the lives of women.]

Bette grew quiet, and then went on in a tiny voice. "I was pregnant during *The Letter,* and Tony Gaudio, the cameraman, kept looking at me sideways. Obviously, I couldn't have the baby and I was upset as hell. I had already had two abortions. I was only thirty-two and thought to myself that, if I married again and wanted to have a baby, my insides might be in such a mess that I couldn't. I cried and cried, but I knew what I had to do. Where was that damn pill when I needed it?

"I went to the doctor on a Saturday and showed up for scenes on Monday wearing a formfitting white eyelet evening dress for a scene, and that damn Tony said, 'Jesus, Bette, it looks like you've lost five pounds over the weekend!' "

She paused, and the way that the firelight caught her face, she looked very old; every wrinkle was outlined in bas-relief. "Looking back, I should have married Willie," she went on dully, "after my divorce from Ham, and taken the chance that it would work out. It just well might have, but, of course, that's hindsight. After four husbands, I know now that he was the love of my life. But I was scared silly. As good as we were together, I was afraid that I couldn't handle the bit at home. I was in no way the hostess that he wanted a wife to be.

"Although I didn't identify him in *The Lonely Life,* I meant it when I said that this man would have run my life from sunrise to sunset, and he would have. I wasn't sure I could take it. Many years later, when I was in Rome before I went to England to make *The Scapegoat* with Alec Guinness, I visited Willie on the set of *Ben Hur,* which he was directing. He was working on one of those huge old frigates, and I climbed up the rigging to get on the boat. It had been some years since I had seen him, and as we talked I still saw that look in his eye! But at that stage of the game, I didn't want to start anything over.

"In 1962 when my book came out, I sent him a copy. Later, when

"I was pregnant during *The Letter*. Obviously, I couldn't have the baby . . . I had already had two abortions." C 1940 WARNER BROS. PICTURES, INC. REN. 1968 UNITED ARTISTS TELEVISION, INC.

I saw him at the Academy Awards, I asked if he recognized himself. It was just like we were back on a movie set; he gave a noncommittal shrug. I tell you, he could be the most maddening man alive!

"But," she went on hurriedly, "having a secret affair in the thirties wasn't easy because of the press. Thank god I'd never been part of the Hollywood crowd, or I'd never have gotten away with it! Willie was closemouthed. If he couldn't communicate well on the set, he sure as hell wasn't going to talk about his private life! And I certainly didn't flaunt any of my lovers. The town was a pretty tight community."

She shrugged. "I suppose it was for the best, at least I kept telling myself. I was always so foolish about men. I'd be perfectly at home as a young girl in society today; everything's so permissive. But Ruthie had raised Bobby and me in such a straightlaced way that we had to get her okay to go to the bathroom. And we were lectured that a girl never, ever lost her virginity before marriage."

Chapter 8

At My Bailiwick, Bette lighted another Philip Morris from the one she was holding. "But the men in my life I didn't marry were the special ones."

"I bet I can name the pictures," I struck out squarely, "when you were in love with either your leading man, or your director."

Her blue eyes widened. "You *can?* Name one."

"Spencer Tracy in *20,000 Years in Sing Sing.*"

She nodded. "Yep. He was a special guy, rugged, so different from my husband, Ham. That was in 1932. Spence and I shared a birthday, April 5, but he was eight years older. He sort of took me under his wing. I was supporting him in the picture. He was crazy about my performance in a terrible, independent potboiler I'd made with Pat O'Brien, *The Menace.* It was the first picture he'd seen of mine—he thought I was different from any other actress in Hollywood. I told him I thought that the picture stunk. 'Yes,' he said, 'but you didn't.' He thought I was sexy!"

[*20,000 Years in Sing Sing,* based on the book by Warden Lewis E. Lawes, was the complicated story of a gangster (Tracy) who goes to the electric chair for the murder of a mobster, who has actually been wiped out by his moll (Davis) whom the court will not believe committed the murder.]

"Spence had made many more pictures than I had. We'd rehearse

"Spence sort of took me under his wing. He thought I was sexy. . . . We'd dream of the big pictures we were going to make." Bette and Spencer Tracy in *20,000 Years in Sing Sing*. LESTER GLASSNER COLLECTION

our big scenes together after hours. Neither of us had made a showing in Hollywood yet, but he said, 'It's only a matter of time with you. Bette, you've got it!' I was so discouraged at that point that his comment was music to my ears. I told him, 'And you're a hell of a lot better than you know.'" She paused. "And he always was.

"Up to the time of *Sing Sing*, only George Arliss had given me encouragement," Bette went on soulfully. "He was a father figure for me, the kindly, gentle father that I'd never had. My own was a holy terror. But Spence and I were smitten with each other before we knew it. He didn't have to pretend he was strong, because he *was* strong, but oh, he could be tender too! All of my husbands were weak, every damn one of them.

"Spence didn't have any pretenses, and for an actor that's like saying that the Hudson River never freezes over. Most of them are so worried about makeup and camera angles that they don't give you what you must have in a scene: concentration. They just stand there and look beautiful. Or, in the case of Charles Boyer in *All This and Heaven Too,* lie there and look beautiful! He was dying, and the gendarmes brought me into his bedroom. Would you believe that he had a mirror concealed in the bed coverings, so he could check himself out?

"But Tracy had no such conceit. For the run of the picture we had this wonderful vitality and love for each other. We had fantasies about working together later, and we'd dream of the big pictures we were going to make.

"He wasn't enamored of the stage. He used to say that 'the theater is either for children or idiots,' and he was right. You reach a certain point where it's insane to put up with those hours, especially when you've been brought up on movies—where you're used to getting up at dawn. In the theater you have to rest all day, then it takes hours to unwind after you finish at eleven o'clock. Then you have to constantly worry about your voice. If it gives out, then where in the hell are you?

"I understand perfectly why Ethel Merman and Mary Martin won't do Broadway again," she went on sympathetically. "They have to give hundreds of performances for the producers to get their money back—the damn shows cost so much today!"

She lighted a cigarette to calm down and then went on softly. "But as for Spence, after *Sing Sing* he went back to Metro and I stayed at Warners." Her eyes grew huge. "I've often wondered if we'd been at the same studio what would have happened?"

[One of Bette's favorite songs was "Someone to Watch Over Me," and it was always her dream to find a man who would take charge and assume what she called "the responsibilities." Yet, the few times in her life when she fell in love with men who had powerful personalities, she retreated in terror after the first flush of romance was over: She could not relinquish the throne. Some of them, like Tracy, were already married. So her dream of finding a "strong man" was actually a fantasy.]

"As it turned out," Bette continued, "Spence and I both won our second Academy Awards in 1938. He got his for *Boys Town,* and I got mine for *Jezebel.* Backstage he took my hand and growled at me, 'We did it!' And you know what? We were both interested in other people at the time, but, strange as it may seem, we still cared.

"Of course Spence ended up with Hepburn. I've always admired her so much. People have said that we're alike in many ways, but I don't think we are really. Our approach to acting may be similar. I understand she's interested in everything on the set, the way I am.

"By the way, a publisher had the nerve to send me the galleys on Charles Higham's awful book about Hepburn for a comment for the advertisements! Can you imagine? I read the thing and I was furious. I telephoned Hepburn at home, and she didn't get my name. I said, 'Bette Davis, you know, like in the movies.' I explained about the book, which she hadn't read.

"I told her that I would send along my galleys, and that what Higham said about Spence's drinking was just terrible. She seemed so disinterested that I said, 'Well, I loved him before you did, and I think this book should be stopped!' " She grinned. "I'd had a few drinks."

She eased down on a chintz-covered chaise longue and frowned. "I shudder every time an unauthorized book comes out about a celebrity. They are mostly crap. I asked B.D. what she would do if a shit book was ever written about me. She said, 'Mother, I would just ignore it!' "

[I was reminded of B.D.'s statement when she published her bilious *My Mother's Keeper* eleven years later. It was immensely saddening that a daughter would write such a travesty of her childhood. After Hepburn had read B.D.'s book she told *Interview* magazine, "What a disgusting thing to do! What a profound betrayal. And Joan Crawford's daughter, too! No matter what the situation, it's family business that should never be discussed. And to sell it is cheap and revolting."]

"Hepburn can be fey," Bette went on. "I can't. I don't like

"Spence and I both won our second Academy Awards in 1938. He got his for *Boys'
Town,* and I got mine for *Jezebel.* Backstage, he took my hand and growled at me, 'We
did it!' And you know what? We were both interested in other people at the time, but
we still cared." Bette and Tracy accepting Best Actress and Best Actor Academy
Awards in 1938. WHITNEY STINE COLLECTION

ruffles and scarves and all of that crap. The closest I ever got to that was in *Skeffington*. Orry-Kelly's clothes made Fanny live for me, they were so right.

"Early in my career, when John Ford made *Mary, Queen of Scots* for RKO with Hepburn, I asked him to cast me in the small role of Elizabeth. The bastard just squinted up at me with his one eye and laughed! He knew better than to even entertain the thought that I would do the picture, because Warners would never loan me out again after I'd made *Bondage* there.

"There is one other Hepburn picture, though, that I would have liked a crack at: *The African Queen*. For a time, after I left Warners in 1949, I thought I might do it for John Huston with Bogey. At that point we were both the right age. We were good together in *Marked Woman*. I laugh when I think about that picture. We girls—Isabel Jewell, Mayo Methot, Lola Lane, and I—were referred to as 'hostesses.'

"Lloyd Bacon, the director, called us girls together before our first scene. He said something like, 'You all know that this story is based on the career of Lucky Luciano and the testimony of prostitutes who sent him to jail. It's up to you girls to show what your profession is in your performances. The script is all innuendo because of the censorship code.'" She laughed. "We made the audiences know that we were whores!

"In our scenes together—Bogey played the district attorney, based on Thomas E. Dewey—he looked at me with such a righteous air that I really felt inferior and that was dead right. In the picture I might have been defiant, but I knew what I was. He helped me considerably, and there was a bitch of a scene in *Dark Victory* that he saved.

"The stable scene?"

She threw me a hard look and nodded. "As written, it was impossible. Bogey playing O'Leary, the horse trainer, had to work with an Irish brogue. Let's face it, he couldn't have liked the role, but being under contract, he had no choice. Judy had come into the stable to check on an ill horse, and she's dressed up after a party and feeling defiant. She toyed with him at first, and he was sort of game. But it was 'Miss Judith this' and 'Miss Judith that.' The boss and her trainer. He kissed her. She asked him if he was afraid 'to burn'—verbally making love to her. Then she told him that she was going to die, and there was a mood change. We acted against the dialogue.

"Bogey and I were good together in *Marked Woman*. We girls were referred to as 'hostesses.' We made the audiences know that we were whores!" Bette and Bogey in *Marked Woman*. C 1937 WARNER BROS. PICTURES, INC. REN. 1964 UNITED ARTISTS ASSOCIATED, INC.

"By the way, did you know they had a different beginning and ending to *Victory?* I should have told you about it for the book. The film took place in a long flashback at the Grand National Horse Show, after Judy's dead. Her doctor-husband, Brent, and her best friend, Geraldine Fitzgerald, are there, and Judy's horse wins the trophy. Then we flash back and return to the Grand National for the ending. The audience surmises Fitzie and Brent are going to end up together. It was all too much, too soap operaish. Thank god Warners had the sense to cut it all out and end with Judy dying."

"Did you think Bogart was a sexy man?"

She pursed her lips. "No, not personally. He could be terribly uncouth. As you know, he played in my first picture, *Bad Sister,* and in several others, so I knew him a long time. But what the women liked about Bogey, I think, was that when he did love scenes, he held back—like many men do—and they understood that. Howard Hughes was the same.

"But up until Betty Bacall I think Bogey really was embarrassed doing love scenes, and that came over as a certain reticence. With her he let go, and it was great. She matched his insolence. Betty came along at exactly the right time for Bogey. He was mature, and she was a kid, and I think he had a ball showing her what life was all about. I had met her once in New York when she must have still been in grade school. She was a fan and I served tea. She was as nervous as a cat, but even then she had a certain quality. She's better than Hollywood thinks she is.

"Bogey didn't have much sympathy with the roles I usually played," Bette went on languidly, "but we were both hell-raisers in our way. We finally had a sort of grudging admiration for each other, Bogey and me. We'd both come up the hard way, and in those days we were married to people that we didn't really have much in common with.

"Ham, being a musician you'd think would have been understanding of my work, but he wasn't. Mayo Methot, Bogey's wife, always underestimated what he could do as an actor. She never gave him any confidence. After hearing about some of their battles, my own fights with Ham seemed like tiny spats! He'd blacken her eyes. Bogey and I never traveled in the same social circles, but we'd have a drink now and then, and bitch about Jack Warner.

"And Jimmy Cagney—we had a lot in common too on the fight front. We were always going on suspension. He never got into the Hollywood whirl. He and his wife, Bill, started out as vaudevillians and

"Did you think Bogart was a sexy man?"

"No, not personally. He could be terribly uncouth. . . . But what the women liked about Bogey, I think, was that when he did love scenes, he held back." Bette and Bogart in the stable scene in *Dark Victory*. LESTER GLASSNER COLLECTION

they never changed, never 'went Hollywood.' They spent a lot of time in the East. When *The Lonely Life* came out, he wrote me a three-page letter and really opened up about his troubles with Warners. I respect him a lot.

"Many of the contract players were more like family to me than my own. I didn't realize this until after I left the studio and went out on my own after being there eighteen years. I missed them all terribly—and you know Hollywood—I never ran into many of them afterward."

"Bette, getting back to romance, what about Franchot Tone?"

Her face softened. "Yes, I did fall for him in *Dangerous* on the screen—and in private life, too. Whereas Tracy was rugged and fun, Franchot was smooth and fun. He was very bright."

[*Dangerous*, the fourth Davis picture released in 1935, was a trifle about a drunken, down-on-her-luck actress, Joyce Heath, who feels she is jinxed, but is rehabilitated through the efforts of a respectable architect.]

Bette went on, "Critics praised my performance in *Dangerous*, but it was a trashy script; and the production values weren't all that great. It was Franchot who made the difference. He'd grin at me and my eyes would light up. Ernie Haller—Old Sober Sides—just brought the camera in a little closer. I never could hide anything from him. He knew. But Franchot gave me the courage to put some of my own character traits in making Joyce human. She was not well defined in the script. I certainly didn't get much help from Al Green, the director.

"Franchot was, of course, married to Joan Crawford. I guess he liked strong women! He was in love with her, so that took care of any feelings he might have had for me! Anyway, he went back to Metro, and I got my first Oscar for *Dangerous*. Of course everyone in Hollywood was infuriated that I didn't get the award the year before for *Of Human Bondage*. At that point they would have given it to me if I'd done *Alice in Wonderland*, which I would have loved to play when I was younger. I looked exactly like the Tenniel drawings of Alice; long neck, blond hair, and big eyes."

"What about your feelings for Anatole Litvak?"

She gave me a long look. "As you know, he directed me in two pictures, *The Sisters* and *All This and Heaven Too*. He was attractive in a different way from Wyler. He was Russian; Willie was German. All they had in common was their accents! You really couldn't call what Tola and I had a 'romance.' We both needed someone at that time."

"I know you didn't have a romance with Herbert Marshall, but you made three pictures with him."

Bette made a helpless gesture. "Bart was far more assertive off camera than on, and quite a ladies' man. He had a tempestuous love affair with Gloria Swanson, for instance. He was a past master at portraying the sensitive type of man and was wonderful in *The Letter* and *Foxes.* He was such an old pro that nothing bothered him. Even Wyler, with all of his retakes, didn't faze him one bit. He would be very charming. "I'd be happy to do it again, Mr. Wyler,' he'd say in his clipped English accent—which got Willie's goat.

"Bart had lost a leg in World War I, but he was so expert at handling his prosthesis, it was really undetectable. Sometimes he would get very weary at the end of the day, the same way that I get tired when I'm filming now. The only scene that I can remember where he had problems was the staircase scene in *Foxes.*"

[Gregg Toland, the cameraman, had just finished shooting *Citizen Kane* with Orson Welles, where he had used "deep focus" lenses that rendered the background as sharp as the foreground. He used the same technique on *The Little Foxes.* In the famous staircase scene Regina is sitting on a settee at the left side of the camera; Horace is on the stairs in the rear right. They quarrel and he collapses, asking for his heart medicine. She ignores his plea, not moving a muscle, while he crawls up the stairs in excruciating pain.]

"I didn't see Bart for many years," Bette was saying, "and his having been my leading man, I was shocked to find him supporting me in *Virgin Queen.* I had run into the same situation on *Pocketful of Miracles,* when David Brian, who was the second lead in *Beyond the Forest,* played a mere bit.

"On *Virgin,* Bart was having problems with his leg; and Henry Koster, the director, set up his scenes where he wouldn't have to be doing much physical action, so his infirmity wouldn't be apparent. I took special care to be nice to him, because at that point, his great career was long over. Remember, he had played opposite everyone from Garbo to Dietrich to Hepburn. Toward the end, he was in a wheelchair and very bitter out at the Motion Picture Home. He died in 1966 at the age of seventy-six."

"What were your feelings about Dennis Morgan?"

"Feelings? None. We only made one picture together, *In This Our Life,* which was a flop. George Brent was more wooden than ever. It

Of Franchot Tone: "Yes, I did fall for him in *Dangerous* on the screen—and in private life, too. . . . Franchot was, of course, married to Joan Crawford. I guess he liked strong women!" Bette and Franchot in *Dangerous*. C 1936 WARNER BROS. PICTURES, INC. REN. 1963 UNITED ARTISTS ASSOCIATED, INC.

was my first modern bitch after a long string of heroines—I never felt Regina Giddens in *Foxes* was a bitch. I was playing young, and Olivia De Havilland, who was eight years younger, was playing old! It should have been the other way around.

"John Huston, our director, was having a romance with Livvie, and brother was she kittenish! He shot loving close-ups of her. After I saw the rushes, he also shot loving close-ups of me! I saw to that. I said, 'No favoritism, John.'" She giggled. "Or words to that effect! Ellen Glasgow won a Pulitzer Prize for her novel, on which the picture was based, but the screenplay was just too hysterical. When I met her later, she said that she had hated what we had done to her book. I had to agree."

Bette snuffed out her cigarette, took a deep breath, and launched into the rest of the account. "Three things about the movie I liked: First of all, it treated the Negro question with dignity and intelligence. A former waiter in Warners' Green Room, Ernie Anderson, played the black boy to perfection.

"Second, I finally got to act with the great Charles Coburn, who played my uncle. We flirted outrageously, as there was an indication of a more-than-uncle-niece relationship. He had a scene that was pure heaven. I come to him for help after I've killed a woman in a hit-and-run accident. He has just learned that he is going to die, and he ignores my pleas. I got goose bumps in the scene. His terror was all in his eyes. I learned a thing or two from him! And third, Billie Burke played my mother, with nary a flutter. She was a fine dramatic actress usually cast as a birdbrain. So, on those three counts, I can't totally write the picture off."

"What about Robert Taplinger?"

She glared at me. "What is all this 'what about' today?" She paused, then, in a switch of moods, went on more kindly. "Well, I might as well tell you, he was romantic. Bob worked for Charlie Einfeld, head of publicity at Warners. He was a smashing guy, a year younger than I. He loved to dance, had a nice sense of humor, and we could be seen in public—because he was my publicity man. After I finished *Heaven* I vacationed in Hawaii, and he went with me. It was the most fun I'd had in years! No stress, no worries, no dodging behind people's backs. It was truly heaven!"

"Maybe you should have married him, Bette."

"*In This Our Life* was a flop. George Brent was more wooden than ever. It was my first modern bitch after a long string of heroines. John Huston, our director, was having a romance with Olivia De Havilland, and brother, was she kittenish." Bette, George Brent, and De Havilland in *In This Our life.* LESTER GLASSNER COLLECTION

She shook her head. "Oh, no. He was too devil-may-care then. I needed a serious husband."

[A year later Bette learned that Taplinger was in Memorial Sloan Kettering hospital in Manhattan, suffering from cancer. After leaving Warners, he had worked for Columbia Pictures and then went on his own, and in 1974, merged his company with Rogers & Cowan. Bette called his room and they spoke briefly over the telephone about the old days at Warner Bros. It was evident to Bette that he would not recover, but she kept her voice light. He died several days later, on November 24, 1975. "It was so sad," Bette said. "It was as if in our conversation he was trying to recapture something that was over a long time ago. He was a smashing guy."]

"You know, I never dreamed that I would marry an actor, much less costar with him. I'd seen Hollywood marriages fail, when the husband's career is in the doldrums and the wife's is hot—or vice versa. *A Star Is Born* is true to life. The Lunts are the exception, but they aren't Hollywood people, and they might have had career problems in pictures. But when I fell in love with Gary Merrill on *All About Eve,* he was not the usual actor. He always kept his Yankee roots, like I did. But, even so, he was disappointed that I didn't keep more of a star image in my private life. He didn't want me to be in the kitchen. He didn't approve of my domestic streak.

"It's true that we made three pictures back to back: *Eve, Another Man's Poison,* and *Phone Call from a Stranger.* People have always surmised that I did the tiny part in *Phone Call* to help his career, but that simply isn't so. I didn't have any offers at the time, and when I was reading lines with Gary at home, I suddenly thought, *I like Marie Hoke, the invalid.* Gary was beside himself. 'It's such a small role!' he exclaimed. 'Yes,' I replied, 'small it may be, but filled with goodies.' I had a terrific bed scene.

"But Gary and I never really made it big as a team, until we toured with *The World of Carl Sandburg.* The audiences loved us as costars and as a married couple. We became friends with Sandburg, who was eighty. He was delighted with us, and Gary did resemble him as a young man. 'You don't know what it means to me,' he said during rehearsals, 'to hear my lines read exactly the right way.' We were so flattered."

And Bette stood up, placed her feet wide apart, wound an imaginary feather boa around her shoulders, and recited in a strong,

Bette chats with a friend while vacationing in Honolulu after completion of filming *The Letter*. WHITNEY STINE COLLECTION

"I fell in love with Gary Merrill on *All About Eve*. But he was disappointed that I didn't keep more of a star image in my private life. He didn't approve of my domestic streak." Top: Bette and Gary Merrill in *Eve*. LESTER GLASSNER COLLECTION. Bottom: And in real life. LESTER GLASSNER COLLECTION

vibrant voice: "'I am Elizabeth Umpstead, dead at seventy-five years of age, and they are taking me in a polished and silver-plated box today, and an undertaker, assured of cash for his work . . .' Now, that is poetry!"

She paused, and went on slyly, "I'm going to tell you about another man but I won't give you his name. He was a different sort than any of my leading men. I fell in love with him. He was ardent, I must say.

"But halfway through the picture I had a sixth sense that I was falling for him because of his character in the film, not what kind of a person he really was. Like me falling for Gary Merrill, and he for me, in *All About Eve,* much later. I had enough sense to cool it with this man. And I've been happy about it ever since. Because we're still friends."

I ventured a name, an obvious choice for me, and Bette colored. "Damn you!" she giggled self-consciously. "Yes, you're right. But if you ever write my story, don't mention his name. Promise?"

"I promise," I answered. "Now, let's have dinner; I'm starved."

Bette served broiled lamb chops, artichokes, a small green salad, and excellent red wine. (Jeremy at that time was importing wine, and she let him select her vintages. He knew what he was doing, after having been involved in several professions. Bette was so proud of B.D. when, newly arrived in Westport, she had introduced herself as Mrs. Hyman, not Bette Davis's daughter, and had handed out Jeremy's business cards.)

Over dinner I asked, "But what about all those difficult roles, Bette, the ones that were badly conceived, like *Dangerous,* when you had to transcend the material."

"What?" Her mouth pursed. "It's not so much transcending, Whitney," she said with a frown. "I don't think anyone has truly transcended a role. Maybe one or two scenes, but not the whole picture. Garbo, of course, transcended—but not the role, because she played only to herself. She was everywhere. In a peculiar way, she was behind the camera, in front of the camera, the cameraman—she was the whole thing. She never fed a line to anyone. She said the line. It was up to the other actor to play off her; she never played off them. But that's a fluke. It never happened to anyone else—except maybe Duse on the stage. She was to theater what Garbo was to pictures.

"You see, the first thing an actor has to do is have the audience accept him in a different part than he ordinarily plays. If they won't, then he's typecast and ends up playing the same role the rest of his life. I was one of the fortunate ones; I've played everything—even old ladies before I had to!

"Leslie Howard, for instance, could play sensitive types and comedy too, but he couldn't do villains; neither could Gary Cooper nor Clark Gable. Leslie was very snobbish about film. He let everyone know he was a stage actor, and only made pictures for money. It has always annoyed me that some Broadway stars treat Hollywood with contempt —as if they are slumming. Of course, sometimes it's not their medium, but it's always been mine.

"Later, when Leslie and I did *Petrified Forest,* he was very chummy. I loved the part of Gabrielle, the painter, but because of the Production Code I couldn't read the line I liked best. Here is this girl, like a fish out of water, stuck in that gas station in the middle of the Mojave desert, and no one but Howard, the vagabond, understands her. And she says, 'My name is Gabrielle, but goddamn wouldn't you know these bastards call me "Gabby"?' She gave her signature cackle.

"When Howard appeared with me in *It's Love I'm After,* he let me know that he wanted real life to go along with the title of the picture. I turned him down flat. It wasn't that he was unattractive, and we did have love scenes together, but he was so promiscuous. He was very nearsighted and wore glasses offscreen. He'd squint about the set, and his eyes would light up at some blurry little blond script girl, and sooner or later, he'd amble over to her; and you could bet he had another conquest. I venture to say that, in his mousy way, he had more one-night stands than Errol Flynn, who was a dreamboat in those days."

"We haven't spoken about Paul Henreid," I said.

"He's one of my favorite people. The part of Jerry Durrance in Prouty's *Voyager* was American. At first I was against the idea of having a man with a foreign accent play him. And when I saw Paul's first test, I was horrified. For some crazy reason that no one remembers today, he was made up with four coats of pancake, his hair was plastered back with brilliantine, and they gave him a smoking jacket to wear! It was horrible, and he hated the way he looked. When I saw how attractive he really was in person, I insisted he be tested again.

"Well, Paul understood Jerry and was a revelation. Our chemistry was just right. He helped my performance immeasurably and we developed a certain style between us. The public all over the world knew what Charlotte saw in this man who was caught in an awful

"When Leslie Howard appeared with me in *It's Love I'm After,* he let me know that he wanted real life to go along with the title of the picture. I turned him down flat." Top: LESTER GLASSNER COLLECTION. "When I saw Paul's first test, I was horrified. When I saw how attractive he really was in person, I insisted he be tested again." Bottom: Bette and Paul Henreid in *Now, Voyager.* C 1942 WARNER BROS. PICTURES, INC. REN. 1969 UNITED ARTISTS TELEVISION, INC.

marriage. So many times foreign actors leer and posture, but Paul was perfectly natural—plus being so good-looking. When he won Charlotte's heart he won every woman's heart in the audience.

"By the way, it was Paul's idea to light two cigarettes from one match. The script had it performed another way that was too cumbersome. Paul made it look as smooth as silk.

"He's a perfectionist, the way that I am, and I had several fights on the picture with Irving Rapper, the director. *In This Our Life* had just come out before shooting began and the reviews were terrible, so I wasn't in the best of moods. I remember putting off Orry-Kelly, who wanted to show me the clothes for tests. Finally, when Charlotte was becoming real to me, mentally, I approved the wardrobe, which was so right. We did all of the scenes with the ugly, fat Charlotte first, so when I did look good for the remainder of the picture, I felt just as liberated as the character. I really had been transformed."

After apple pie for dessert, Bette stretched her back and mixed herself another scotch, which surprised me because she did not usually drink after dinner. "It's a wonder I didn't become an alcoholic after Vik left," she said. "I was here in the house alone and it got on my nerves. And I wasn't making any money. I've put Twin Bridges up for sale. As it turns out I owe Harold Schiff fifty thousand dollars, and since I'm scared to death that something will happen to me before I can pay him back, I had it put in writing that he will be paid off when the house sells."

She turned out the light beside the sofa. "I'm very tired," she said. "You always make me tired, because we talk so much and it's hell remembering—usually. But, I still think we should get married, and tell the rest of the world to go fuck themselves!"

Chapter 9

B ette and Dick Cavett, whose autobiography had just been published, were asked to perform at the ending-night banquet of the American Booksellers Association annual convention—that annual mating dance between publishers and bookstore owners—May 13 through 15, 1974, at the Shoreham Hotel in Washington, D.C.

They were to create a short version of his television talk show. It had also been arranged for us to appear on one of Cavett's ninety-minute "Wide World Specials."

Our publishers had arranged for Robert Andrea to drive Bette, Jim Neyland, and me to Washington. Bob could also double as a body-guard, if necessary. The limousine was a sleek, silver Fleetwood Cadillac, with curtains, mink pillows, a telephone, tape deck, and a bar. On the center footrest an engraved silver plaque gave the information that this was Miss Bette Davis's car, which was a nice tribute to Bette and probably brought Bob some additional business as well.

As we were discussing the Cavett show, an idea occurred to me. "Bette, you know he's very informal. Since your big films were in black and white, wouldn't it be great if we did the show in evening clothes?"

"Great idea!" she exclaimed. "I have a new backless, black chiffon evening gown with coq feathers. We'll all be in black and white for color television! I'll tell Dick."

She gave me a conciliatory look. "While we're on the subject of television, never have a drink before a show. You've got to have all your wits about you. Anyone who has even one drink deserves exactly what they get. Television is a very peculiar medium—even more revealing in many ways than film. Because there are no retakes, you've got to be sharp. What you are inside comes out over the tube more forcefully than through a camera on a set. By the way, Cavett is famous for his unexpected questions. On my first ninety-minute show, out of nowhere, he asked when I lost my virginity! I told him on my wedding night. It was the truth. It was a shit question, but I answered."

We had almost reached Washington when Bette asked Robert to stop at the next gas station because she had to use the rest room; her kidneys, which she had once alluded to as "trusty as a camel's," were not. Twenty minutes went by and we had yet to reach a facility. She became desperate and, sighting a fire station nearby, asked Bob to stop.

We got out of the limo. Midwife Jim sprinted over to the fire station to get permission for Bette to use the rest room. But she could not wait until the astonished firemen cleaned the facility, and when Jim returned, I was patrolling the pavement, and Bette was whizzing in the tall grass!

Then she good-naturedly signed autographs for the firemen, and we proceeded to the Madison Hotel.

The next morning, with a dozen people about, Bette, full of glee, recounted her misadventure on the parkway with surprising gusto! The account spread, and everyone had a good laugh at what could happen to a famous star in dire straits.

Bette wanted to look as good as possible for the evening's entertainment, and since she had decided to wear "straps," which she could not manipulate herself, her makeup woman, Margaret Sunshine, flew in from New York. Bette wore the same long, gauzy, blue Chinese dress, with a silver-filigreed collar, that she had donned for her show in Denver.

The Shoreham Ballroom was filled to overflowing for the dinner dance. At ten o'clock Cavett was introduced and a few people in the audience stood up. "Well," he said with a grin, gazing out over the throng, "that's the first partial standing ovation I ever saw!"

Bette, Dick Cavett, and Whitney Stine at the American Booksellers Association banquet, May 1974. ED SEGAL/CAPITOL PHOTO SERVICES.

The crowd laughed, and then he introduced Bette to loud applause. She bowed and carefully arranged her dress as she sat.

Cavett glanced shyly at Bette. "Well, we're out here hustling our bodies," he quipped, "to sell books."

Bette laughed. "Yes," she agreed, "and it's fun. We don't have to worry about being bleeped if we say something we shouldn't. On our ninety-minute television show, you asked me when I lost my virginity, remember?"

"Yes, but did you ever answer?"

Bette leaned back and reflected. "Why, yes, when I was first married. I had to be taught." She paused and then went on slyly, "When did you lose *your* virginity, Dick?"

Cavett blushed to the roots of his hair. "That's a question, for gosh sakes, I don't think a man should have to answer."

The audience booed good-naturedly.

Bette raised her eyebrows and surveyed the crowd knowingly. "A double standard, eh?" She laughed.

They spoke about leading men in Hollywood, and when Bette took out a Philip Morris and leaned forward, Cavett struck a match. "I get hate mail when I light women's cigarettes on the show," he commented. "I'm accused of trying to keep women in their place, and liberated women are just awful to me."

"Well," Bette replied quickly, "those women know where they can go, don't they?"

The audience applauded loudly.

"Do you ever get any hate mail, Bette?"

"No, I can't say that I do."

"I get it all the time." Cavett went on blandly, "In fact, just last week I got a fake telegram printed in crayon, which read: *Fuck you. Strong letter follows!*"

There was such an explosion of laughter that it seemed as if the roof of the Shoreham Ballroom rose two feet before it settled down sedately again.

Conversation switched to the stage. Bette shrugged. "I think the theater can be the refuge for those who don't like themselves. I was never very fond of myself. But I've played so many different women in my life—some of them I was very fond of—so I guess everything evens out."

"What about Baby Jane?"

"I knew her very well, but I didn't like her very much." Bette then looked out over the audience and sang "I've Written a Letter to Daddy," a cappella. It was a special moment during a special evening.

When we got back to our hotel Bette inquired, "Do you have any plans for tomorrow?"

"No."

"I'd love to see the Kennedy Memorial at Arlington Cemetery." Since Bette was a staunch Democrat, and I was a staunch Republican, early on we had agreed never to discuss politics.

It was arranged that Robert would pick us up at the Madison the next morning, and we took a leisurely tour of the city monuments. Bette pointed to the White House. "I was there for the first time to visit F.D.R.," she said quietly. "I had written that I wanted to see him, and in due time an invitation arrived.

"I was lined up with a lot of people and when the president saw me, a look of disbelief passed over his face, and he asked me to stay and talk with him a bit. He mentioned that he was going to Warm Springs in a few days. I told him that I was staying in Phenix City and had just come up to see him. He asked me to come to dinner at Warm Springs, which was nearby. I was glad that he did not ask me why I happened to be in the vicinity."

She grinned. "It was during a squabble with Warners after *The Corn Is Green,* and I had taken a house so I could be near my boyfriend, Lou Riley, who was stationed at Fort Benning. Bobby was with me, not only as a companion but as chaperone. No one in Hollywood knew that I was having an affair with Lou." Bette reflected with a sigh, "The president was dying. You could see it in his eyes."

"Bette, why didn't you marry Riley?"

"Because he never asked me!" she retorted. "I had met him in Hollywood and we had gone out quite a bit. He was a big guy but not handsome in the Hollywood way. In fact, he sort of looked like Sherry. I kept thinking he'd pop the question. Maybe he was scared to marry me and then go off and maybe be killed, I don't know. Anyway, he was quite a smashing guy. People thought that just because he was only a corporal, he was middle-income, but the truth was he was a multimillionaire. His family had something to do with the development of Acapulco as a resort area. He was very clever. Eventually after he went overseas, I got tired of waiting and broke it off."

"There's something, then, that you don't know, Bette," I said.

"The owner of a bookstore in Hollywood told me that he was in the service with Riley and had met you in Georgia. He was among the soldiers you entertained at the rented house. It was fun, he said, to wear the plaid shirts and jeans that you bought the guys so that they wouldn't have to be in uniform when they visited. In fact, he was overseas with Riley when your 'Dear John' letter arrived. Riley took it very badly, and my friend was with him for three days of drinking. It took Riley a long time to get over you!"

"My god," Bette cried, "then Lou *did* love me! I wish I had married him instead of Sherry. He got me on the rebound."

She giggled girlishly. "There's a funny story about Lou and me. He handled my fame fairly well, but once, we wanted to hide away for a weekend. We decided to go to the Mira Mar Hotel in Santa Barbara. Perc Westmore made me up with a darker skin and a black wig. I was ecstatic at my appearance; we would show the world! Before dinner we went into the bar for a drink, and a woman next to me said, 'It's no good, Miss Davis, you aren't fooling anyone.' When I gave her a blank look, she retorted, 'It's your *voice*. You can't change that!' I just packed it all in, went up to the suite, took off the wig and makeup, and came downstairs as myself. Lou took it all very well, I must say."

"Riley must have liked actresses. He married Dolores del Rio," I said. "They have been married for many years."

"He did?" Bette replied. "Is that so? I knew her slightly at Warners. She was so beautiful."

Bette glanced back at the White House, and then continued in a confidential voice. "I was twice investigated by the FBI, you know. The first was during the Hollywood Red Scare in the late thirties. There was this man—supposedly a bodyguard—who hung around for a week or so. I later found out he was checking on all of my movements and telephone calls and so forth. Well, he didn't find anything, naturally. If I am nothing else, I am patriotic. I believe in this country."

[During World War II Bette had appeared at several political rallies that supported Roosevelt, and she was active when he ran for a third term. She also endorsed John Kennedy and various other Democrats, including Jimmy Carter and Adlai Stevenson, whom she admired greatly. Although she could be outspoken about various candidates, she had nothing to do with Hollywood politics.]

"Then during the McCarthy era," Bette went on blithely, "I was investigated again. This time I learned the report said that I was hyperthyroid and had a heart of gold. Well," she laughed, "I am not hyperthyroid and I don't have a heart of gold!"

When we reached Arlington Cemetery I went into the information booth to ask for a pass.

After the guard came out to the limousine to convince himself that it really *was* Bette Davis inside, we were issued a VIP pass, the guard was given an autograph, and Robert was presented with directions to the tombs.

He parked to the right of the memorials, and because of the large crowds present, I asked him to keep the door of the limo open in case we had to make a run back to the car. However, an amazing thing happened: While Bette was recognized immediately, no one approached, nor were any photographs taken, although most of the gathering had cameras. They respected her privacy, and the memory of the man whom she had come to visit. We paid our respects at the JFK memorial, and then walked over to Bobby's tomb, which is nearby. She said a prayer at both crypts. This was a spiritual side of Bette that I had never seen before.

The taping of the Cavett "Wide World Special" went well, and amid much publicity, the show was scheduled to be shown on August 8, which happened to be the night that President Nixon gave his farewell speech. Our show was cancelled. "Damn him!" Bette raged. "To be upstaged by a Republican!"

We were rescheduled for September 19, and while the reviews were good, and helped sales of the book, it did not achieve the ratings that it would have if shown earlier.

As it happened I never got to see *Miss Moffat,* which closed in Philadelphia after fifteen performances. Bette's back, which had been broken in a fall in 1957, flared up again. On August 28 she went into the Columbia Presbyterian Hospital, and her leg was placed in traction. The original opening for the production was rescheduled for December, in Philadelphia.

When Bette was well enough to return to rehearsals, Josh Logan, the director, was upset because she still carried a script, which she only put down for the preview; it was her security blanket. Her ovation that night was so long and so vociferous that it even dumbfounded Logan, who with forty stage productions and ten movies had a few opening nights in his memory.

I heard no more from Bette for several weeks, but an old friend of mine went to the opening. "She's incredible," she told me. "The audience is with her all the way, even when she flubbed—which was frequently. She lost her way more than once. She's not giving a real performance, but it's probably just jitters. She received more curtain calls than I could count. But it's a good thing you weren't there; I don't know what you would have said to her backstage."

Bette had no understudy, because she was in almost every scene. The public wanted to see *her* onstage, not someone else. "I've never had such pain," she said on the telephone. "On matinee days I wear my corset from afternoon to midnight, because if I take it off between performances, my flesh swells. They keep switching lines around. I asked Logan to go easy with changes. My god, we have months on the road before Broadway.

"I want time for everything to jell. I keep missing lines. One or two performances were all right, but I know it will all work out on the road—that's why you tour in the first place. Anyway, I was in such agony on October 18 that the doctor gave me something—I don't know what—but it lessened the ache, and I sang like a bird."

The next day, Bette was in such a state that she lay flat on her back in bed. "My great energy had deserted me," she said later, "and I was exhausted. For the first time I realized that I was an old woman. Oh, the pain was indescribable. The doctors said I couldn't go on and that was that! I felt so awful—all that money, all that wonderful cast, all that effort. We had a potential hit, houses sold out on tour, and I was screwed by my damn back! Just when I not only needed a hit, but money!"

Bette called me at the end of October from Connecticut. "I'm home," she said. "I will never again act on the stage."

Bette removed the back brace just before Christmas, and on New Year's Day, while walking friends to their car after dinner, she waved gaily, turned, then fell on the ice at the back door, fracturing an ankle. "What *else* can happen?" she asked when I telephoned. "I crawl on my hands and knees to get up the stairs to the bedroom. B.D. brought over a portapotty for me to use downstairs. It's so dreadful looking—I've covered it with a pretty shawl."

* * *

In January, Bette came to the Coast again to inaugurate Humphrey Bogart posthumously into the Hall of Fame, at the behest of Lauren Bacall, who had another commitment. She was wheeled to the Palladium where the event was telecast, and gave the presentation, seated on a stool. The home audience was unaware of her physical condition.

Since Chuck Pollock's house had just been completed, Bette gave a rather large party, and the guest list included several of her old Warners cohorts. She wore a white silk blouse with long sleeves and a floor-length yellow tapestry skirt that concealed her cast. With her hair swept back, she looked rather like an older version of Charlotte Vale.

Ingrid Bergman, who was appearing in *The Constant Wife* at the Shubert Theatre, let it be known through a secretary that she would like to attend the party. But since she had also broken *her* ankle and was playing the show in a wheelchair, it was thought it would be the better part of valor not to have *two* screen queens in the living room vying for attention with their ankles propped on stools! Bette was not about to be upstaged.

"Swedes have a very cosmopolitan attitude about sex," Bette said. "One thing I'll never forget. When Roberto Rossellini first came to town, Ingrid gave a party for him, and although she and I had never met, he requested that she ask me to attend.

"Ingrid's husband was insipid and glacial, and in a way I could understand her attraction to a supposedly hot Italian. It was certainly obvious to everyone at the party. He wasn't even good-looking!

"During the evening Rossellini asked me outside to have a cigarette, and remarked that he had a script that he thought I might be interested in! Here he was—with his lady love in the next room— intimating that he wanted to work with me! I never felt that was right."

[However, Bette loved Bergman's 1978 film, *Autumn Sonata*, and thought she should have won an Oscar. When Bergman portrayed Golda Meir on television in 1982, Bette sent her a letter of congratulations to the hospital where she was dying of cancer, saying how marvelous she was as Golda. Bergman wrote a touching note of thanks.]

At Bette's party Lisl Henreid wore a burgundy-colored dress that matched my velvet jacket, and carried a mink coat, which she promptly threw on the hearth. Bette, who imitated her voice so well, was exactly on target.

When a little man entered the room, Bette gave a whoop, and fell into his arms. It was the first time that she had seen Henry Blanke, her old Warners producer, in over twenty years. They both had tears in their eyes.

In the Spring of 1975, Bette took her one-woman show to Australia: Sydney, March 8–9; Melbourne, 15–17; Brisbane, 18–19; and Perth 20–21. She doubled back to Sydney 23–24, because the first two shows had sold out and there was a clamor for tickets for the two additional performances.

Bette went to see Glenda Jackson in Ibsen's *Hedda Gabler* at the Elizabeth Theatre. "I know the play backward and forward," Bette told me later. "It was one of the plays that Blanche Yurka presented in repertoire when I did *The Sea Gull.* Glenda moved around flapping her arms so much, it annoyed me, so when I went backstage I didn't quite know what to say. So I just held out my arms to her and said, 'Great,' which got me off the hook.

"Then she took me around to meet the rest of the cast. I know she likes the stage, but I have a feeling that film is her medium. She was wonderful in *Women in Love,* and when they asked me to present the New York Critics' Award to her for that picture, I was delighted. I said that I felt a little like Margo Channing in *All About Eve,* giving her award to Eve Harrington. And she was equally good in *A Touch of Class.* She's much more disciplined on film, and it may be that she needs a director around all the time. But I do admire her. And there is no one in Hollywood who's quite like her. Like me, she was never a glamour puss."

Bette's left ankle began to swell during the last leg of the tour, and since she had to spend an hour walking back and forth on the stage every performance, she saved her strength and arrived in Brisbane in a wheelchair with the ankle wrapped. "I had visions," she said, "of wheeling myself about the stage every night, answering questions— which would have been a riot."

Chapter 10

*B*ette checked into the Bel Air Hotel to meet the clothing coordinator for *Burnt Offerings,* a new film she had just contracted to do for a United Artists release. Dan Curtis, who specialized in suspense films, was the producer and director. I had a room-service lunch with Bette at the hotel.

"I told Curtis," Bette said, "that I wouldn't even consider the script if I disappeared in a sneeze, and he assured me I wouldn't. I play an old auntie, fairly normal. It's a spooky, supernatural story of the effects that an old house has on a family of renters. They all have personality changes, and as the house becomes newer and newer, I become older and older. It's not strictly a horror picture, although I have a smashing death scene—if the damn thing comes off. It's not a film I would choose to do, but at this point I want to keep working."

She wore a new, tightly curled, short blond wig, and a white-and-blue dress that made her aquamarine eyes stand out. She was trying to cut down on smoking and snubbed out her cigarette in a large tray. Over coffee she took a deep breath, and I knew that she was about to start on a monologue. "I don't like to smoke on the screen," she grimaced, "but if the character calls for it, I do it. It can create a problem for the film editor later, if it's not done right. You have to match the shots—light up before a certain word and snuff out after another word. If you do a lot of takes, it can become confusing, so you have to remember what you've done. Many actors light up and then put the cigarette down, then go on with the scene; it's easier that way.

"I was always taught to repeat everything exactly for each take, so the editor can match easily. Today, some of these kids I work with have to be watched carefully. They will do something slightly different, which just means that in the cutting room, the editor will discard that shot and use a close-up of the other person appearing in the scene, and dub the other actor's voice over it. And these kids then complain that their scenes are being cut, which in many cases is their own damn fault!"

After several friends had dropped by and then left, Bette took off the wig and combed her hair long around her shoulders. She had always been unselfconscious with me about her grooming habits. "Growing old is hell," she said as she glanced into a hand mirror. "If I was just a housewife, I wouldn't mind, but it's going out in public that gets on my nerves. People who've just seen you on television the night before in *Victory* or *Voyager* or *Eve* expect you to look the same, and sometimes you can see the disbelief in their faces."

"Bette, do you know what I tell people who ask me, 'What does she *really* look like?' I say, 'If you put Bette Davis in a room with a dozen sixty-eight-year-old ladies, she would look incredibly young.' And I mean it. It's only when confronted with your collective past does the public feel you haven't aged well."

When *Burnt Offerings* was released, Bette was revolted. "It's such a hideous mess!" she exclaimed. "God, if I didn't need the money! Jane was fine, Charlotte was great, and Nanny was okay, but dear god, I can't keep on playing these crazies! But I still have to pay for Margot's school, and even though I live simply, expenses pile up."

"At last I'm going to do a good movie," Bette enthused a week later from Connecticut. "I'm going to play the Hermione Gingold part in *A Little Night Music* with Elizabeth Taylor. I'm her mother, a wise and crusty old courtesan. I can't wait to get to Europe where it will be shot. Elegant clothes and silver wig and wonderful lines."

But Hal Prince, the producer/director, decided to go with Gingold herself, and Bette struck out again. Then Bette went to England to tour her one-woman show. When she returned a date was set to do *The Mike Douglas Show,* to coincide with publication of the paperback edition of *Mother Goddam.* Our co-host was Tony Randall,

"People who've just seen you on television the night before in *Victory* or *Voyager* or *Eve* expect you to look the same, and sometimes you can see the disbelief in their faces." Left: Bette as Margo Channing in *Eve*. LESTER GLASSNER COLLECTION. Right: And in 1978. LESTER GLASSNER COLLECTION

When *Burnt Offerings* was released, Bette was revolted. "It's such a hideous mess!" she exclaimed. "God, if I didn't need the money! Jane was fine, Charlotte was great, and Nanny was okay, but dear god, I can't keep on playing these crazies!" Bette with Lee Montgomery in *Burnt Offerings*. LESTER GLASSNER COLLECTION

who was in Philadelphia filming intros for his new television sitcom. Mike began the show with a song, then Randall, an aficionado of old tunes, sang, "Annie Doesn't Live Here Anymore."

Bette came out to a huge ovation, and the interview proceeded. Also on the show was throaty singer Kim Carnes, with whom I had shared a limousine to the studio. Kim remarked hopefully that her new recording would make the charts. "I need a hit so badly, and maybe this is it!"

Bette was intrigued with Kim. "What's wrong with your voice? Do you have a cold?" she asked after the number.

"That's just me." Kim laughed.

Bette giggled. "You sound like you just swallowed a safety pin!"

[A few months later I gave a dinner party for the writer Anaïs Nin, who called at the last moment to ask if she might bring along a houseguest, singer Jackie De Shannon. She turned out to be a vivacious redhead with a delightful sense of humor. Upon leaving, Jackie took my hand. "I loved *Mother Goddam,*" she said, "and I'll never forget the look in Paul Henreid's eyes when he lighted those two cigarettes in the ending of *Now, Voyager.* I want to write a song about the great Bette Davis." I told her, "Good luck!" and I promptly forgot the incident. But true to her word, Jackie, with Donna Weiss, wrote "Bette Davis Eyes," a song Kim Carnes recorded seven years later in 1982. At long last, Kim finally had the hit of her life.]

Back in Weston, Bette heated Stouffer's stuffed shells as the entree for dinner. Then she brought up the idea of a face-lift again.

"You know I'm such a coward when it comes to things like that," she said, "but I'm so tired of wearing straps I could vomit! I wonder if Dietrich has had a face-lift?"

"I assume so," I said. "According to Fritz Lang, Josef von Sternberg taught her to use straps even in the thirties. He once made a very telling statement: 'The only way to succeed is to make people hate you. That way they remember you.'"

"He was right and he was wrong," Bette said. "I've always said that you get more with being all sweetness and light, but I never had the time. I'm afraid more people hated me than loved me.

"It can also work the other way around—this love and hate business. A good example is Ruth Chatterton's performance in *Dodsworth.* She hated Willie Wyler, and he was as nasty to her as he could be. The wife in the movie was having a mid-life crisis. Ruth was forty-two and having a mid-life crisis herself. She was the discontented wife both on screen and off. But her hatred for Willie helped her performance, I'm sure. It kept her on edge.

"One director that I truly hated was Michael Curtiz, who could be loathsome. By the time he directed me in *Elizabeth and Essex* he was really vile. Looking back, I guess our mutual antagonism helped my performance—the queen was so volatile. I didn't like the picture very much, but the color is still spectacular, one of the best Technicolor movies of all time in my opinion." She downed her scotch. "It's been a long day."

"Yes, and I'm pooped," I replied, and kissed her good-night.

When Mike Douglas's name came up later, Bette always changed the subject, but it was not until many years later that I learned the reason for her disenchantment. Through a bookkeeping error she was personally billed for the rooms and food we had enjoyed at the Bellevue-Stratford. "I was furious," she said, "and when Harold Schiff complained, the producer of the show, and even Mike himself, sent notes of apology, but this was a mistake that should not have been made. I'll never do the damn show again." And she didn't.

But it was never easy to book Bette on a talk show. While she liked Cavett, and had appeared with Jack Paar, Steve Allen, and Dinah Shore, she was not enthralled with Merv Griffin or Johnny Carson, although she occasionally did their shows. Later, she did get to like Carson, and some of her most riotous appearances were with him.

Nor did she care for Barbara Walters, and when appearing on the *Today* show, she insisted upon being interviewed by Gene Shalit. However, after Walters began taping specials, in which she interviewed such diverse people as Cher, Angela Lansbury, and Fidel Castro, Bette developed a certain respect for her. Eventually she shared an hour with Elizabeth Taylor and Deborah Winger in 1988, which was shown after her appearance on the Academy Awards.

Democrat Bette was ecstatic that, after Gerald Ford's occupancy of the White House, Jimmy Carter was elected president, and she was invited to the inaugural.

Jim Neyland, a confidant of Miss Lillian, and also a rabid Democrat, was writing and photographing *The Carter Family Scrap-*

book. When he called Bette at the Watergate Hotel, she was enthusiastic. "I'd love to meet Miss Lillian. What a woman she must be!"

Jim replied that he would be happy to introduce them. Miss Lillian wanted Bette to portray her if her book, *Away From Home: Letters to My Family*, was filmed for television.

Jim telephoned both Miss Lillian and her daughter, Gloria Spann, to tell them that his tickets to the inaugural gala had not arrived, but hotel security would not put the call through.

When Bette learned of this mishap, she threw up her hands and said, "Please, take my tickets to the ball. The crowd will be too hectic for me. I'll see you at breakfast."

Gloria Spann approached Bette at the affair, but the noise in the ballroom was deafening. Above the tumult Gloria introduced herself, but Bette, not connecting the name with the president, cut her off. "I don't care who you are," she announced testily, "I want to meet Miss Lillian!" Stung with Bette's abruptness, Gloria went back to her table.

Bette finally was introduced to Miss Lillian, and they had a nice chat. She was never formally approached about *Away From Home*, because by the time that the project was ready for development, Carter was running for a second term. The networks felt that the television film would be propagandistic and force them to give equal time to the president's opponent.

In late February 1976, I visited Bette for a weekend at My Bailiwick, and she was in a quandary. "The American Film Institute is going to honor Willie Wyler," she said, "and I don't know whether to go or not."

I was shocked. "Didn't they send tickets?"

"Of course, my airfare and hotel will be paid."

"Then I don't understand your hesitation. You must be there," I urged. "Of all the stars he directed, you were the most important to him—for many reasons, not the least of which was *Jezebel*."

She frowned. "I suppose you're right," she said reluctantly.

I was peeved. "Bette, I don't understand your attitude."

"Well, you don't need to get mad about it!"

"I'm not mad, just perplexed."

She mixed us drinks. "I'd just feel strange, that's all."

"Is it because you were lovers?" I asked. "Why should that make any difference? If you were receiving the award, wouldn't you be insulted if he didn't come?"

"I suppose you're right." She brightened. "I've got a new cape with mink tails. I'll wear that and my straps."

"I'll tell you what, Bette," I said the next morning, "I'll remain in New York for a couple of days and go with you on the plane."

"Oh, would you? You know, I don't like to travel by myself. Oh, that would be wonderful. You can go to the affair with me if you like."

Two days later, Bette called me at the Sherry Netherland, and her voice was muffled. "I can't go, Whitney, I've got a terrible cold."

I was unmoved. "What you mean to say is that you've got what Vik used to call 'a Bette Davis cold,'" I said without raising my voice. "Can't you see that it will be a slap in Wyler's face if you don't appear on the show?"

"I've made up my mind."

"I'm very sorry," I said, "and I think you will be too." I hung up the telephone, not waiting for her reply.

A few days later Bette called as if nothing had happened, and I did not bring up the incident. The tribute to Wyler was heartwarming. Audrey Hepburn, charming and dignified, flew in from Switzerland and stole the spotlight that rightfully belonged to Bette.

There had been many plans to film the story of evangelist Aimee Semple McPherson. Frederick Brisson had once wanted to star his wife, Rosalind Russell, in a production, and in the fifties Bette was interested in a similar project. "Well," she said, "better late than never. Now, I'm going to play Maw Kennedy, Aimee's mother! Isn't that a riot? It's a play for television called *The Disappearance of Aimee,* and it only concerns the episode when Aimee walked into the ocean in Santa Monica and turned up three days later in Carmel. Faye Dunaway plays Aimee."

Bette came back to the Bel Air Hotel for a few days before going on to Denver for the rest of the shoot. "The costumes are fantastic!" she exclaimed. "It's really going to be period. Edith Head has found authentic 1920 clothes. I wear furs and hats and dresses that will make the role. The first scene was filmed at the beach, with me wearing big wireless earphones." She recreated a famous photograph of the real Maw Kennedy at the ocean's edge.

In the cast was James Woods, who formed a solid friendship with Bette. When *Life* magazine devoted its spring 1989 issue to Hollywood,

Bette appeared with Woods in color photographs on the cover and a two-page inside spread.

"Faye is making the mistake of a lifetime," Bette complained from location. "She's really not even trying! It's a great role, and I don't even think she did any research! Parts like this don't come along every day, but she seems so uninterested. Anthony Harvey, the director, is good, but she's not giving him feedback! Damn! If I was thirty years younger, I'd play the part myself!"

Bette was in unusually good spirits and being the "old pro" on the film. She concealed her resentment of Dunaway, who was being blasé about the production. Once she threw a rose at Davis after a scene, and Bette drew herself up to her full five feet, three inches. Then gracefully bending down to the flower, she said very softly, but so that the cast and crew could hear, "Thank you—now I know how to behave like a star."

When Dunaway was late on the set one day, keeping two thousand extras in the galleries waiting, Bette pitched in and kept the crowd entertained until she showed up. She even sang a chorus of "I've Written a Letter to Daddy."

[In June 1976, Bette was honored with a Doctor of Letters degree from Columbia University. "Can you believe," she said, "Ashley calls me Doctor Grammas!"

[It was the highlight of her summer.]

Bette, feeling that she should promote the film in any way possible, made a personal appearance at the opening of the Rowe-Manse Emporium in Clifton, New Jersey, on October 14, 1976, to celebrate the first showing on NBC on November 17. "Well," she said philosophically, "I've done everything else, so now I'm cutting red ribbons!"

Bette was about to enter one of the most interesting periods of her career: She was to receive a major award, change residences, and appear in a motion picture, made especially for children, from the studio that made Mickey Mouse famous.

Chapter 11

I was a fool about real estate out here," Bette replied hotly when I mentioned that I had moved into a small clapboard house on Bellingham Avenue in Studio City after doubling my money on the previous house. "Congratulations! When I first came to Hollywood in 1930 I said that I'd never own a house, that I'd always keep a suitcase packed, so in case film acting didn't pan out, I could go back to Broadway.

"The years went by, and if I had bought every house that I rented, I wouldn't have to accept some of these lousy scripts I have to take just for the money! God! I could have bought the Camino Palmero house, where Gary and I lived when we were first married, for fifty thousand dollars. Now there's a huge apartment house on the property worth hundreds of thousands.

"Oh, if I'd only had a business manager who had invested my money in the thirties and forties! Bob Hope and Bing Crosby and those other multimillionaires didn't make their fortunes in pictures, but land. Of course during World War II the government took 90 percent in taxes. After supporting Ruthie and taking care of Bobby and my husbands, and then later, Margot, I guess, thinking back, there wasn't all that much left. I wish I'd had Harold Schiff; during those money-making years, he would have given me such good advice."

She rolled her eyes and laughed heartily. "Did I ever tell you how I met Harold? I was at a party and I saw this interesting man in the corner of the room and asked someone who he was. When I was told he was a lawyer, I introduced myself. "I want you to handle my affairs," I said. "He sort of blushed and stammered."

Schiff was floored several days later when several packing cases of records landed at his office on Fifth Avenue.

"The first thing he found," Bette went on intently, "was that Seven Arts owed me a lot of money on my percentage of *Jane*, and he literally camped out at their offices for a week until he got the check. He's saved my life more times than I can count! It was a sizable chunk. Robert Aldrich was a fool, though. He sold his TV residuals to Seven Arts for $200,000. That film will be shown forever on television."

In Spring, 1977, Bette stayed at the Sheraton Hotel, located next to Universal Studios. She was sixty-nine years old. This was a nostalgic time, because she could look out of her ninth-floor minisuite at the modern entrance to the studio—drastically changed from the low, two-story buildings with the pseudo–Spanish fronts that she remembered from when she first arrived as a contract player in 1930.

Her view was only slightly marred by the new "black tower" that housed the MCA brass. "They fired me," she said simply. "My first picture, *Bad Sister,* in 1931—where I played the good sister—was awful. So was *Seed*, and my loan-out pictures were not so hot, all four of them. So from my window I look from Universal over to Warner Bros., which became my alma mater."

Bette arrived on the Coast to film *Return to Witch Mountain.* She took pains to state to anyone who would listen that she was "not portraying the title role."

"At this stage of my career, doing a picture for Disney is the nuts," she said, mixing me a bourbon and 7up when I came to call. "For the first time, Ashley, at age nine, is impressed to think 'Grammas' is working for Uncle Walt!"

"What's the part like?"

She laughed. "Don't ask! I play a kind of funny villainess, Letha Wedge, and I'm going to look as good as I can, no horrible death scenes. My leading man is Christopher Lee. He's very menacing in the script. If this picture is ever remembered, it will not be because of me, but the special effects—things flying through the air. They treat you wonderfully well at Disney, a very pleasant atmosphere to work in, and," she sighed, "the money is good, and I just may reach an untapped audience out there. Children, for obvious reasons, are not drawn to my pictures. I usually don't attract them until puberty, and sometimes beyond!"

Cinematographer Frank Phillips had difficulty shooting Bette. He finally achieved the best results by placing banks of "fill light" in front of the camera, the same way that James Crabbe had photographed her in *The Disappearance of Aimee,* which flooded her wrinkles with light. Color film also softened the high-key look.

Bette had brought as her companion for the shoot Gary Merrill's sister Rosemary, a charming lady with whom she had remained friends. I asked them to come to dinner, along with George Hurrell. The girls, dressed in evening clothes, arrived via limousine. After looking over the house, Bette pronounced it was "just her style."

She talked about the old days at Warners that she had shared with Hurrell. "How did we do it, George? All those pictures? I went from one to another sometimes without a break, and the costume fittings, and the makeup tests, and the fan magazine interviews—and the fights, always the fights, over the scripts."

Hurrell stroked his beard and laughed. "And don't forget the days spent in my portrait gallery, not only the publicity pictures on each film, but the fashion layouts."

"My god, I'd forgotten about those." She turned to Rosemary. "In the thirties and forties, besides everything else, we had to pose in the latest fashions for the fan magazines and sometimes *Vogue* or *Harper's Bazaar.* It was ironic for me to be photographed in high-fashion stuff, considering that I was never a clotheshorse in private life. Crawford and Dietrich always looked like they'd stepped out of bandboxes, with mirabou and satin and four-inch heels. I didn't have the time, and I wasn't the glamorous type, anyway."

She leaned forward confidentially. "George, after all these years, I'm going to tell you something. When I heard that you were under contract to Warners, and Hal Wallis was praising you to the skies, I raged at him: 'Hurrell can't do any more for me than any other photographer, and I bet he's a bore to boot.' I'd seen some of your work, and I thought, *God, what that man has to put people through to get those effects must be torture!*

"I put off the sitting as long as I could, and finally I couldn't delay it

"My first picture, *Bad Sister,* in 1931, was awful." WHITNEY STINE COLLECTION

any longer. I came into the gallery in full war paint and an evening dress and furs, ready to take my medicine. Ready for an all-day ordeal. You had the lights all set when I came in, and you said good morning so cheerfully that I almost retched.

"'I brought up a sofa from the set that I thought would be comfortable,' you said, and I thought, *He's worried about comfort, when we've got a job to do?'* You asked me to recline on the sofa. *Recline?* I thought. *Doesn't he know that I'm not the reclining type? He can't make a glamour girl out of me.* But I did as you asked."

George grinned. "As I remember, you were tense that first time."

"I'm certain I was very uptight," Bette agreed. "Then you put on a samba record—how you knew I was going through a samba phase just then, I'll never know—and you started to dance with my fur all over the studio. I was fascinated and laughed at the sight of you carrying on like a kid with a new toy. In one of your passes around the couch you placed the fur on my shoulders and in a minute or two, you said, 'Thank you, Miss Davis,' and I asked, 'What for?' And you said, 'For posing for me.' And I replied, 'But Mr. Hurrell, I haven't even started yet,' and you said, 'But I've already taken the shots.'

"You could have bowled me over with a feather. I'd been in the gallery for no more than half an hour. I thought to myself, *Brother, are these shots going to be a mess, and I'll have to do it all over again later.* And, I'm afraid, I stomped out."

Bette's eyes grew big and her voice softened. "When I saw the pictures, I flipped. It was really a new me. Not only did you make me look gorgeous but I looked so natural. From then on, I was putty in your hands. How many shots did you take of all the Warners stars, do you suppose?"

George shook his head. "At least two hundred thousand—maybe more, including all the executives and department heads and visitors like Doris Duke and some of the Roosevelts."

"Which reminds me, I need some new fan pictures. Can I come to your studio?"

He raised his eyebrows. "Times have changed, Bette. I don't have one," he said soberly. "But I'll bring my lights and equipment to your place."

Bette looked off into the distance. "It's not like the old days, is it?" she said quietly. "Female stars really had it so much rougher than men

"In the '30s and '40s, besides everything else, we had to pose in the latest fashions for the fan magazines. It was ironic for me to be photographed in high-fashion stuff. . . . I wasn't the glamorous type." (All) WHITNEY STINE COLLECTION

then. We had the heavy pancake and the hairdos and the manicures and the pedicures and all of that crap that took so much time in wardrobe and makeup, besides the acting, which is what we were there for in the first place.

"The men at Warners had it easy—except Muni—his makeup for his historical roles took longer than mine, even in *Skeffington*. But Flynn and Robinson and Bogey could dash into makeup and out again in ten minutes. I looked forward to the photos in the gallery, George; you made that part of it so much fun."

"Thank you," Hurrell said modestly. "But I just shot photos of brass during the war, while you formed the Hollywood Canteen."

"Yes," I put in, "and don't forget all those Liberty bond tours."

"Yep," Bette replied, "that took a lot of time too, but I never resented those years. The Canteen was my baby, but by then I was down to one or two pictures a year, which gave me more time to play."

George grinned. ". . . and the studio?"

Bette threw back her head and chortled. "I'm certain, at that point, they were just as glad to get rid of me for six months a year. Jack Warner, many years later—we were at some charity event—got rather nostalgic and said, 'Bette, I miss scrapping with you. You were hell on wheels, but the studio was never the same after you left. It was too damn peaceful.' "

She sighed. "It was strange. He was an old man then in his eighties, and he couldn't walk very well, and I thought to myself, *Age catches up to us all.* He was my father figure all those years, and then later, so much water had gone under the bridge. All my lovers and four husbands . . ."

"By the way, what ever happened to Ham Nelson?" George asked.

"Well, after our divorce he married again and had a son. What happened to him was weird. He was up on the roof of his house putting up Christmas lights when he lost his balance and fell on his head. That was some years ago, and he's still in a wheelchair. He doesn't know anything. When I was at the Bel Air Hotel a couple of years ago, his son called and asked to see me. He said he wanted to know what his father was like when he was a young man. I chickened out. I just couldn't see him. I didn't want to dig all that up again; it's been buried for so long. Ruthie always said, 'Let sleeping dogs lie.' That was one time when I followed her advice."

Bette was in England when her first husband Ham Nelson died. "It was spooky," she told me. "I happened to be staying at the same inn where Ham and I had lived on the seacoast at Rottingdean, when I had fought my battle with Warners in 1935. Talk about déjà vu! I walked along the beach and thought back over our marriage. After all, he was my childhood sweetheart." Bette and Ham Nelson in England in 1935, visiting a cobbler's shop. WHITNEY STINE COLLECTION

[Bette was in England when Ham Nelson died. "It was spooky," she told me later. "I happened to be staying at the same inn where Ham and I had lived on the seacoast at Rottingdean, when I had fought my battle with Warners in 1935. Talk about déjà vu! I walked along the beach and thought back over our marriage. After all, he was my childhood sweetheart, and I mourned a little. It was sad. All these years later I was alone, without a man."]

While Bette was filming *Return to Witch Mountain*, she went over to see Riverbottom, the house on Rancho Avenue in Glendale that she had bought in 1939 and where she had lived while married to Arthur Farnsworth. The place was still in pristine condition, but the lot containing the riding ring had been sold.

She also took Rosemary and me to Hollywood Hills Forest Lawn where Ruthie was buried. The cemetery, located on the steep side of a mountain, contains an exact replica of both Boston's North Church on one side and the Church of the Hills nearby, a little New England–style place of worship, where Bette planned to have her funeral service.

[The Davis plot, directly in front of the left side of the mausoleum, featured a large statue of a woman, gazing out over the Warner Bros. back lot. When Bobby died of cancer in October of 1979, she was placed next to Ruthie. When Bette visited she always placed hothouse violets, her mother's favorite flowers, on the memorial.]

The climax of *Return to Witch Mountain* was shot at the mammoth waterworks at Huntington Beach, where the villains have fled. The script called for Bette and Christopher Lee to be suspended on a scaffolding high in the air. Bette told John Hough, the director, "I'm not a stunt woman. I won't get up there."

"I'd rather not use a double, Bette," he pleaded, "it will be too obvious."

"To hell with you!" Bette retorted angrily. "Get together with the cameraman and work out the angle." They used a stunt double who grasped the ropes holding the scaffold in such a way that it hid her face, but it was evident in the finished film that it was not Bette teetering in the air.

Hal Wallis sent over a script called *Whitewater*, which was to costar Katharine Hepburn, with whom Bette had always wanted to work. The story concerned a good woman and a bad woman in a Texas town. "She's the goodie and I'm the baddie," Bette said. "The only trouble with the script is that the two women never meet. Now if you have Davis and Hepburn in a film together, you better damn well have a confrontation! The script was rewritten by the writing team of Lawrence and Lee, but Wallis can't get the financing. Can you imagine this genius not being able to raise money for a picture?"

Bette groused about *Witch Mountain* being shot in color. "I know it's a fantasy," she said, "but it would be more Gothic if it was shot in black and white.

"The beautiful part about makeup for black-and-white films is that you can use all shades of gray. For instance, there was never a color picture made that could really show a devastating illness. Everything is prettified.

"In these later years, when I'm filming, young crew members often come on the set with stills for me to autograph. Usually there's a photograph of Mildred in stark black and white, and I think, *Boys, before you were born, I played the first real bitch ever portrayed on film.* Dietrich had come close in *The Blue Angel,* but she had looked divine without color.

"Another thing about black-and-white films, dramas should always be stark. Warners had the right idea. They used color only for spectacles, never on anything serious. Of all of my films, only *Skeffington* should have been in color. Fanny would have been more beautiful. But can you see *Dark Victory* or *Jezebel* in color? The audience knew Julie's dress was red, even in black and white."

[In 1986, when Ted Turner added color to *Dark Victory,* Bette was furious. "Orry-Kelly must be turning in his grave!" she raged. "The colors they chose for my clothes were all wrong! Kelly would have designed me a totally different wardrobe if it had been shot in color. It's insane! And it's so murky, when the original was sharp and clear." When I told her that *The Catered Affair* was to be colorized, she hit the ceiling. "Damn! If there is one picture in the world that doesn't need color, it's that picture. My god, it's got to be drab—that's what the story is all about in the Bronx!"]

"People said Warners let me have *Jezebel* as a consolation prize for not giving me Scarlett O'Hara," Bette said. "That's simply not true. Warners optioned *Gone with the Wind,* and Selznick later offered it to me and Errol Flynn. I couldn't play opposite him in that role. He was totally wrong. The public wouldn't have accepted an English actor as

Bette denied that *Jezebel* was a consolation prize for not getting Scarlett. C 1938 WARNER BROS. PICTURES, INC. REN. 1965 UNITED ARTISTS TELEVISION, INC.

Rhett, the way that they accepted Vivien Leigh as Scarlett; in toto, they wanted Gable, who was born to play it.

"John Hough on *Witch Mountain* is an instinctive director. Many aren't. Tola Litvak had everything worked out on paper, and on *The Sisters* and *All This and Heaven Too,* the camera couldn't deviate one inch from its position, ever. If something didn't go right in the blocking, we did it over and over again, trying to make it work for the camera. Wyler would have said, 'To hell with it, let's put the camera over *there* and have her come in *here.*' Litvak was a slave to his preconceptions. All of his work took place the night before with his blueprints; he didn't do anything spontaneous on the set. That's why all of his pictures moved so slowly, and were so ponderous."

Now, given a director who didn't know what he wanted, who hadn't done his homework, Davis could be derisive, to say the least. It was her nature to be critical, but she was just as demanding of herself as of others.

Most often, if there was good rapport with a director, a picture would start promisingly. Midway through, she would be responding well to the director, but usually by the end he was a bastard. She always, consciously or subconsciously, compared them to William Wyler, whom she believed until she died was the greatest director with whom she had ever worked. She did not consider the fact that, because of her love for him, she was more malleable under his guidance than with any other director.

Bette was on the phone late one evening. "Well, the Hymans have moved to a farm in Pennsylvania," she said wearily, "and the house is very small. Since there is really no place for me to sleep when I visit them, I guess I'll give them the money to add a large suite. B.D. will work her fingers to the bone, but they'll have horses and livestock. It will be good for Ashley."

She brightened. "By the way, did you know that of all of my pictures, B.D. likes *All This and Heaven Too* most of all?"

"How strange," I replied. "I would have thought she might like almost any of your other pictures better." Yet, perhaps B.D. had always wanted her mother to be as undemanding and quiet as Henriette, the twenty-five-year-old governess she played. There was a part of Bette's personality that *was* sweet and undemanding; she could be warm and wonderful and kind and gentle. But there was also part of her personality that could be strident and demanding and critical and uncompromising and astringent.

Bette was thirty-nine when she had B.D., and she was proud of the fact that, after her abortions, she could have a baby at last *and* a career, because her mother had always insisted that she couldn't have both. She never tired of reminding Ruthie that she could be a mother *and* an actress.

When B.D. was in her teens, Bette was in her fifties. Bette was not working all that much then. Bette and Sherry had lived at Laguna Beach when she made *Winter Meeting* and *June Bride* (1948); *Beyond the Forest* (1949); and *Payment on Demand* (1950–51). Some of the time Bette stayed in town during the week when she was working and went home on weekends, but she did not neglect her child.

After *All About Eve* (1950), when she married Merrill, they lived in Malibu, adopted Margot and Mike, and took the brood with them to England to make *Another Man's Poison* (1951–52). They returned to the States to move to a house on the corner of Franklin Avenue and Camera Palmero in Hollywood while Bette filmed *Phone Call from a Stranger* (1951–52) and *The Star* (1952–53), after which they switched the household to New York while Bette appeared on Broadway in the musical, *Two's Company,* in the fall of the same year.

After Bette's jaw operation, which closed the show, they bought Witchway on Cape Elizabeth, Maine. Bette did not work at all during B.D.'s fifth through eighth years. For the next eight years before B.D. married, her mother made only ten pictures, mostly shot in a month to six weeks. Guest appearances on series television took only a few days, so Bette was not away from her children for long periods. She spent far more time with them than the average working mother with a full-time job.

Bette was ecstatic when she learned in January 1977 that she was to be the first woman named by the American Film Institute to receive their Life Achievement Award. She had been working very little and felt this acknowledgment by Hollywood of her contribution to the industry had come at exactly the right time.

Also, she was honored to be the first woman to be given the award. "And this has nothing to do with women's lib, either!" she exclaimed.

"But women have been too long ignored in some areas of this town when it comes to their achievements."

I received a call one afternoon when she was in town, house-guesting with Chuck Pollock. "What are you doing right now?" she asked in her characteristic way. When I said I had finished my pages for the day, she asked, "Can you come over? I want to discuss something with you."

She was dressed in a bright red pantsuit. "I'm wearing this," she explained laughingly, "to keep up my courage." She mixed us a drink as the "sun had gone over the yardarm." "I woke up in the middle of the night, crying," she exclaimed, "thinking, *What in the hell am I going to say to that audience at the banquet?* AFI have told me they will give me a speech writer, but I refused because I want you to do it, if you will?"

"Of course, Bette, but . . ."

She didn't let me finish. "Okay. I don't want you to do it for free. Whatever you want, I'll see that Harold Schiff pays you."

"Bette, you interrupted me before I could say that I'd do it only on one condition."

"And what might that be, pray tell?"

"That I do it for *you*. No payment."

"Well, I think you're a damn fool." She grinned. "But, okay. What shall we say? I don't want to thank everyone in Hollywood."

"You don't have to," I replied quickly. "Let's start with the people you *can't* leave out. George Arliss, because he gave you your first real break; Hal Wallis, because he was in charge of all your box-office films at Warners; William Wyler, your first great director. The women? Olivia De Havilland, not because she's your closest woman friend, but because she won the battle you started when Warners sued you in England."

"Jesus! That's half my speech right there!"

"Then because you're the first woman to receive this award and also because you're Bette Davis, the audience is going to expect a little philosophizing—not much, but a tad."

"Yes?"

"The AFI will certainly give you a list of people that are going to say something about you, so you can acknowledge their comments."

"I want to say something about Ruthie, too. Oh, how her eyes would have sparkled if she could be there!"

"That's great, Bette. We'll use that."

"Now, I'm going to La Costa to get in shape and lose ten pounds. I've got to look my best before all those people and the others watching on television, too. I'm going to get a new dress and I'll wear straps!"

"Bette, I'll bring the speech down to you at La Costa."

Geraldine Fitzgerald was to appear with her one-woman song show at the Backlot Theater, on March 8, 1977, and Bette chose to introduce her. "I owe it to Fitzie," she said. "She's been my friend since *Dark Victory*, and the club is a stone's throw from Chuck's." As it happened, after the introduction, Fitzgerald turned the tables on Bette and gave her a long and generous tribute.

In the audience was the impressionist Charles Pierce. His most famous characterization was Bette, partly so successful because they were both blond and had many of the same features. His show was funny, simply done, and risqué. For many years at the start of her career Bette was upset that no one gave an impression of her. Then Arthur Blake, who regularly appeared at the Bar of Music nightclub on Beverly Boulevard, started to "do" her, and Bette would occasionally attend his shows. She felt he was the best impersonator of his era.

"You know," Bette exclaimed, "I never knew that I moved my elbows that much—until I saw Arthur. He satirized me just enough to point it out. I watched it after that, I can tell you!"

When she met Charles Pierce, Bette said, "I understand that you're very good." He was quite flattered.

[His wit and talent were most extraordinary, and later Lawrence Christon noted in the *Los Angeles Times*, March 5, 1980:

Among Pierce's personalities he spotlights: Marlene Dietrich ("I'm going to do a few numbers I did during the war. Some are in the audience tonight."); Joan Crawford ("Your bathwater is ready, Christina. I've been boiling it for two hours."); Mae West ("I feel like a million tonight, but I'll take one or two at a time."); Katharine Hepburn (who straightens her wattles under her scarf and tells us "A Lion in Winter" was choreographed by Helen

Keller, "whose favorite color was corduroy"). . . . Others are given a one-line sketch (about Rose Kennedy: "She drove that night, you know"). Occasionally, an incredulous Jack Benny creeps in to register his quiet dismay.

[His one-liner about Bette brought down the house: "I'd like to do a scene for you from all of my films!"]

Chapter 12

ette's room at the La Costa resort was done in shades of calming blue. As always, the children's framed pictures were on the bureau. She was dressed in a yellow sack dress over black leotards and wore her usual billed cap. "We'll eat by the pool," she said gaily. She was in good spirits.

I laughed. "If you don't think there will be a commotion."

She gazed at me steadily. "No, these people are down here for the same reason I am. We see each other every day in the sauna and the Jacuzzi and on the pounding table. They don't bother me. The routine here is gargantuan, I exercise six hours a day, with lots of pool time."

As we were going to the patio, a middle-aged woman was trudging slowly and painfully up the walk. Bette took her arm. "Is this your first day?" she asked kindly.

The woman nodded, her eyes almost closed with exhaustion.

"We've all been through it, my dear," Bette said sympathetically. "In a few days you'll be just fine."

The woman recognized her, smiled wanly, and tried to straighten her back as she walked away, but she was too bone weary.

"It's murder here at first," Bette said, "but, oh god, you can conquer the world when you leave!" She paused. "My first drink—only one—is at six o'clock."

She went on conspiratorially, "I've ordered regular food for you." We sat down poolside and she continued, "But I'm on six hundred calories a day." Luncheon proceeded uneventfully, and we were ignored after the first few stares. Over decaffeinated coffee Bette read the first draft of the speech. "It's exactly right, except you don't have a closing."

"I was going to ask you about that," I said. "I think it should end on a light note. How about giving your favorite line from *Cabin in the Cotton,* like you do on tour?"

She considered the suggestion. "Perfect! That's great. I don't want them weeping in the boondocks!" She grew wistful. "Say a prayer that I don't make an ass of myself—cry and ruin my makeup."

The AFI award ceremony was held at the Beverly Hilton Hotel on March 1, and telecast on the twenty-first. One long wall of the banquet hall was filled with nineteen huge blowups from *Dangerous, Of Human Bondage, The Little Foxes,* and *What Ever Happened to Baby Jane?* Dressed in black net over nude chiffon, Bette sat at a table opposite the stage, with Chuck, George Stevens, Jr., director of the AFI, Robert Wagner and Natalie Wood, Celeste Holm, Olivia De Havilland, and Geraldine Fitzgerald.

Between film clips, several stars gave comments about Bette, including Olivia De Havilland, Paul Henreid, Peter Falk, Celeste Holm, Geraldine Fitzgerald, Henry Fonda, Joseph L. Mankiewicz, Liza Minnelli, Cicely Tyson, Lee Grant, Robert Wagner, Natalie Wood, and William Wyler, who said: "She was difficult in the same way I was difficult—she wanted the best." Then he averred that she would at that very moment be willing to go back to Warners and reshoot the renouncement scene from *The Letter.* Bette nodded her head forcefully.

After the film clips, George Stevens, Jr., introduced the guest of honor. "There is a saying," he said, "first spoken by a man, I believe: 'It is less difficult for a woman to become celebrated for her genius than to be forgiven for it.' So tonight, we are here to celebrate, and forgive, a woman of uncommon originality and distinction who, throughout a bold career, dared to be different—in fact, insisted on it . . .

"She dared to appear before the camera—long before fashion wished it—with cold cream on her face and curlers in her hair. She dared to stand her ground, becoming one of the first women in motion pictures to shape her career by using the power her talent gave her. She dared to test her range as an artist, illuminating for audiences all the women she found within her—a mother, a moll, a dowager, a spinster, a queen, a lover, a shrew, a wife, an actress. She sang, cried, screamed, raged, and killed. Yet, always there was something withheld, some emotion in the shadows which gave dimension to the portraits in the Bette Davis gallery.

". . . Before we call her forth let us once more see the faces of Bette Davis as she will be seen now and tomorrow and forever."

With the strains of the theme from *Now, Voyager* coming from the orchestra, there followed a series of dramatic close-ups of Bette, closing with the ending misty shot from *A Stolen Life,* showing her long hair blowing out from her face.

Bette came to the podium and acknowledged a standing ovation that lasted for four and one-half minutes. Then she put on her glasses and read her handwritten speech from eight-by-ten shirt cardboards:

> At the beginning of my career, over forty years ago, how could I have possibly imagined I would be standing here tonight, the recipient of such fabulous compliments for my work? I am truly overcome. The American Film Institute Life Achievement Award is to me the frosting on the cake of my career.

I found myself mentally going over each word, then smiled at my uncertainty. I admonished myself: Of course she would give the proper reading!

At one point Bette paused and looked up at the audience. "I see one earring has dropped off. I might as well take the other one off, too!"

I was impressed with the way that she smoothly integrated the comments from the other participants of the evening. It appeared effortless, and yet, she had not once lost her place, a difficult feat reading from a handwritten script with all of Hollywood in attendance. Those tours with her one-woman show had given her the confidence to be able to ad-lib adroitly. She was giving a polished performance.

In 1926 there was a young girl from Lowell, Massachusetts, who had a dream. She wanted to become an actress. Her name was Ruth Elizabeth Davis—commonly known as Bette. She was not beautiful. She was not tall and willowy. She had a tiny, high-pitched voice that would not have been heard beyond the first row in any theater. But she did have drive and ambition. She did not know whether she had talent or not. She had a great champion, who worked and slaved for many years to help her dream come true. Without this great champion's belief in her, there would never have been the great success she finally attained. The champion's name was Ruth Favor Davis. She was her mother. How her eyes would have sparkled if she could have been here tonight.

I am proud to be privileged to join the ranks of my four predecessors: John Ford, Orson Welles, James Cagney, and William Wyler. I will take second billing to any of them, any time. As I say "good night," I would like to quote my favorite line from all of the pictures I have made: "I'd love to kiss you, but I just washed my hair!"

There was a tremendous standing ovation. At one point Bette choked up a bit. Because of the current drought, the hotel had not served water at tables. Friends handed her a glass of wine, but she whispered, "Not until I'm through will I have anything. Then I shall probably get very drunk!" Jane Fonda gave her a glass of water, and the show continued.

Later when she was handed the award, the star dropped the trophy, and when George Stevens, Jr., retrieved it, Bette held on to the base for the photographers.

The next day, Bette was still aglow. "It really was the capstone so far," she said of the AFI affair. "If something positive careerwise doesn't happen now, it never will!"

Film offers did not pour in as expected. Irving Allen, the British producer, hoped to sign Bette to star with Glenda Jackson, Vanessa Redgrave, and Diana Rigg in *The Family Arson*, a film to be made abroad, but unfortunately the financing fell through.

She was also offered the title role in a remake of the classic 1938 British film, *The Lady Vanishes*. "I loved Dame May Whitty in the original, but I don't think the part is quite right for me. She should be a plump, sweet old lady." Angela Lansbury inherited the role.

Bette had been scouting for a condominium, but nothing struck her fancy. One day Roddy McDowall called her at Chuck's. "I'm coming to get you, Bette. I think I've found a place that you will like."

As Roddy turned from Sunset onto Havenhurst Drive, Bette

"I'd love to kiss you, but I just washed my hair!"
Bette with Richard Barthelmess in
Cabin in the Cotton. C 1932 FIRST NATIONAL PICTURES, INC.
REN. 1959 UNITED ARTISTS ASSOCIATED, INC.

started to giggle. "I know where you are taking me," she said. "I bet it's the Colonial!"

He could not hide his surprise. "You're terrific. How did you know?"

"I know the place well," Bette answered quickly. "When Ham and I were first married, we had a tiny apartment next door. Isn't this a coincidence?"

Roddy shook his head. "Isn't that something else? I'm into real-estate investments and we're turning the Colonial into condos, which will be ready in a few months."

Bette chose a large two-bedroom floor-through. "It's perfect! Now, if Harold Schiff says yes, I'll take it."

Schiff said yes. "With real estate escalating in Los Angeles, how can you lose with a $125,000 condo?" he asked.

Bette waved her arms at the empty rooms. "This is my last home!" she exclaimed. "They can just carry me out the door when it's over and take me over to Forest Lawn, where, if I wasn't dead already, I'd die from the fumes of the freeway below!"

Death on the Nile was Bette's first feature film in three years, and after Peter Ustinov, who was playing detective Hercule Poirot, she shared all-star alphabetical billing with Mia Farrow, Olivia Hussey, George Kennedy, Angela Lansbury, David Niven, Maggie Smith, and Jack Warden, among others.

I had a note from Bette, on location in Egypt, saying that she was full of holes, being bitten by Nile flies, and that scotch cost eighty dollars a bottle! It was so hot her makeup was always running. Director Anthony Shaffer wanted her to ride on a camel for a scene in which the principals traveled up to the Temple of Karnak. Bette walked. They filmed for several days there, but she said that, even with the heat and the flies, it was worth the trip just to see the pyramids. She called them awesome.

When Bette returned from Egypt, she invited me to dinner at My Bailiwick, West. "How did it go?" was my first question.

"Well, it was an experience. Most of it was filmed on a tiny, antique, paddlewheel steamer. There was no room to move. It was only a hundred and thirty feet long. The camera crew was on another boat, tied alongside the steamer. Lord Snowden took some breathtaking still photographs. Imagine Queen Elizabeth's brother-in-law on our picture!

And that Jack Cardiff, that incredible cinematographer who is so great with color, would be photographing me at this age. Too bad he wasn't around to shoot me when I was young. He makes the girls look so beautiful."

"How was Maggie Smith to work with?" I asked.

Bette threw me an amused look. "Great. But on the set she is so sour, so depressed, there's not a laugh in her, I swear. She's strong, though; I had bruises from a scene where she whirled me around. Niven is a delight, but he wasn't himself. His daughter had a terrible automobile accident in Switzerland. She was in a coma, not expected to live. He flew there every spare moment, and if you look closely at the film, you can see him age. Poor man, he looks grayer and grayer. Thank god, the girl recovered.

"And Ustinov is full of stories, mostly good, but some terrible. It was a treat to see Mia, whom I've known since she was a little girl, when her father directed *John Paul Jones*. She's a sweetheart. Angela, whom I adore, is fantastically funny. She's a riot. She broke us up time after time. It was almost impossible to play a scene with her without cracking up. She and Niven do a tango that is the funniest thing since Rudolph Valentino. She plays a writer who is bombed all the time and lurches about in the most incredible costumes imaginable! In fact, all the costumes are pure twenties. I know, that's when I grew up!

"Anthony Powell, the designer, found wonderful things. I have a lace cap in my opening scene that is hysterical. The fabrics are old and delicate. You know me, when I dress in authentic clothes for a movie, the period just rubs off and adds to my performance. I remember, I had a few words with Mary Wills, who designed *The Virgin Queen*. I had a scene in my bedroom and I wanted my nightgown lined with silk. It gave me a certain security to hear it rustle, a sound picked up by the camera. I always wanted lots of petticoats when I wore hoopskirts. They make you walk a certain way that helps the character.

"Niven, even if he was subdued, was very witty. One day all of us were talking about actors our age dying off. Most of my costars are gone.

"Anyway," Bette continued, "we were all in our cups thinking about the dead, and Niven pops up with a quote from Noel Coward: 'I'm delighted if my friends last through lunch!' " Bette screamed with laughter.

"But seriously, we had filmed all of our individual scenes, and the entire cast had three weeks on one set—the salon of the steamer— while Poirot solves the crime. I jokingly told everyone: 'This is so static, look out. I'm going to use every trick in the book to steal scenes!' I think some of the youngsters felt I was being serious! But it is so boring, the same makeup, the same wardrobe, the same seats day after day. We couldn't move an inch or the shots wouldn't match."

Bette settled back into her chair on the terrace. She had cleaned the trophy room that day, and placed her Oscars as temporary door stops in the dining room.

The 1938 *Jezebel* Oscar was bright gold, but the 1935 *Dangerous* Oscar was metallic-gray, the gold having been rubbed off during the last forty-five years.

"Why don't you have the Academy regild the statuette?" I asked.

She grinned. "Oh, I'm rather fond of him that way. It shows that deep down he's a fake." Bette glanced at the twin men with a jaundiced eye. "This Academy voting business has always been a mess," she reflected. "So political! The original founders, led by Louis B. Mayer, ruled the Academy for years. Cedric Gibbons, the art director over there, even designed it! And Mayer's attorney drew up the bylaws.

"Until the awards made a lot of money being shown on television, the Academy was funded by the studios, so their block of votes went to pictures they wanted to be nominated. It was a very 'inside thing.' It makes my blood boil when I think of the stars who never received Oscars. Garbo—the greatest screen actress who ever lived—should have had a closet full, and she ended up with an honorary. That's a guilty-conscience award. Chaplin finally got his. Poor D.W. Griffith was doled out one the same year I won for *Dangerous*. He was a sad old man, forgotten by Hollywood. He didn't need an Oscar, he needed work! Whitney, if I ever receive an honorary—you can pick it up for me. I won't!

"And *Dangerous*—shot on a tiny budget—was my reward for *Bondage* the year before. Claudette Colbert, who won for *It Happened One Night* when I wasn't even nominated for *Bondage*, was embarrassed to win. She deserved an Oscar later on but not then, and she knew it! Politics! The other actresses nominated that year were Grace Moore and Norma Shearer in roles that were ordinary. In those days, only three actresses were nominated, but the Academy had it

"I jokingly told everyone: 'This is so static, look out. I'm going to use every trick in the book to steal scenes!'" Bette, with the cast, in *Death on the Nile*. LESTER GLASSNER COLLECTION

within its power to nominate up to five if the situation warranted. So it was a double blow to me.

"Well, but really, what could I expect? RKO wasn't about to submit my name because they'd borrowed me from Warners, and when I came home to Burbank, Jack Warner let it be known that he didn't want me nominated. He hated *Bondage,* only because he hadn't produced it. All the reviews said I deserved better parts and only RKO recognized the fact. Jack was chagrined, plus he was afraid I'd raise more hell than usual—which, of course," she laughed, "I did! I made his life hell for a few years!

"Anyway, industry people whom I didn't even know rallied around me. Joan Blondell—Rosebud from my John Murray Anderson days in New York—turned into a hellcat. I think she got on the telephone to everyone she had ever met in Hollywood. Without the big blocks of studio votes, I knew I didn't have a Chinaman's chance. But the Academy membership was also way, way down. Frank Capra told me once that when he went in as president in 1935, membership was down to forty!

"The sad part of the whole voting system is that the voters try to make up for past sins. When I picked up my award for *Dangerous,* I beat Katharine Hepburn out for *Alice Adams,* a great performance, but she had won for *Morning Glory* a couple of years before. So each sin is compounded. Years later, her *Lion in Winter* was a good choice for an Oscar, but then she won again the next year for *Guess Who's Coming to Dinner*—only because everyone knew she had nursed Tracy through the film. Sentiment!

"It's unending, these battles. For years they didn't even give supporting-actor awards, or for the musical score of a picture!

"With *Victory* I knew I didn't have a chance against Vivien Leigh in *Gone with the Wind.* When Ginger Rogers won the next year for *Kitty Foyle,* it should have gone to Joan Fontaine for *Rebecca*—but she got it the next year, a guilt award. But, thank god, Mary Astor got the Supporting Award for *The Great Lie.* She deserved it! She told me that I gave the picture to her on a silver platter. Hell! It was the part that did it!

"I would have liked to win for *Voyager,*" Bette added pensively, "but there was no way I could beat out Garson for *Miniver.* It was wartime, and we were in love with Great Britain. But, by the same token, Paul Lukas won for *Watch on the Rhine.* He was wonderful but

"The Oscar for *Dangerous*—shot on a tiny budget—was my reward for *Bondage* the year before." Bette and Franchot Tone in *Dangerous*. C 1936 WARNER BROS. PICTURES, INC. REN. 1963 UNITED ARTISTS ASSOCIATED, INC.

not liked much in Hollywood and wouldn't have won if the picture hadn't dealt with the Nazis.

"Then with *Jane*, I was almost sure I'd win, but Crawford, who hadn't been nominated, had a hunch I'd lose. That bitch telephoned all the nominated women. She asked if she could accept the award for them, if they couldn't attend the show. When Anne Bancroft won for *Miracle Worker*, Joan would have spit in my face if she could. She pushed me aside backstage, and the triumphant look she gave me as she pranced out on that stage I'll never forget. Oh, she was in her glory! She carted that Oscar around for a long time on her Pepsi tours, before she finally gave it to Bancroft.

"But the saddest incident concerning the Academy occurred when I was elected president in 1941 — the first woman. I was damn popular then, and box-office at last. But I was blackballed. I sailed into the first Academy meeting with a fully prepared agenda. It was time for changes and I was going to make them! My first suggestion was that, because of the war, I felt the Oscar ceremonies should be held in a theater — instead of the Biltmore Bowl or the Coconut Grove. Tickets should cost twenty-five dollars apiece to help British War Relief. You would have thought that I had roasted a sacred cow!

"I also suggested awards for costume design and makeup. Another silence! When I suggested that Rosalind Russell, an excellent hostess famous for entertaining, would be a good choice as chairman of the awards dinner, Mervyn Le Roy, who'd had that job for years, walked.

"'And,' I said, 'the Irving B. Thalberg Memorial Award for the best producer of the year should go to Orson Welles for *Citizen Kane*.' There were agonized gasps from the board. They wanted Walt Disney!

"They almost had apoplexy in toto when I suggested that extras — who were not professional actors and made up about two-thirds of the voters — should not be allowed to nominate actors and actresses for Academy Awards. This was logical to my way of thinking, because if some of them did not like you, they wouldn't vote, or if a star treated them to something special, he or she would get the vote. Most of the time they didn't even see the top films."

Bette rolled her eyes to the ceiling and reached for a cigarette. "I stood it for eight weeks, but I knew that I was fighting a stone wall. I was to be a figurehead only. When I resigned in fury, Zanuck told me that I would never work in Hollywood again, can you imagine? He was a fighter and knew that I was a fighter, too. He had built my career at Warners before he left for Fox. Yet, because I was a woman, I had to be controlled. Oh, it's all hopeless, hopeless." She pointed a finger at me. "Of course, later, my suggestions were incorporated by the Academy."

A while later, Bette called me on the telephone. "I called to say that I'm giving myself a seventieth birthday party. Just a few of the people closest to me, not the Hollywood crowd. And the house rule is no presents. I don't want to be gifted on my day of mourning."

Bette was not joking. When I showed up on April 5, 1978, there was a large, black wreath on the door. Bette answered the bell herself, dressed entirely in black, including blackface and a short, black curly wig!

"I'm grieving!" she exclaimed, and cackled. Among those present were Bertie Strauser, lately of I. Magnin, who had sold Bette her personal clothing for many years; Peggy Shannon; girlhood friend Robin Brown, who had flown in from Westport; Chuck Pollock; George Gaines, the set designer; the Lennons from San Diego, who were longtime fans; and Bette's manicurist. Bette was relaxed and witty, and the evening was a smash hit. It wasn't a bit morbid.

Bette had not found a person Friday since Vik had left, and it became increasingly apparent that she needed an assistant. She interviewed several women but was most taken with a stunning-looking brunette from San Bernardino, Kathryn Sermak. She turned out to be a twenty-two-year-old Libra, although the agency had added a few years to her résumé. Eventually Kath became Bette's surrogate daughter.

What was most endearing about Kath was the fact that she knew nothing about Hollywood and had not seen any of Bette's great films. She liked Bette for *herself*. She read *Mother Goddam* and *The Lonely Life* to help understand her employer better. Besides being beautiful, she was selfless, clever, sympathetic, efficient, and, best of all, possessed a remarkable sense of humor.

While Elizabeth Taylor was playing Regina Giddens in the play *The Little Foxes* in Los Angeles, the Filmex Society of the Los Angeles International Film Exposition invited Bette to present her with an award.

To introduce Taylor, Bette wore the blue-brocade dress designed for her for the Jack Warner tribute several years earlier. She said: "Elizabeth Taylor is a survivor, and one helluva dame." She paused meaningfully. "May one little fox present another little fox the Filmex award?"

Up flew the screen, the curtains swung back, and Taylor came forward, wearing a violet jersey gown and sparkling with diamonds. She was delighted to have her idol present. "I don't know how to cope with all this," she said, eyeing the audience in awe. "I was listening backstage. And you know, I kept thinking I was *dead*. I've never been so eulogized in my life . . ."

Bette, who had received so many awards over her lifetime, laughed with me later on the telephone. "It was great to present an award to someone else for a change! I admire Elizabeth. With all of her health problems and thin and fat and married and unmarried and with all those hits and stinkers, in a way, she's still a little girl. She still has enthusiasm."

Bette had never been bothered with eccentric people troubling her, but one day the doorbell rang and, assuming it was one of the neighbors, she opened the door to a middle-aged woman who croaked: "I am your daughter, don't you recognize me?"

Shocked, Bette could only answer, "You are not my daughter."

The woman pressed forward. "You are my mother and Anthony Quinn is my father!"

Shaken and frightened, Bette slammed the door and called the police, who found the woman loitering in the vicinity. They couldn't arrest her because she did not have a weapon, but the officers warned her to stay away from Bette.

The next day, Bette was about to enter her car in the parking lot below, when the woman accosted her again with the same story. At this point Bette hired twenty-four-hour bodyguards and took the woman to court. The judge admonished her to stay at least five hundred feet away from Miss Davis, but when he asked her if she understood, she replied, "Yes, but can I talk to my mother now?"

"Can you imagine?" Bette said on the telephone. "Of all people to hook me up with, that woman chose Anthony Quinn! I've never even met him, much less gone to bed with him!"

* * *

When Edith Head died, Bette, dressed in a black dress with a black hat, gave the eulogy at the Good Shepherd Catholic Church in Beverly Hills.

"A queen has left us," Bette said to the mourners. "She will never be replaced: her contributions to our industry in her field of design, her contribution to the taste of our town of Hollywood, her elegance as a person, her charms as a woman." Bette then spoke about Edith's dressing her in *All About Eve,* which won one of Head's eight Oscars.

Old Hollywood was present in abundance: Elizabeth Taylor, Roddy McDowall, Ann Sothern, Jane Wyman, Loretta Young, Janet Leigh, George Peppard, and Bette's old agent, MCA Chairman Lew Wasserman.

Looking at the orchid-covered mahogany coffin, Bette murmured, "Good-bye, dear Edith. There will never be another you. Love from all of us, Bette."

Chapter 13

The poignant *Strangers: The Story of a Mother and Daughter* was the best script that Bette had been offered in a very long time. She played an embittered sixty-year-old widow living on the Rhode Island seacoast, whose forty-year-old daughter returns home after many years. The success of Bette's character depended a good deal on who was cast as the daughter.

Bette read with every available actress in that age group, including Cloris Leachman and Ellen Burstyn, but it was Gena Rowlands, married to the late director/writer/producer John Cassavetes, who was the most impressive. Rowlands not only resembled Bette somewhat, but possessed the personal warmth necessary for the role.

"It's a hell of a part for me, this dame," Bette told me on the telephone from location in Mendocino, a small town two hours north of San Francisco that was doubling for Rhode Island—the same area where the Cabot Cove scenes for *Murder, She Wrote* would later be filmed. "And I'm a little afraid of it. A lot of me is going into it—much more than I had planned.

"What is peculiar about the roles I've done lately is that more of me goes into them. Of my films in the forties, only Maggie in *The Great Lie* and Kit in *Old Acquaintance* resembled me."

"And Charlotte in *Now, Voyager*," I ventured.

"You would say that because it's your favorite film of mine. I did love the character, and certainly understood her. She was from my neck of the woods. But she was noble in the same way that Judith was in *Victory,* and after she had undergone psychoanalysis—which was skirted in the film—Charlotte sublimated her love for Jerry. I could never do that." Bette laughed deep within her throat. "Besides, being perfectly honest, and not detracting one whit from the role, Charlotte Vale was an undersexed Bostonian!

"Mendocino is so like the summer beach villages where Ruthie, Bobby, and I spent our summer vacations in the twenties. We've had fun dressing this woman in old hats, slacks, and canvas shoes; and you've seen me that way a million times, but the public hasn't. And her mental makeup is so much me. If I had a daughter who hadn't kept in touch, then came back because she hasn't anywhere else to go when she knows she's dying of cancer, I'd react the same way. After she worms her way into her mother's heart—and it takes a while—she tells her she has actually come home to die, and I shout 'You bitch!' and slap her. It's exactly right.

"And the script! The lines are pure murder. The dialogue is brilliant, and the writer has put words in different sequences than usual, so we have to go over each line again and again to get it just right, but I admit it sounds natural.

"And the director, Milton Katselas." Bette was enthusiastic. "He's sooo good. The best I've worked with since Wyler. Gena, well, she's something else. God, she's got talent. If she only had my ambition at that age she'd go right to the top. But she doesn't, and then a lot of people in the industry think she'll only work for her husband. She won't fight for parts the way I did. Only the first couple of days did we have a little problem, which I think was attributed to Cassavetes's 'at-home' advice. Then Michael won her over. If this was a feature picture, she'd win awards."

On a Monday, the last week of shooting, the producers announced that because the production was over budget due to the lost time because of bad weather at Mendocino, they would close down two days early, and told Bette which pages would be cut. "But those are the goodies!" she cried. "Those touches are what people will remember."

She spoke to Rowlands, then came back to the producers. "Gena and I have agreed that, if necessary, we'll work without extra pay until midnight each night to shoot those scenes."

"Sorry, Bette," she was told, "but we'll have to pay overtime to the crew."

"*Fuck* the overtime!" she shouted. "Gena and I are working *free.* Find the money for those men!"

They shot the scenes. *Strangers* wound up receiving rave reviews and scored the highest ratings Bette had ever received on television.

Both Bette and Gena Rowlands were nominated for Emmys for *Strangers: The Story of a Mother and Daughter,* but Bette was in England filming the night of the awards. It was not explained why she was not present to receive the trophy; consequently, some Hollywood people felt that the television award was beneath her. "I had to explain," she said later, "that, quite the contrary, since I've worked a very great deal in television, I long ago changed my mind about the medium." No longer did she tell interviewers that "television was a great way to ruin your career."

For over fifty years Bette had often been listed on various nationwide polls, usually among the best actresses. However, in the 1979–80 season, she appeared on a stinger: She was counted among the ten worst-madeup by cosmetologist Livia Sylva. With her on the list were Nancy Reagan (who was thought to "need brighter cosmetics"); Jackie Onassis ("lips too thin, thick brows give a hard look"); Phyllis Diller ("Why-oh-why did she ruin her face with a lift?"); Ingrid Bergman ("She should accentuate her gorgeous eyes more and use lots of moisturizer to eliminate the taut look"); Queen Elizabeth ("too pasty, too dull. Her face is lifeless, dried out"); and Barbra Streisand ("I know it's her trademark, but if I were she I'd have a nose job.")

Ms. Sylva remarked about Bette: "One can't live on past fame, so stop saying 'This is the way I am.' She's a mess, needs everything from a facial, to a lift, to a new coif and different makeup."

Bette, who usually took such comments with a shrug, was furious. "Who is that dame?" she demanded. "What right does she have to criticize me?" Then her anger vanished and she chuckled deep within her throat. "I guess I'm not in such bad company, am I? It's the first time that I can recall ever being on the same list as a Queen!"

Three months later the National Mother's Day Committee selected Bette as one of the top seven mothers of 1980. Among her associates were: adoption pioneer Dorothy DeBolt; actress Anne Jackson; political activist Coretta Scott King; newscaster Pia Lindstrom,

Ingrid Bergman's daughter; Thurmon Munson's widow, Diana; and Olympic champion Wilma Rudolph.

Bette was thrilled by the honor. "Every one of those women have proven themselves in their fields. They were professional women, and still had time for their children. It's wonderful."

Bette telephoned Henry Fonda, since she had heard he'd undergone cosmetic surgery. She explained her dilemma to her old friend, whom she had known since 1927. "Hank, who should I go to?" she asked. When there was a long pause at the other end of the line, she knew that she had made a mistake in calling him for advice. He hemmed and hawed and finally admitted that he had had his eyes done ten years before, but couldn't remember the name of the doctor.

In late March 1979, she flew to New York with Peggy Shannon and interviewed three top plastic surgeons. She finally chose a doctor who had utilized the wood from the side of a New England barn for a wall in his reception room. Bette snickered, "Being from Down East, I knew he had to have some sensitivity!" As it happened, she was scheduled for surgery on April 5, her birthday.

She called me the next day. "It's done," she cried, "one of the great face jobs of all time. My eyes look like they used to look twenty years ago, and my 'chicken neck' is gone! I didn't let them smooth my mouth, because that would look phony, or do anything to my forehead."

"Are you black-and-blue?" I asked.

"Surprisingly not. Just a touch, and all the stitches are hidden in my hair. The results are so natural, I'll look like I've rested for years! My face is still numb, and my right eye is out of kilter, but the doctor says that it will straighten out when the swelling goes down. It's amazing. Every day's progress is like a month."

When she got out of the hospital, Bette invited me to dinner. I carefully examined her face. As usual, she was not wearing any makeup, except lipstick. The most noticeable improvement was her eyes: The extra skin on the upper lids had been trimmed away, and the fat pockets underneath excised; her neck was smooth, her jawline pronounced. She appeared ten years younger, and she did not look pinched or pulled. She had refused a skin peel, which would have produced the unwanted porcelain-doll effect.

Bette discarded the wigs in which she had been appearing in public for years, and Peggy Shannon often did her hair, which was somewhat thin. "I lost the wonderful thickness I had always had," Bette told me, "after Tennessee Williams wanted me to dye my hair that harsh red color for *Iguana*. After I left the show and went back to my natural color, my hair was never the same."

Five weeks after her surgery Bette was interviewed in her living room by Mike Wallace for a segment on *60 Minutes*. She served sandwiches and coffee to the thirteen-man crew. Her face was still slightly swollen, and she wore a hat with a green snood drawn over her ears. Wallace casually asked during the interview: "Bette, you've always said that you'd never have a face-lift, yet . . ."

Bette held up her hands. "Stop the cameras!" she exclaimed, and took Wallace into the trophy room. "Mike," she said in a low voice, "professionally, I had to do it, although it personally went against my grain. The way they shoot today everything is catch-as-catch-can, and they don't take time to light older people properly. And some of these television cameramen don't even know what a 'key light' is! I'm at the point where I can't wear straps for fifteen hours at a time, and my skin can't tolerate makeup an inch thick. It's difficult enough to get parts at my age. Without lifts I looked a hundred and ten on camera."

Wallace nodded. "I know what you mean, Bette," he said, and, being a gentleman, did not mention her face job on the show.

The *60 Minutes* segment was supposed to be a brief rundown on her career. A scene was shot at the Warner Bros. wardrobe department, where Bette told about coming there for the first time in 1931 for *The Rich Are Always with Us*. One of the wardrobe ladies then brought out a dress Bette had supposedly worn in *The Private Lives of Elizabeth and Essex,* but hadn't; Bette exclaimed over it as if it were the original.

Another scene was shot near the back-lot gate, where Bette, Henry Blanke, and a prop man had gotten drunk on her last night at the studio after *Beyond the Forest* had been completed, which finished her eighteen-year contract with the studio. These two sequences were deleted before the telecast.

One scene that was included: Bette took a wreath up to her mother's tomb at Hollywood Hills Forest Lawn, overlooking Warners. It was a windy day and the wind blew off Bette's hat and wig—much to her amusement.

The segment ended with a scene with Bette, B.D., the children, and a horse, taped at the Hyman farm near Camptown, Pennsylvania.

January 20, 1979: Bette with Mike Wallace on *60 Minutes,* after her face-lift. LESTER GLASSNER COLLECTION

Both B.D. and Mike were interviewed. Wallace told Bette privately: "Your kids are certainly protective of you!" After B.D.'s book was published, CBS ran the *60 Minutes* show again.

The first film for television that Bette made after her face job was *White Mama,* directed by Jackie Cooper. Principal photography was begun on November 5, 1979. The story concerned an indigent elderly widow, Estelle Malone, who takes a streetwise black teenager, B.T. Williamson, into her home in exchange for welfare payments. What she and the boy learn about life, and each other, is the crux of the plot. Near the end, after the boy has taken all of her belongings, she is thrust out on the streets as a bag lady, but the boy rescues her for a semihappy ending.

Two weeks into filming, when Bette had a day off, she called me. "Well," she said breathlessly, "we're shooting in the most disreputable neighborhood in East Los Angeles. If I thought the locations were crummy on *Witch Mountain,* they're worse here. And it's exactly right. You wouldn't believe the graffiti on some of the buildings. They had to clean it up! And I'm learning a thing or two. Ernest has the part down pat. He's so streetwise and arrogant in the role, it's easy to play my scenes with him, because I truly am naive about this segment of society.

"Jackie is so helpful to him, and understands the problems of a young actor. Also, the role gives me pause. I was thinking the other day that what happened to this woman could happen to anybody. If I'd had another kind of life, I might be in the same situation." She gave her Baby Jane cackle. "Who knows, I still might.

"You know, I was thinking last night, Whitney, that the first film of mine all shot on location was *The Star.* That was twenty-seven years ago. Yet, I haven't gotten used to being scooted all over town! But that picture had something to say about Hollywood. What does an actress do when she no longer has a public? I've been lucky with my stories lately, but what will I do when no parts come along? I've often said that I would end up as an old woman on a hill. I may end up as an old woman at the Colonial!

"Margaret Elliott in *The Star,*" she continued nervously, "was saved by a man. But I don't have a man, and it looks like, at my age, I won't—ever! Sterling Hayden was great as the guy. He was so beautiful as a young man—a blond Adonis, but at his age then he had this wonderful, weather-beaten face—a Maine fisherman look. And Natalie Wood was so fine as my daughter, and to think that she's still my friend as a grown-up!

"But, that auction scene, where Margaret's belongings are sold, gave me chills. I'd seen it happen to some actors I knew well. And when the relatives come and ask for money! I'd supported my own family for years! Anyway, after all this time, I'm still doing location work. 'Be modern,' I keep telling myself."

Chapter 14

I had dinner with Bette on May 13, 1980, at My Bailiwick, West. She had prepared her elegant lamb curry and we sat at the lazy-Susan table over coffee. She was wearing a pale blue denim dress and a new blond-streaked wig, styled in a pageboy bob with a right side part.

"I haff saved ze best for ze last," she said, in her Lisl Henreid voice, as Kath washed dishes. "I'm going to Love Field, Dallas, to do a TV film. Can you guess who is directing? The least likely person in Hollywood."

I laughed. "Don't keep me in suspense!"

"Remember that boy, Richie Cunningham, on the *Happy Days* television show? Well, he is no longer a lit-tle boy. I guess I've come full circle, first Jackie Cooper and now this youngster. The producer is a boy too, Anson Williams who played Potsie. It's called *Skyward*, and I play Billie Dupree, a former barnstorming pilot—somewhat like Pancho Barnes—who runs a diner at a small airfield. Honestly, after all these years," she snickered, "I'm a waitress again, just like Mildred in *Bondage*. Not bitchy, just quite a bit older and more crusty around the edges!"

She lighted a Philip Morris from a pale blue Bic that matched her dress. She had given up kitchen matches when one had flipped out of her hand and caught a sofa pillow on fire.

She went on quickly, "The story is about a girl, a paraplegic, who wants above all else to fly, and I help her. They've promised me I won't have to go up in a plane; they're going to shoot all my cockpit stuff on the ground. One thing has me worried though, and that's the girl. Howard insists on using a real paraplegic, Suzy Gilstrap, and that's all right if she can act. I have it in my contract that if she can't, then she'll be replaced." She gave me a long look. "I'm not being mean about this, it's just that I believe actors should act. I'll keep you posted on what happens."

The next week when Bette arrived at Dallas's Love Field ready to work on *Skyward*, the temperature was 108 degrees, so hot the soles of her tennis shoes melted on the tarmac. As Ron Howard walked out to meet her, she asked Howard Hesseman, who played a washed-up pilot, "Who's that kid?"

"That," Hesseman replied suavely, "is our director."

"How was Howard?" I asked, when she telephoned from location.

She chortled. "He's all right. I should have known that he would be, after all he's been working since he was six months old. I didn't realize that he was also the kid who played Opie on *The Andy Griffith Show*. My kids used to watch that program all the time. He's got savvy.

"Naturally, he started calling me 'Miss Davis' right away, and I called him 'Mr. Howard.' You know me, I've had directors in their fifties who have called me 'Miss Davis' all through a picture. He asked me to call him 'Ron', and I told him that I didn't know whether I liked him or not just yet. At the end of the day I would know what to call him. The next night I thought he would faint when I said, 'Good night, Ron, see you tomorrow.' I gave him a little pat on the butt." She chuckled deep in her throat. "After that it was 'Bette' and 'Ron.' Frankly, I wouldn't mind being directed by him again."

"How is Gilstrap?" I asked.

"She's okay. Nervous as hell at first, probably because of me. When she found out I wasn't a monster, she warmed up and our big scenes—where we fight—are good. She has some nasty lines to say to me, and I told her, 'Go ahead. Remember, I'm on your side.'

"One thing I found out was that it would have been difficult for an ordinary actress to do the role. She would have to learn how to get around in a wheelchair convincingly, lifting herself up and so forth—on a short shooting schedule. It would have taken a lot of practice. It's going to be kind of an inspirational movie, and then of course, I've never played a pilot before."

The plucky Gilstrap, a sophomore at Irving High School in California, had been paralyzed from the waist down after a freak accident three years before, when a eucalyptus tree had fallen on her back. After the film was completed she appeared on *Little House on the Prairie* and *Real People*.

Skyward had the distinction of premiering at the Film Institute Theater at the Kennedy Center for the Performing Arts in Washington. The principals from the film held a press conference in Bette's suite at the Watergate Hotel, because she felt that the others should have as much press coverage as she. But it didn't work out that way. As usual she was the star attraction. And she was not pleased that more space was devoted to her than to them.

"It's the same old story," she complained. "When I made films like *The Empty Canvas* and *The Scapegoat* overseas, I had small parts, and yet the press treated me as if I was the major star. You can't win. I've never wanted to be more important than I was in the script. Often, the picture would end up on the marquee with my name first! I must say that Mr. Guinness, as in the case of *Scapegoat,* could not have been pleased with that billing. My key scenes were cut out of the film!

"I'm not for special billing when I do a small part. It's like Ethel Barrymore with her name above the title, when she actually supported."

Then Bette giggled. "For some reason I'm thinking of Joan Crawford in *Mildred Pierce*. She had a hell of a time *looking* like a waitress—apparently, she had done everything in her life but wait tables!" she howled. "I had turned down *Pierce*. I didn't want to do a rags-to-riches melodrama. And I couldn't stand to work for Curtiz again. So I did *The Corn Is Green* instead. An interviewer once asked if I regretted not doing it, and I said no. The timing was right for Crawford to get an Oscar. She'd left Metro because she wasn't getting worthwhile parts—something I well understood myself, and her gutsy quality was just right for the role.

"But, Joan herself, in *Jane,* was the challenge. I've run into this situation many times since, when I was playing with someone—Claude Rains comes to mind—when I was challenged to give more, to be better. It's stimulating as hell. It happens all the time on the stage, when you're out there and you're building a scene with someone, the audience catches the sparks. But with film, and so many technical aspects to worry about, it doesn't happen as much. A good director will pull everything in the book to create this atmosphere of tension. But, by

"I had turned down *Mildred Pierce* . . . I couldn't stand to work for Curtiz again. So I did *Corn* instead." Bette in *The Corn Is Green*. C 1945 WARNER BROS. PICTURES, INC. REN. 1972 UNITED ARTISTS TELEVISION, INC.

the same token, a bad director can confuse you by running a set like it was all sweetness and light. Some of the worst movies of all time have been shot on 'happy, fun sets.' Now I'm not saying that you can't have fun while working. I've always believed in practical jokes and keeping everything 'up' as much as possible.

"And I don't believe in bad-mouthing someone behind his back. If I have a problem with a director, out it comes. It is discussed, a solution worked out, no hard feelings, and back to work. People forget this is a business. All those sixty technicians on the set are there for your ultimate good. They want you to succeed. If you are happy, they are happy. On a TV series, if you fail, so do they because they won't have jobs.

"I truly believe you only have big fights with little directors. The big directors sit down with you and discuss all the aspects, they listen to your suggestions, you listen to theirs, and you work it out. Mankiewicz gave me one line that told me exactly what kind of a dame Margo Channing was in *All About Eve*. He said, 'She treats her mink coat like a poncho.' Pow! Lightning struck. They also always have a reason for you to do something."

She paused in her monologue. "How in the hell did we get onto that subject?"

"We were talking about being helped by unseen forces."

"Oh, yes! Some people call it inspiration. A critic will say that so-and-so gave 'an inspired performance.' Hah! It's hard work, but you sure do get help from somewhere! So many times people have asked me about my 'theory for acting.' I wish I had one to give them, but I don't.

"Acting ability can't be acquired. You can get better, however. On the stage, you learn the basics, how to move, how to speak, how to fall down gracefully, how to project—and in pictures you learn where the camera is, and how to hit your marks, and get your voice level and all that—but those things only help you to look at ease before the camera. After that, you're on your own.

"When it comes to acting, it's up to you, and you either have it or you don't. The director can tone you down or plump you up—but eventually he has to turn you loose. That is what's so consuming about doing a television series every week. You have to play yourself basically, or you'd go mad. Good actors I've worked with all started out making faces in a mirror, and you keep making faces all your life."

* * *

"Mankiewicz gave me one line that told me exactly what kind of a dame Margo Channing was, in *All About Eve*. He said, 'She treats her mink coat like a poncho.' Pow! Lightning struck." Bette, Gary, Anne Baxter, and George Sanders in *All About Eve*. LESTER GLASSNER COLLECTION

I picked up the *Los Angeles Times* on July 28, 1981, to read that William Wyler had died. I telephoned Bette at once. "I'm so sorry," I said.

Her voice was very low. "I've been thinking of him all morning. His wife, Tally, called me yesterday with the news. She didn't want me to hear it on television—or read about it in the papers. When someone like Willie dies, it comes home to you that it may not be long for any of us when we get this age. He was the love of my life. I do so regret that I didn't show up when the AFI honored him. You should have *made* me go!"

"You know very well," I answered quietly, "I—or anyone else, for that matter—have never been able to *make* you do anything."

She gave a deep chuckle of agreement, not humor. "I suppose you're right, damn it. But Willie was so special. I won't be the only one in this town who'll miss him. He helped so many of us get Oscars. Some of his actors still hate him, but by god he made them work. No one ever left a Wyler picture without having learned more about their craft."

Bette went to be with Mrs. Wyler at the wake. The two women sat side by side. As the visitors thinned out in the afternoon Bette turned and said, "Here we are, Tally, the two women who loved him most." She lowered her voice. "I want you to know that after you married him, Willie and I never had anything to do with each other."

"Yes, I know," Mrs. Wyler replied quietly.

And they cried together.

Bette was on the telephone. "People have been calling me about a song about my eyes that they've heard on the radio. Do you know anything about it? It's by someone called Kim Carnes."

"Don't you remember her, Bette? She's the gal who sang on our Mike Douglas Show."

"Oh, my god!" Bette exclaimed. "The one with the funny voice!"

Bette found out a great deal about "the girl with the funny voice" during the next few weeks. The song "Bette Davis Eyes" was destined to remain number one on the charts for nine consecutive weeks. I was fascinated that the song was written by Donna Weiss and Jackie De Shannon, and that long-ago night with Anaïs Nin on Oakshire Drive came back to me.

"I'm a hit with the younger generation!" Bette exclaimed enthusiastically. "Ashley loves rock and roll and thinks the song is the nuts."

After hearing the lyrics several times, Bette wrote Carnes a note: *How did you know so much about me?*

It was inevitable that Bette and Kim would meet again. *People* and *Rolling Stone* magazines published articles, the latter featuring a photograph of the pair by Hurrell. Said he: "The camera was all set up in Bette's living room and Carnes was forty-five minutes late. That didn't set too well with Bette, but she didn't show it. I half expected her to say, 'Young lady, the first thing you learn about being a star is to be on time!' "

Bette was thrilled when Carnes won a Grammy Award for the song and watched her exuberantly pick up the trophy on television.

When Bette was honored along with Clint Eastwood and Julio Iglesias with an achievement award, the capstone of the evening occurred when Kim Carnes sang "Bette Davis Eyes" to Bette in person.

Chapter 15

*S*cripts were piled on the chaise longue when I came for dinner the next week after Wyler had died.

"They're all awful and back they go!" Bette exclaimed vehemently. "Murderesses and lesbians and dotty old ladies with ghosts! Why can't someone write me a part that I can play? One is good: I'm going to do *Little Gloria . . . Happy at Last*, about the Vanderbilt custody trial. I will play Alice Gywnn, the matriarch."

She had sent Kath to Hawaii for a long-deserved vacation, and Peggy Shannon was keeping her company. Before Kath left they had taken care of a mountain of fan mail. "It keeps coming in droves," Bette said, then added, "I'm not objecting, you understand. I spend a lot of time on it, because if someone writes you, it's only fair to answer. But, oh, I miss those wonderful people at Warners who took care of it for me. Every new picture brought scads of requests for photos. Then, when you were in the news on a personal level, you got more.

"When Farney died I was so touched. Thousands of letters of condolence arrived from all over the world. And so many from widows who had lost their husbands and were commiserating with me. I couldn't answer them all, so I had a card printed up."

"I know," I broke in. "It read: 'Bette Davis thanks you from the bottom of her heart for your kind expression of sympathy.' I have one in my scrapbook."

She looked at me out of the corners of her eyes. "And all these years later, you and I are here together. Isn't that strange?" She paused and then exclaimed over the Dustbuster vacuum I had brought along for her birthday. I had stopped sending flowers on special occasions—except Mother's Day because of *Mother Goddam,* and Valentine's Day—several years before, because she received so many tributes that her condo looked like a florist shop. Bette was so pleased about the appliance, you would have thought I'd given her a new Rolls-Royce.

"I think I've reached some sort of peak," she laughed. "I've just been interviewed by *Playboy,* which is a first. The writer followed me around for three days. I thought I'd go nuts, but it's exposure that I need. Men read that magazine, when they won't read anything else."

As it happened, the *Playboy* piece gave Bette more exposure than she had bargained for, and aroused a hornet's nest of publicity. Bette had casually mentioned that at age sixteen she had posed in the nude for an elderly Boston sculptress and her male assistant. The piece was entitled "Spring," and she had accepted the assignment because Ruthie needed the money. "It was lovely, beautiful," she said. "I had the perfect figure for it. I've heard it's still up there in a park someplace."

Once the magazine was on the stands, the search began. Phone calls came in by the dozens to newspapers in Boston, each suggesting a different piece of art. Every park and museum that played host to nude female statues even remotely suggesting a resemblance to Bette were laboriously scrutinized. Wire services and weekly magazines picked up the item, and foreign publications printed stories.

Bette gave her Baby Jane cackle. "Can you imagine an innocent remark of mine resulting in so much flak? They even contacted Mike in Boston. You can guess how embarrassed he was! Really, I've received Academy Awards that have gotten less press!"

Michael suggested, in order to find the statue, "Why don't you have a park statue contest?"

Finally, on June 15, 1982, Florence Wolsky, an ardent researcher, found a statue named "Young Diana" in the storage room of the Boston Museum of Fine Arts, and thought it must be Bette because "the statue's unusually expressive face, with its large eyes, does look much like a youthful Bette Davis." The find was quite as sensational as the discovery of the nude Marilyn Monroe calendar thirty years earlier.

"Young Diana" had been sculpted by Anna Vaughn Hyatt Huntington in 1924. Newshawk Ray Richmond was pleased to observe that prudes and defenders of Bette's honor would be happy to note that her pelvic area was clothed in bronze drapery and her breasts were inconsequential; that it was her eyes that identified the model.

Little Gloria . . . Happy at Last was based on the 1980 best-selling book by Barbara Goldsmith and detailed the 1934 custody battle between Little Gloria's mother, Big Gloria, and her aunt Gertrude Whitney. The producers hired an all-star cast that included John Hillerman as columnist Cholly Knickerbocker, who originated the "Poor Little Rich Girl" sobriquet for Little Gloria; Maureen Stapleton as Nurse Kieslich; Martin Balsam as attorney Nathan Burkan; Glynis Johns as Laura Morgan; and Barnard Hughes as Justice John Francis Crew. And as the Vanderbilts: Lucy Gutteridge as Gloria; Bette as Alice Gwynne; Christopher Plummer as Reginald; Angela Lansbury as Gertrude; and Jennifer Dudas as the ten-year-old Gloria.

The four-hour miniseries was to be filmed partly at The Breakers, the former Vanderbilt mansion at Bar Harbor, but residents put up a successful fight against the production, ostensibly because of the summer traffic problems. A similarly large house on Long Island was found for exteriors, and then the production moved to Florida for the rest of the shooting.

"It's the nuts," Bette said, "the whole production is a class act from start to finish. And I get to wear great period clothes—all black. After her husband died Alice Gwynne wore mourning for the rest of her life, never modernized. The only trouble is, black is damned hot. All the other women in the cast get to wear cool, summery things."

The first two hours of *Little Gloria . . . Happy at Last* debuted on NBC on October 24 and concluded the next night to good reviews, and a Supporting Role Emmy nomination for Bette.

"I've got a wonderful movie," Bette said on the telephone, her voice high-pitched and nervous, "but the best part of it all is that Jimmy Stewart is going to be in it with me. It's called *Right of Way* and it's for HBO. None of the public television networks would go for the story because it deals with euthanasia.

"Since I've done everything else, I might as well do pay television —that's where the future is going to be. Maybe if I step into it, some of the other holdouts will come in, too. It's doubly good for us because we get paid well. We each get two hundred and fifty thousand. It sounds better if you say a 'quarter of a million.'"

"That's a blessing," I said.

"Well, it's about time! Think of all the millions that kids not even wet behind the ears are making today! Jimmy and I made lots of money in the old days, but Jesus, nothing like the salaries today."

"What's the story?" I asked.

"This elderly couple, who live in Santa Monica, want to die together because she has terminal cancer. He doesn't want to face a convalescent home by himself."

"It doesn't sound very commercial."

"It is and it isn't," she replied. "This 'right to die' question is becoming more important every day."

"I'm all for it," I replied. "I don't want heroic measures to be taken if I'm dying."

"Me either," Bette agreed. "Who wants to live attached to some goddamn machine, when the brain is gone? But, this couple have a daughter, an artist from Carmel, played by Melinda Dillon, who interferes—and the audience is treated to what happens when bureaucracy is turned loose, with social workers and lawyers and interfering neighbors—all very realistic. They simply can't understand why the old couple don't want to go on living."

I posed my old question, "How are you going to look?"

"I felt this woman wouldn't go to a beauty parlor," she answered, "and would have her hair cut short so she could take care of it herself. Peggy Shannon has found me a white wig. I like it so much, I had a blond one made up for myself."

"And what's the character like?"

There was a pause. "Cute," she said finally. "Cute. She's had a doll shop in Santa Monica and still makes miniature dolls. In fact, that's her name, Miniature Dwyer. Mini's uncomplicated. No temperament. A woman who loves her husband above all else." She laughed. "Do you know that Jimmy and I have a scene in bed together? At this stage of my career, imagine me doing a bed scene! It's important to the story and at our ages, not sexy at all."

Most of *Right of Way* was shot on location in Santa Monica in late 1982. I asked Bette how it was going. "Fine," she said, "just fine. Jimmy has a hearing problem and has trouble learning his lines. But oh god, is he good. If they gave Emmys for HBO, he'd win one. It's the best part he's had in years and he says it's going to be his swan song. We also have to work with a lot of cats; and they are named Robert De

Niro, Paul Newman, Robert Redford—and other top actors—cute touch.

"Between the cats misbehaving and Jimmy, we have to do take after take. It doesn't bother me. I'm very calm about it. I just wait until everything works, because it's worth it to be with him. We were talking the other day about how marvelous it would have been if we'd been able to do a comedy together when we were younger."

A week later Bette was on the phone and angry. "One thing I hate about the film is the dolls they've found, the ones I'm supposed to make. They are huge and ugly. One of the doll scenes was the first to be shot, and I'd just got back from New York and I hadn't seen the dolls until I showed up on the set. The woman's name is Miniature, for god's sake, and the dolls are supposed to be tiny. One other thing that got my dander up; one of them is the image of me, the public Bette Davis—long hair, lipstick, eyelashes. About the way I looked in *All About Eve,* and there's no rhyme or reason for it! But we're on a little budget, and there isn't time to change the dolls. I know a woman who makes tiny, tiny dolls that would have been perfect, but I guess you can't win them all."

I was invited to the screening of *Right of Way* at the Screen Director's Guild on May 6, 1984. Coming into the lobby I heard Bette's chortle; she was joking with Johnny Carson and wearing her red Valentino dress.

The ending of the film was unsatisfying. The daughter, who has been visiting them, finally realizes it's best not to interfere with their wish to die, then on her way back to Carmel, changes her mind, turns the car around, returns to Santa Monica, and calls the paramedics, who remove her parents from the car and take them to the hospital.

After the screening I went up to Bette, who was sitting in the back row of the theater with Kath. "You were wonderful," I said, "you've used things you've never used before."

There were tears in her eyes. "You think so? It was an ordeal," she whispered, looking around. "It's murder seeing a film with a lot of people." She paused, and shook her head. "And, I suppose I've got to get used to seeing myself look that way!"

As Bette was leaving, director Richard Brooks, who had guided her through *The Catered Affair* in 1956, told her he liked what she had done with Minnie Dwyer. Brooks had never forgotten that in his film with her, Bette had made herself look like his mother.

"Jimmy has a hearing problem and has trouble learning his lines. But oh, god, is he good." Bette and Jimmy Stewart in *Right of Way*. LESTER GLASSNER COLLECTION

I hadn't seen Bette on her birthday, because she had been shooting that week, so I had brought along a gift, which I placed in her limousine. I had found a set of dishes featuring a New England farm scene done in the primitive Grandma Moses manner.

By the time I got home that night, Bette had left a message on my machine. She loved the dishes and told me to call the moment I got in even if it was late.

I called her at eleven-thirty. "I'm really furious about the ending!" she exclaimed. "It wasn't the way that it was supposed to be."

"It bothered me, too."

"It was a cop-out!" she cried. "Jimmy and I didn't know that they had shot all that stuff with Melinda coming back. The old people should be allowed to die! I suppose it's too late for them to change it. Damn!"

As it happened, the producers saw the light, and although the film was shown on HBO as previewed, when Metromedia picked it up for showings on commercial television, the ending was changed. The old couple was allowed to die, and then the camera panned over the doll collection for the ending.

Bette lounged on the sofa in my living room at Whistling Chimneys, my new house located at the foot of Mount Baldy, where I had moved the year before.

It was St. Patrick's Day, 1984. Kath had driven up from Palm Springs, where they had spent ten days in the sun. Bette was dressed in a smart red pantsuit with a matching red hat and wore soft shoes. They arrived just before lunch, and Bette looked around the den, then headed for the bar. "You know me!" she laughed.

"Indeed, I do," I said. "There's vodka and orange juice in the refrigerator."

I told Bette how good she looked. She glanced in the mirror, grimaced, and freshened her lipstick. "Not bad for an old dame," she laughed, then looked at me seriously. "Actually, I think I photographed pretty well until I was about forty. *Winter Meeting* was the turning point. I look around today at the women between forty and fifty who're still going strong and I think, *Jesus! How lucky can you get!* There are plenty of roles in that age group. Not back then, I can tell you! Of course, with plastic surgery it's easy to look young today! And the men," she scoffed, "they look just darling with smooth cheeks and jowls pulled back!"

"We're having soup and salad for lunch," I said, "so you can keep your figure."

"Figure? You know I don't usually have lunch. I eat a slice of bread or some cheese standing up, then a nice dinner. So many people who drink don't eat, and that's a mistake."

Bette exclaimed rapturously over tossed green salad and waxed poetic over the homemade vegetable soup. I was accustomed to extravagant praise from her, as were all her friends. Anything that those close to her accomplished was always the best, whether it was roasting a joint of beef, writing a book, making a film, or cleaning a mirror.

After lunch, while Bette was freshening up, I drew Kath aside. "You're awfully thin," I said, "you hardly touched your soup. Doesn't she make you nervous?"

"I cope," Kath replied quietly. "I cope."

I thought what a strain it must be to live twenty-four hours a day with a powerhouse personality. I loved Bette, but spending more than a couple of days with her was exhausting. An actress must live on the outside; a writer must live on the inside. That was the difference between our mental makeups.

I guided Bette into the living room. She glanced at the cover of a magazine featuring Joan Collins on the cover. "Beautiful girl! She's finally made it in *Dynasty* at fifty. Bless her. When she played with me in *Virgin Queen*, I was forty-eight and she was an ingenue. I looked at that blank face and thought, *Fox will cast her in nothing roles forever. She hasn't a chance. She won't fight for the good roles.* And she didn't. She was a sex symbol then, and by god, she's come back as a greater sex symbol twenty-five years later! Good for her. I was doing frump roles at the age she is now. That was all right then, I didn't have a choice, but then I was never a glamour girl. But the sexual situations on TV are getting to be too much.

"I've always hated censorship, because it affected so many of my pictures, but now, it's gone too far in the other direction. Sex should be private. Get in bed, kiss, and then dissolve. Let the audience fill in the details. I can tell you that people's imaginations are hotter than any sex on the screen. There's only one film I can name that it was justified at all, and that was *Coming Home*. In that, the paraplegic has an affair,

"Beautiful girl! She's finally made it in *Dynasty* at fifty. Bless her. When she played with me in *Virgin Queen,* I was forty-eight and she was an ingenue. I looked at that blank face and thought, *Fox will cast her in nothing roles forever.* She was a sex symbol then, and by god, she's come back as a greater sex symbol twenty-five years later!" Joan Collins and Bette in *The Virgin Queen.* LESTER GLASSNER COLLECTION

and the soldier and the girl have to very tenderly work out the logistics. But they went too far, even though they used another girl's body for Jane Fonda's in the bed scenes."

She lighted a cigarette, and puffed energetically. "*Deception* would be a great movie today. Then, we had to pussyfoot about the sexual relationship between Christine and her old lover, Hollenius. Claude Rains rightfully stole the picture. It was up to him to work against the dialogue and to make the audience understand, through his jealousy, that they had been having a hot affair, and that he was not just her piano teacher. He worked like ten men on that movie.

"We were caught between the devil and the deep blue sea. The plot was certainly very French—like the playwright! Paul Henreid and I tried, but even the ending defeated us. When I killed Claude and had to give myself up to the police, it was too damn noble.

"Another movie I wanted to make at about the same time as *Deception* was the Sarah Bernhardt story. I would have played her just before she had her leg amputated and up until her death. Warners would have let me do it, too, but there were lots of legal problems. Madame Sarah's daughter, Lysiane—who wanted me to play her mother—tried everything in her power to get clearances, but couldn't. Then years later, Glenda Jackson did it brilliantly on TV."

She sighed at another lost opportunity and then went back to the subject of Claude Rains. "We were friends for over thirty years. After we both moved East, I'd go visit him in Bucks County and he'd come up to Maine to see me. But, he held on too long. When I saw him at the Westport Playhouse in *Darkness at Noon*, he was having trouble with his lines. I was shocked. He was frail and should have packed it in. But it's easy to say that about someone else. I suppose there are a lot of people who think I should call it quits, but as you grow older, what is there besides work? If a woman doesn't have a man, what does she do with her later years? For me, work is all that counts now. I thought about Claude when I was losing lines in *Moffat*."

Bette got up from the sofa, and her cigarette case slipped on the floor; when I retrieved it, she showed me the inscription inside: *An actor is something less than a man, and an actress is more than a woman.*

She lighted up, then laughed. "That about says it all, doesn't it?"

Before dinner we sat in the living room and chatted over drinks. "By the way," she laughed, "did I ever tell you about the scene between

Susan Hayward and me on the last day of shooting *Where Love Has Gone*? We could have been good friends, but she was aloof.

"I was only ten years older than she was, and with even a wig my own color, I looked too young in the camera to be playing her mother. So I had to wear that damned white wig. Even so, I looked good—I knew it; I was wearing straps.

"The essence of the picture," Bette expounded, "was the very complicated relationship between mother and daughter—otherwise it was just too hysterical. In our scenes together I had to have a certain reserve because of this grande dame I was playing, but I wanted some affection to show between them—the kind of thing that two actresses can do between the lines. It would have given more dimension to our roles. This would have raised the quality of the picture. It wouldn't have turned out so trashy.

"I'd admired Hayward for years. Her *Smash-up, the Story of a Woman* was simply wonderful, but she wouldn't give me anything in our scenes. It was like playing to a blank wall. After weeks of this, keeping my temper and being polite to her on the set, I'd really had it. Everyone else on the picture was great. Mike Connors played her husband, and he was so good. Anyway, after my last scene, just before I went into my dressing room, I took off the wig and threw it at her. 'Fuck you, Susie!' I said and that was the last time I ever saw her.

"I don't know what to think about actresses like Hayward," Bette went on dully. "The audience has to understand women in a different way. We can interact in scenes in a way that men can't. Gable and Tracy, in their buddy pictures, were the exceptions. They were so secure in their masculinity, they could show affection for each other between the lines. It established a wonderful quality in their pictures together. And, I don't mean that men have to hug—the way so many characters do on television—to show they like each other.

"Anne Baxter in *Eve* was superb, but if she had had an attitude like Hayward, the picture would have turned out a big flop. Of course, Mankiewicz wouldn't have stood for it. But Margo and Eve's relationship worked on two or three levels. She was really playing a double role: one thing on the surface, another underneath. I called it the 'sweet bitch.' Her part was more difficult than mine. She worked all through the picture; I only worked three and a half weeks.

"I wanted Norma Shearer so badly for *Old Acquaintance*. I'd admired her for years. It would have been a different picture with her in it, instead of Miriam Hopkins. But Shearer was forty-three and didn't want to come out of retirement. She'd always been the Queen Bee at Metro, and Warners must have seemed like a comedown.

"Even today you get that kind of snobbery. People who live in Bel Air and Beverly Hills slum by 'coming over the hill' and working in the valley! Then too, Shearer had all of Thalberg's money. It also might have been that she was scared of working with me. Plus the fact that she played a bitch. She was used to playing the heroine. Actresses! If I live to be a hundred, I'll never understand them!

"Meryl Streep is probably the most versatile of the current crop," Bette went on quickly. "She's always good, and a past master of accents. But you've got to have good parts in hit pictures, and many of hers fail, and that's too bad. It's not her fault—she can do anything, but it's the material that has always counted and always will. Debra Winger is wonderful, too."

[Streep's career was contrasted with Bette's in the spring 1989 issue of *Life* magazine, which celebrated fifty years of films, 1939–89. The headline read, "Meryl Is Magic, Best in the Business, But Maybe Bette Was Better." The statistics noted that Bette had made forty-one pictures from 1931 to 1939, and Streep had appeared in fifteen from 1977 to 1989, and was five years older than Bette when she had made her first picture, *Julia*, in 1977. Also, Bette was making $40,000 per picture (upgraded to 1989 inflation prices to $365,000), while Streep was earning $2 million to $3 million per film. Bette had two flops among her forty-one films, while Streep had four among her fifteen.]

"When a script is handed to you," Bette was saying, "you don't dare fall in love with your character. If you do, you won't see how other characters relate to you. You may end up with good reviews—but the picture stinks. There's nothing wrong with playing odd types. I made a career out of them, but you can't do it all the time. Every now and then, you've got to play a heroine."

"I always liked you in romantic parts," I said.

She grinned. "Well, if you're in love with your costar, it helps. But if you're wildly in love with someone else while you're making a romantic film, it's far more difficult.

"Love relationships are really the nuts at any time. You know, even after Ham's blackmailing and the trauma of our divorce, would you believe that we almost went back together? We met in an elevator in, of all places, New York. We ended up spending the weekend together. We had both changed. He was more mature. But instinctively, I knew it wouldn't work, any more than the first time, when I had simply outgrown him. We parted friends. That was the last time I saw him.

"Then, after Charles Higham's book about me came out, Ham's wife called me. I invited her for tea and we talked. She is a nice woman. I liked her. Those last years with him in a wheelchair—not knowing anything—couldn't have been easy. Thank god, she had a good job as a television executive. Isn't life strange?"

She snubbed out her cigarette, and went on contemplatively, "I think I have a good chance of making eighty if I don't get a heart attack or a stroke; that's what seems to down most people in their seventies. I've lived life the way I wanted. I like to drink. I've always smoked up a storm. Never actually kept very good care of myself, but so far, so good."

At that point I announced dinner. Bette rhapsodized over the pot roast with browned potatoes and carrots and swore the bread pudding was the best she had ever eaten.

After dinner we had coffee in the living room, with Bette curled up on the sofa. She was so relaxed and at ease, seeming much younger than her years. "You look terrific," I said, "so tiny, so feminine."

"Thank you!" she exclaimed. "You know Lauren Bacall can sing 'I'm One of the Girls Who's One of the Boys,' and be sensational, but it's not my type of song. I could never be one of the boys!"

The next morning at eight, Kath fixed two three-minute eggs and a piece of toast for Bette and brought the tray upstairs. Bette wore a white frilly lace nightgown, a short type that she had made famous in *Old Acquaintance*. Her wearing of the shorty nightgown created a rage in 1943, much as Madonna's "Merry Widow" in 1985. She was looking out the window, over the lemon grove at the mountains. There was snow on Mount Baldy.

Later she came downstairs, dressed in a white cap, jacket, and trousers. "We're going to leave early," she said with a laugh. "I don't mind having people for houseguests, but I want them to leave before the glow wears off. Usually, in two days you've said everything you want to say. When you start repeating yourself, it's time to get out."

She grinned. "It's the same when I have guests for dinner, after they've drunk and eaten and had dessert and coffee, I want them to leave pronto!

"When I visit B.D., I only stay two days. For one thing, it's so damned expensive. It costs about three hundred for the limousine, and then I usually bring presents for the kids."

I kissed Bette on the cheek, and we posed for Kath's camera at the door; then I saw them to their car. My quiet neighborhood had suddenly come alive. Men were ostensibly polishing cars, women were poking around in flower beds, and more than one silhouette could be seen behind lace curtains. Bette Davis had never visited Upland before.

Chapter 16

*I*n 1934, when Frank Capra was casting *It Happened One Night,* he asked Jack Warner to loan Bette to Columbia for the role of the effervescent heiress opposite Clark Gable. The studio had just loaned her to RKO for *Of Human Bondage* and turned him down flat.

Forty-eight years later, Capra was presented with the AFI Achievement Award on the fourth of March of 1982. Bette, giving a nod to Kim Carnes's hit, came to the podium with a snapper that brought howls: "I'm an actress, not a *song!*"

She told the audience: "A great director like Frank gives the audience a new way of seeing the world. Most of all he needs guts. . . . He has to tell the front office we'll do it *my* way, and to admonish the actors when they're not good enough. It's rough because moviemaking isn't a popularity contest; what counts is what's up there on the screen when the audience sees it. As for Capricorn, let's get more corn back into the business."

"I wanted to appear for Frank," she told me later, "because he's practically the last one left of the old directors who were truly geniuses."

"But you had such a problem with him on *Pocketful of Miracles,*" I reminded her.

"Well," she replied pensively, "sometimes you have to forget. He was a monster, but I didn't know until I read his book what he had to put up with to get the film made in the first place. Horrible. And then he had cluster headaches that almost did him in. Ruthie died at that time, so I probably wasn't myself, either. Actors are spared so much when a movie is being made. We only know our part of it, our problems. I wasn't used to the ensemble playing that you get on the stage. *Miracles* was an ensemble acting film.

"As I look back at the way I was then," she continued quietly, "Capra had to take Bette Davis and put her in the film, and make it work. If it was difficult for me, it had to be doubly difficult for him. It was a fairy tale."

"Bette," I laughed, "you are mellowing!"

"Mellowing!" she cried. "Mellowing!" She went on gruffly, "Maybe you're right. God knows, I've been through enough."

"As long as we're talking in this vein," I urged, "what do you think of the horror now in *Hush . . . Hush, Sweet Charlotte*?"

Bette rolled her eyes to the ceiling. "At the time, I was shocked about the head rolling down the stairs. I thought that was a bit much, but in light of all the gore on the screen today, it doesn't seem so repulsive. Charlotte was much more difficult to play than Jane, who was a child in a woman's body. But Charlotte had an innocence about her that I found appealing. In a way, she was another 'fairy tale' character who had a lot in common with Blanche in *A Streetcar Named Desire*. She was an unfortunate, sad woman."

Bette was on the telephone again the day before her birthday, April 5. "Another's gone," she said sadly. "Swanson died today."

"A spectacular Aries," I said.

"Was she? Then that explains so much. She was a true star. It's funny, but stars are really America's royalty. Europeans have theirs by divine right, over here we have nothing. It's important for people to look up to someone. Hollywood gave the public royalty about the time that Swanson came along. Mary Pickford was another role model—a little girl who never grew up. You know, I was never invited to Pickfair; I never traveled in those circles. But after Pickford died, I went to a charity affair there, and I thought, *This is the house of a true queen.*

"It's wonderful to have glamour in our lives. That was the true meaning of the star system. Now we know everything there is to know about celebrities—who they go to bed with, their illegitimate children, everything. There is no mystery anymore. We need heroes, too. Franklin Roosevelt was a hero in my day, Babe Ruth, Clark Gable, a few great others. Name one today! Michael Jackson?

"I wouldn't have minded losing the Oscar to Swanson if she'd won for *Sunset Boulevard*—coming back after all those years, playing a woman that she must have known well. But to lose to Judy Holliday, that was a shocker.

"When stage stars redo a role in a movie, it is completely opposite from creating a role from scratch. See what happens when two older stars like Swanson and me compete? We both lose. Then we also had Anne Baxter who insisted that Fox put her up for nomination, too. Years later, she told me that she shouldn't have asked them to do that. She was my costar, but the picture was mine. The votes were obviously split. Well, Aries or not, Swanson was very special. What they should do is put Lillian Gish and me in the same movie, while we're still alive!"

[In 1987, Gish and Davis costarred in the acclaimed *The Whales of August*, which turned out to be their last film.]

In the spring of 1983, Bette was feeling lackluster; her famous energy was well below normal.

Within the course of three months—March, April, and May—she was presented with several awards. "It's like I'm going to die and everyone's trying to honor me before it happens! If you last in this business, you begin to get trophies for surviving." She laughed. "But it's been fun."

There was a pregnant pause, during which her mood changed. "Actually, this award business can get out of hand, too. Most are legitimate, but some organizations, I swear, look around and find someone who's been in the business for forty or fifty years and who isn't working. They then give them an award, just to get people to come to the affair!

"It costs the recipient—especially if it's a woman—a lot of money. You've got to get a new gown for one thing. And makeup and hairdressing people are not cheap. Then, sometimes they don't even pick up the limousine tab! Then you've got to give some kind of acceptance speech, so you try to say something that hasn't been said a dozen times before. All of this takes time. When you receive three or four of these awards, it can cost thousands.

"If you say that you can't attend for one reason or another, they give the award to someone else, who can!" She drew a deep breath. "I'm off to New York, but not to accept an award this time! I might do the Tonys, if I'm still in New York." She paused. "Did I ever tell you about the last time I did the show?"

"No. What happened?"

"Well as you know, Paul Newman and Joanne Woodward live in Westport, and although we don't move in each other's circles, we have talked on the phone. I truly loved it when a reporter once asked Joanne if she would like to meet me, and she said, 'Why?' That shows you how laid back we are in the East!

"Anyway, I was backstage at the Tonys and Paul Newman was in front of me waiting to go on, and I asked very innocently, 'Mr. Newman, what are you going to do?' And he answered, 'I'm going to go out there and take down my pants!' I was shocked, but not amused!"

Bette left for Manhattan for the summer and I did not hear from her until August 21. I was not alarmed; often, if she was making a film, I wouldn't hear from her for twelve weeks or so. Finally, I got a call from her. "All hell has broken loose," she said in a desperately strange and weak voice. "I've been terribly, terribly ill. Have you heard?"

"No!" I managed to say at last. "I've been holed up in my writing room for months on a deadline and haven't heard a word. Otherwise, I would have called Harold Schiff and asked for news."

"I had a mastectomy on June 9." She paused, then went on in an uncharacteristically resigned way. "And that's not all . . . nine days later, strokes. It was in the *National Enquirer,* naming names and dates."

Her words came back to me: *I think I have a good chance of making eighty if I don't get a heart attack or a stroke . . .*

I was shocked and very concerned. "How *are* you?"

"Well, it all started in May, when I was visiting Anne Baxter in Connecticut. I was dressing one morning when I felt this lump in my breast. It scared me half to death, so I went into New York for a checkup, including X rays. The doctor said that the breast should be removed. All those awards had been scheduled to be presented in Hollywood, so I went back for them. Then I returned to New York for the operation. Thank god the doctor got all the cancer; it was localized."

"But why didn't you tell me that you were going into the hospital?" I asked, somewhat miffed.

There was a long pause. "I didn't think it was something that I should talk to you about." Her voice sounded muffled. "It's a very personal operation. I assumed I would have it done and no one need be the wiser."

"But the shock, Bette, the shock!"

"Well, let's face it, I'm never going to have another lover, and thank god that this didn't happen to me years ago. Aren't you glad you didn't marry me? Look what you would have had to put up with! A woman in her seventies can handle this kind of operation better, but think what young women must go through!

"But there I was, after the stroke, paralyzed, couldn't move a muscle, and I was terrified. The doctors thought I was a lost cause—that if I did recover I'd never work again. I lay there night after night, and thought of Ruthie, just tired and deciding she didn't want to live anymore. And Bobby dying of cancer, and trying to put up such a brave front for me the last time I saw her. I thought, *Why me? I'm not brave. If I die, well, no one can say I haven't had a full life, really.* But I couldn't get used to the idea of death, then. It was all so new.

"Days went by. Then, Kath, who was sleeping in my room, god bless her, was adjusting the sheets and saw my little toe move, and she ran out into the hall to get the nurses. It was then the doctors knew that there was hope for me. They started the therapy. It was a joyous moment for me, and I knew that there was a possibility that I could come back.

"The first thing my doctor asked was: 'What is your name?' I was furious and shouted 'Bette Davis.' And he asked me if I knew where I was, and what day it was, and my birthday. I screamed the answers to all of his questions. It was just like the competency hearing in *A Piano for Mrs. Cimino*, when the judge asked exactly the same questions! Talk about déjà vu!

"Well, very gradually, the muscles in my face came back, and then my right side. My left arm is still giving me problems. Then that damned *Enquirer* ran the story about my illness—with mistakes, as usual—and printed my room number. Then the telephone calls and letters and flowers began to arrive by what seemed thousands. And here I was so helpless. Kath kept saying, 'We'll make it . . .' That really pulled me through.

"The therapy was—and is—agonizing. Anyone who hasn't been through strokes like these has no conception of what it's like. The exercises in themselves are not difficult, it's just that you can't see any progress being made. Of course you are making progress, but it's so slow, so infinitesimal.

"Then I was so listless because of the drugs, and finally Kath told the doctors, who were killing me with kindness, 'No more drugs.' Then I began to improve.

"B.D. came to visit me once, and I was glad to see her, and we chatted. She brought me up to date with the family, but I was so tired after she left. All my energy was gone.

"While I was in no way feeling good, I was beginning to be myself. When I would scream at someone, Kath knew I was getting better!

"I'm cranky and hard to get along with and depressed much of the time," she continued, "and you know that's not like me at all. I get to the point sometimes, when I think, *Is it really worth it?* I told a friend, 'I'm afraid I have a short fuse.' He replied, 'You've always had a short fuse!'

"In the hospital, I'd think about the tragedies in my life. All the mistakes I've made. And then I got to the point where I looked at death in a different way. And I thought, *If my time has come, it's come.* And I really wouldn't have minded all that much. The world was out there and I was in here. I was very calm about it inside.

"I'm still in therapy here at the Lombardy. Kath helps me dress; I still can't move my arm and leg very much, and it takes me an eternity to move. But I'll make it somehow. Bye." She hung up.

That was the first time that she did not end a telephone conversation with "I love you," and I was sad, because I knew that she was still very ill. When Bette did not make a production out of something, the handwriting was on the wall.

When I called Bette back a couple of days later, Kath answered and said that Miss Davis was resting. "I'm glad I have you alone," I said. "How is she *really* doing?"

Kath sounded worried. "Not good."

"What about the therapy?"

"Well, she does the exercises, but . . . I just wish people wouldn't keep telling her that she's a strong person. That's disheartening. She's been through so much and she's scared to death she won't be able to work again, and you know that's the biggest part of her life."

"Is she drinking?"

"Only a wine spritzer before dinner, no scotch."

"Smoking?"

"Vantage cigarettes, no Philip Morris."

"Do you think she'll be able to go back to work?"

Kath paused. "I hope so, but it doesn't look likely in the foreseeable future. She has to be able to do it physically."

"You mean . . . she's impaired?"

"Well," Kath hedged, "she's getting better and better, but it's very slow."

Bette moved to Malibu for the summer, and Kath took an apartment nearby. She had fallen and broken her hip at the Colonial, and the doctor told her that walking along the beach, digging her toes into the sand, would be most helpful in regaining her balance. When her feet grew tired, she would get down on her hands and knees and crawl, then rest, and laboriously get up on her feet again. Strength gradually came back into her legs, although she would always walk with a slight limp.

While at the beach she made her first appearance in public at a Jimmy Stewart dinner party given at a restaurant in Topanga Canyon, not far from the beach house. No photographers were present.

When she returned to the Colonial, I called her. "How's it going?"

"All right, I suppose," she replied, "but my energy isn't what it was. Anyway, I have a script. Remember Henry James's *The Aspern Papers?* It's now called *Burning Bridges* for the film version. Producer Mark Reichert wants me to do the one-hundred-and-eight-year-old woman, with Anthony Hopkins."

[Forty-one-year-old Agnes Moorehead had worn a hideous rubber mask and gloves when she played the same role in *The Lost Moment* in 1947.]

"I'll be in a wheelchair," Bette went on, "and it won't make any difference how I look. . . . They're going to shoot it on location, but how they are going to make Yugoslavia look like Venice is beyond me. I just may do it if they can raise the money."

But the deal fell through, and Bette was secretly relieved. In her first appearance after her illnesses she wanted to look as good as possible, and she was afraid that the public would think that she actually looked that old and fragile.

Bette's voice over the telephone was edgy and tense. "I'm very nervous," she said. "I've decided to go to England for a Miss Marple Agatha Christie TV movie with Helen Hayes.

"It's called *Murder with Mirrors.* Sir John Mills plays my husband. We start filming in November and should end up before Christmas. It's actually a small part and not demanding. I play a character called Carrie Louise, who is being poisoned." She added cryptically, "So they don't expect me to look like Margo Channing! But I don't know whether I can take those hours on a set yet, and I'm not sure I can remember the lines."

I knew that it was the old insecurity eating at her. "Bette," I said reassuringly, "you always say that at the beginning of a movie. Think about *The Virgin Queen,* when you hadn't worked in three years."

"This is completely different!" she answered tartly, "and don't you dare say that I'm Aries and strong enough to do it!"

"Bette," I replied firmly, "the director is not going to expect either you or Helen Hayes to do somersaults. After all she's older than you, eighty-four! And Sir John is your age."

"I'm still very apprehensive."

And well she might have been. The woman who played Carrie Louise did not look like the Bette Davis they knew, and it was no fault of the cameraman.

Although Bette had never been beautiful in the Vivien Leigh mold, there was a period of about ten years—from 1937 to 1947, from *That Certain Woman* through *Deception*—that she often gave the illusion of beauty.

So Bette, having been photographed by Ernie Haller, Tony Gaudio, and Sol Polito, had a complex about the way she looked on film in the seventies and eighties. Spoiled by these men who could only be called film cosmetologists, she was never satisfied with the current crop of directors of photography and often threatened to have them replaced.

For *Murder with Mirrors,* Bette felt the chatelaine of a great English manor house would have dyed brown hair. A suitable wig was chosen. Since all the other females in the film wore very little makeup, a

Although Betty had never been beautiful in the Vivien Leigh mold, there was a period of about ten years—from 1937 to 1947, from *That Certain Woman* through *Deception*—that she often gave the illusion of beauty. Bette in *Deception*, 1946. C 1946 WARNER BROS. PICTURES, INC. REN. 1973 UNITED ARTISTS TELEVISION, INC.

line was added about how Carrie Louise always took great care with her appearance.

"Kath has been such a godsend to me," Bette said from the Lombardy upon her return from Hertfordshire, England. "She's going to be billed as my assistant. We filmed at a thirteenth-century estate called Brocker Hall. Gorgeous. And the countryside is so beautiful. How are you doing?"

"Right now I'm reorganizing all my material on you."

"Well," she said brightly, "when I'm gone, tell the truth in your book."

"I will. I've taken notes for years." I asked her how *Murder with Mirrors* went, and she said to me, "Well, the experience wasn't as bad as I thought it would be. The first day was hell. But when they started to shoot, my blocking came out naturally and the lines were there."

"How did you like to work with Helen Hayes?"

There was a meaningful pause. "She's *all right*. But, I've never cared for her very much, you know. She's tiny, like me, and she's a pro, and our scenes together, which were shot on the last day, went fine. I would have appreciated a little more rehearsal, though. Helen gives you everything you need in a scene. But we didn't get chummy. I came on the set and did what I had to do, and that was it! But, I must say, I was not thrilled when she was interviewed in New York after coming back from England and she told the press that I'd come back too soon!"

A few weeks later Bette received a note from Hayes, saying how nice it was to work with her, and that she had learned so much about how to conduct oneself on the set. Bette sent her an engraved silver mirror.

Both Harold Schiff and Kath knew that B.D. Hyman, who had converted from agnosticism to Pentecostalism, and had moved with her family to the Bahamas, was writing a book about her life with Bette. They said nothing, because it was essential that she finish *Murder with Mirrors* without being emotionally upset. The film was crucial for her mental well-being, and it was essential that she realize that she could work again after her illnesses. Before the last two days of shooting, just before she left London, afraid that word in the trade would reach her about the book, Bette was told. She was incredulous.

"What kind of a book could B.D. write?" Bette asked me on the telephone, after she had arrived in New York. "She's become a born-again Christian and this is supposed to be her statement?"

"I'll try to get a copy of the bound galleys," I said.

B.D. had received a $100,000 advance from Morrow, the publishers of *My Mother's Keeper*. When the softcover rights were auctioned later, Berkley Books won with a $605,000 commitment, according to *Publishers Weekly*. The English rights went to Michael Joseph for $57,000.

On February 19, 1985, ABC aired David Hartman's interview with Bette on *Good Morning America*, her first public appearance on a talk show since her illnesses. She was fond of Hartman and knew that he would not ask embarrassing questions. Her main purpose in doing the show was to tell about her recovery.

Her appearance was a shock to the public. She was gaunt, and the side of her mouth, pulled down at the corner, gave her a pathetic look. Her brownish wig was not becoming. She resembled the elderly Fanny Skeffington. But when she spoke of her recovery some of her old fire came back, and for a moment or two, she was the Bette Davis of old.

A *USA Today* (April 30, 1985) review of B.D.'s book appeared alongside an interview with Bette, both by Giselle Galante, the daughter of Olivia De Havilland. Bette had given very few interviews since her illnesses and did not want to be questioned about the book. De Havilland had brought her daughter to meet Bette in February at the Lombardy, and she had agreed to be interviewed.

When Galante asked about B.D.'s book, Bette replied, "I had no idea she was writing a book. It astonished me . . . I have not even read it yet. I give her the benefit of the doubt. I adore my daughter and I think she loves me, too. I think I have been a good mother and I hope that she agrees with me."

The review began:

There are no wire hangers in B.D. Hyman's *My Mother's Keeper*, a memoir of her mother, Bette Davis. But there are beatings and drunkenness, jealousy and rage. It all adds up to a portrait as disturbing and bitter as Christina Crawford's *Mommie Dearest*.

Rather than loving her daughter too little, as was the case with Joan Crawford, Hyman writes that her mother, now 77, loved her too much—to the exclusion of almost everyone else. Hyman, 38 this week and Davis's only natural child (she adopted two others), writes that her mother often said that "B.D. is the only thing I have ever really loved . . ."

Commented columnist Radie Harris of *The Hollywood Reporter,* May 6, 1985, who had known Bette for over forty years:

I have just finished reading it and am still reeling from the shock. Compared to Christina Crawford's revelations about *her* famous mother, Joan Crawford emerges like a Rebecca of Sunnybrook Farm, while B.D.'s description of Bette's booze and battling treatment of her, makes her sound as monstrous as Annie's orphanage mistress, Miss Hannigan.

The week of Mother's Day, *People* magazine hit the newsstands with a cover illustrated with a prestroke color photo of Bette, and an interview with B.D. inside. The article by Andrea Chambers, speaking of B.D. and Jeremy Hyman, concluded with:

As they face the future, they may need a guardian angel. "The first precept of any religion is honor thy father and mother," says Gena Rowlands, who played Davis's daughter in the 1979 TV movie *Strangers: The Story of a Mother and Daughter.* Readers may loudly echo that sentiment. Yet Bette Davis's bold, possibly foolhardy daughter insists she has carried out "a Christian act, not a betrayal."

Time magazine, August 19, 1985, said of the book:

Scandal began with the first motion picture, but the modern sharper-than-a-serpent's-tooth era can be traced to 1978 and the appearance of *Mommie Dearest,* the harsh memoir of Joan Crawford. *My Mother's Keeper,* by B.D. Hyman, is even more acrimonious. Joan Crawford was dead a year when the revenge was taken. Bette Davis is still alive and ticking. B. (for Barbara) D. (for Davis) Hyman declares that the front door is always open to her estranged mother. But only a masochist would enter after the appearance of this seething volume.

Bette was absolutely numbed. "What do you think about the book?" she asked.

"I'm in shock. Speechless. I still can't believe it," I answered.

"It's not written by the B.D. that I knew inside and out," Bette said. "It's unreal. I haven't read it all, I can't, but a few pages here and there . . . It's all so twisted, so distorted."

"I know," I answered heatedly. "I was aware of some of the incidents she described, because I was with you in Westport during those times. A bit of truth is there, but molded out of shape. It's the surly, mean-spirited, ungrateful attitude that surprised me most of all."

"Yes," Bette said, "not one compliment. Not one accolade. Oh, I just can't talk about it, I'm so shook up."

"What are you going to tell the press?"

"Nothing. I will not comment. For me, the book does not exist."

And Bette stuck to her guns.

Support for Bette came from diverse quarters. Gary Merrill (who was destined to write his own book in 1989, *Bette, Rita, and the Rest of My Life*) picketed a bookstore in Portland, Maine, and took out an advertisement in *The New York Times*, which read in part, "Greed was B.D. Hyman's guide when she wrote *My Mother's Keeper*, the scurrilous new book about B.D.'s mother, actress Bette Davis. And anything for a buck is what William Morrow & Co. must have said when they published it." Merrill went on to give Harold Schiff's address and urged readers to write to him and support Bette. "Tell her you are boycotting the book. You'll both feel better. A message from Gary Merrill, Bette's friend and former husband." And he gave his address.

"Well," Bette said, "while I do thank him, I don't feel he did it strictly for me, since from what I understand, he also fared badly in the book."

B.D.'s book was on several best-seller lists. In Los Angeles on a promotional tour, she was interviewed by Roderick Mann of the *Los Angeles Times*, May 18, 1985:

Someone asked, "How could you write a book like this? It will destroy your mother." My answer is that it will take more than my book to destroy my mother. She's indomitable."

B.D. went on to say that her mother would eventually capitulate and contact her and that "will be the start of true communication between us. As I say at the end of my book, the door will always be open."

Bette's voice was never the same after the strokes. She had learned to project on the stage, and that training came back when she recovered. Her voice seemed to come from deep inside, an effort. And, her gaiety, one of her most outstanding personality traits, would never be the same. She would laugh and carry on as usual, but there was a new fragility, even when she was angry.

She was suddenly an old woman.

Never again would she cackle like Baby Jane.

Chapter 17

Retrospectives of Bette's classic movies were organized in several parts of the world during the late 1980s, and her films were regularly shown on public and cable television stations.

"In a way, it's like I'm being exhumed, when they have these festivals that show my old films," she said dourly, then brightened. "It's a great tribute, of course. But when the pictures are shown, the public sees only what's there, which was the Wyler and Capra and Mankiewicz points of view. If they knew what transpired while they were being made—they just wouldn't believe it!

"I saw *The Bride Came C.O.D.* the other night on television, a film no one remembers, my first out-and-out comedy. It was released before *Foxes*. I only had ten days' vacation over the Christmas holidays, after I'd finished *The Great Lie,* and I married Farney to the surprise of everyone—including me. He was a Yankee, and I think that's why I fell in love with him. He was low key, and by today's jargon, I guess you'd say he was 'laid back.' He was a corduroy and pipe man, and the handsomest of all my husbands.

"The best thing about *Bride* was the casting of Jimmy Cagney as my boyfriend. He hadn't done a comedy in years, either, and we both needed a change of pace at that point in our careers.

"Farney went with us to Death Valley for the outdoor stuff. I think the fact that I was in love gave the picture a certain sparkle. It was by no means a 'Bette Davis film,' and Hal Wallis hoped that Cagney fans would come in droves."

She blew a puff of smoke through her nostrils, and inhaled again. "Farney had never been treated to my kind of fame—the way that actors are treated by the cast, reporters, the crew, and fellow actors. He only knew me tramping around New Hampshire, with my hair up and just lipstick on. He was the manager of Peckett's Inn in the White Mountains. Ruthie loved him, and in fact it was she who introduced us! Being the husband of a famous woman is not what any man should endure, actually. Often, it's hell.

"I tried to prepare him, and he was cordial with everyone. Since we were really on our honeymoon we were given more privacy. The picture was so-so—but made money I guess—and Jimmy and I had fun. After I left the studio, I didn't run into him often. He was such a private person. The last time I saw him was at the Radio City Music Hall's *The Night of a Thousand Stars,* which everyone dubbed *The Night of a Thousand Face-Lifts!*

"They placed Jimmy's wheelchair in the stage's basement on an elevator for the finale. When all the stars had already gathered onstage, he was brought up on the lift. As we were hailed and given a standing ovation, Jimmy began to cry. It was heartbreaking. This old man, who had been so active, a singer, a dancer, a dramatic actor even, turning sentimental. It gave me pause. The way that Jimmy tackled his roles—and *C.O.D.* was no exception—he was never less than a man."

"How about your other comedy with *Bride* in the title? *June.*"

"With Robert Montgomery?" Bette paused meaningfully. "He was something else! I had known him for years, since summer stock days, and liked him. But my god, he was a teaser. Now, don't misunderstand, I love practical jokes, but he deviled me from the beginning of the picture to the end. I was under a great strain, because *Winter Meeting,* which I had just finished, was such a dog. We both needed a good picture. His career had gone downhill after he came back from the war. This was a very funny comedy, and I was bound and determined not to show how miffed I was at his attempts to upset me."

"You mean he was nasty?" I asked. "Montgomery is quite funny in that drunk scene when he falls into a snowbank."

"You don't understand," she went on quickly. "He was exactly right for the part, and our chemistry was great. He had been through

"The best thing about *The Bride Came C.O.D.* was the casting of Jimmy Cagney as my boyfriend. He hadn't done a comedy in years, either, and we both needed a change of pace at that point in our careers." Bette and Cagney in *The Bride Came C.O.D.* LESTER GLASSNER COLLECTION

"Robert Montgomery was a teaser. He deviled me from the beginning of the picture to the end. I was under a great strain, because *Winter Meeting*, which I had just finished, was such a dog. We both needed a good picture. His career had gone downhill after he came back from the war. I was bound and determined not to show how miffed I was at his attempts to upset me." Bette and Montgomery in *June Bride*.
LESTER GLASSNER COLLECTION

the studio wars, just like I had. He was just unprofessional, that's all. He tried to outsmart me at every turn. Like Bogey, he was a needler, and he had intelligence and wit, too, so I wasn't dealing with a numbskull.

"When it came to shooting close-ups—best shot in the morning when makeup is fresh—as a courtesy the women always do theirs *first,* since the cameraman has to fiddle more with the lights.

"Well when I went to see the rushes, I was flabbergasted. He reacted differently in his close-ups than I had in mine! This meant that the film cutter would use his close-ups only; mine would not fit.

"It was similar to what I had to put up with concerning Dick Barthelmess in *Cotton,* who waited for the close-ups to do his real emoting. As a supporting player I didn't have any clout then, but I had now. Very graciously, I said, 'Bob, since you are my costar, and a guest artist not under contract to the studio, I waive my right to shoot my close-ups first. Be my guest.' He smiled and bowed, but he knew damn well that I had won. He was a bit more docile after that."

"We haven't spoken about scene stealing," I said, "excepting Miriam Hopkins."

Bette rolled her eyes. "She was the worst. She had studied the camera and had worked out little bits of business. In a 'two shot,' when one character is speaking, it's bad form for the other character to distract from the dialogue. But she would pat her hair, fondle a button—anything to attract the audience's attention.

"Another thing, she seldom looked at you directly, because she was always showing as much of her face to the camera as she could. All actors have to *cheat* a bit, so you won't show your profile all the time—you learn how to do it gracefully, but she was impossible. She finally ruined her career because people hated to work with her. She only made a few films after *Old Acquaintance* and was effective only in the two made with Wyler, *The Heiress* and *The Children's Hour.* By then, she was supporting. Willie liked her work but wouldn't put up with her crap.

"But I never worked with people who were real scene stealers. The films that I did with female costars you can bet the director was careful to give us equal footage. I would have hated to work with Peter Lorre or Sydney Greenstreet, for example, because they would pull everything in the book. Lorre's famous trick was to blow smoke in your eyes. I think it was Mary Astor who slapped his face once after he had done that to her. Greenstreet's was to giggle. Even Walter Brennan, a notorious

"Miriam Hopkins was the worst at scene stealing. She would pat her hair, fondle a button—anything to attract the audience's attention. Another thing, she seldom looked at you directly, because she was always showing as much of her face to the camera as she could. She only made a few films after *Old Acquaintance*. William Wyler liked her work but wouldn't put up with her crap." Miriam Hopkins and Bette in *Old Acquaintance*. LESTER GLASSNER COLLECTION

scene stealer, was a joy when we did *Stolen Life,* but he took all of his scenes in *To Have and Have Not* from Bogie and Bacall."

Bette was wound up like a top. I fed her the line, "What about your other comedy, *The Man Who Came to Dinner?*"

"I needed a short part after *Foxes,*" she replied gamely, "to lighten my schedule. But since I had star billing, they built the role by adding some romantic scenes with Richard Travis. But I'm all for a small part if it helps your image. That was the only time I got to play with Ann Sheridan and Jimmy Durante. He always called me Bett. Some of the lines are still hysterical after forty years or so!"

[*The Man Who Came to Dinner* dealt with a famous radio personality/lecturer, Sheridan Whiteside, who is invited to the home of an Ohio couple for dinner. He slips and breaks his ankle on their doorstep and convalesces with them, riotously taking over the household.]

I laughed. "The ending was hilarious, with Whiteside falling on the doorstep *again* after his recovery. The audience knows that the entire scenario will be repeated. Don't forget Eleanor Roosevelt's voice over the telephone for the last shot, saying 'Sherry, Sherry . . .' while he is flat on his back on the ice at the front door!"

Bette threw back her head and laughed. "That's ideal comedy. But it was Monty Woolley's picture. He had played Whiteside on Broadway for *years.* Would you believe he had taught at Yale? He knew Alexander Woollcott, on whom the character was based.

"As good as Woolley was, I knew John Barrymore would be better. He tested for the part, and since his memory was shot with all that booze over the years, he had to read his dialogue from 'idiot cards.' I would have put up with that—and much more—if he had won the part. But the studio was afraid he couldn't keep the schedule; he was in almost every scene. It would have revived his career. But seeing the great Barrymore fumbling around those last years, parodying himself, was not pleasant. I don't want that to happen to me!"

I was visiting Bette at the Colonial for drinks, and she had settled back in an easy chair. I knew she was nostalgic and was about to launch into one of her famous monologues.

"The difficult thing about film was, in my day, of course, that you never knew which take they'd print. By the second week of filming, you didn't even dare to think about what your performance was going to look like up there. You were in the director's hands completely. He had the final cut, and if the cutter had any sensibilities at all, he brought out the best that you'd put on film.

"But the editor can't do anything about it—after all, he gets the film last, so if he doesn't have enough other stuff to work with, he's hamstrung. They always said that Hitchcock 'cut his films in the camera,' so that if he died before it was cut, the editor had to put it together as he had planned.

"My favorite editor—and Wallis's too—was Warren Low. He cut *Voyager* and *Heaven* and *The Sisters* and many more. He saved a lot of my films, because he knew how to cut me in and out at exactly the right moment. For instance, one goddamn close-up held too long can absolutely ruin a particular scene, or if it isn't held long enough it can spoil the effect. Usually there were too many close-ups, anyway. Close-ups are very special and must be used sparingly. *The Corn Is Green* was a good picture, but Rapper used too many close-ups, and they intruded on the performance.

"An actor's timing is one thing, but when a film is cut into pieces and pasted back together again, it may be altered, sometimes saved, often destroyed. A performance can be negated by what's done to a film. Maybe we'd done two or three other films by the time the one we'd put all our hopes in came out.

"Well, my dear, you'd go to a screening and the picture is so different. After all, there's lots of scenes in which you didn't appear, so you didn't know how they went. And the extra stuff, too, like the titles, that set the mood of the film. When you see it for the first time altogether, it's usually hell. And every once in a while, you just gloat, because it's so right.

"It's all different now doing small parts, because you simply show up and do your scenes and hope they'll use the best takes. But when you were a star in those days, you were responsible for the whole picture in the eyes of the public. They never knew about all those crappy things that took place every day when you were making a picture. So I was put out when stupid mistakes were being made. I'd made all those shit pictures with crappy stories and crappy directors when I first started out. I didn't have any say-so at all then, so I just went home at night and screamed.

"So when I had the power, I used it, and I got a reputation for raising hell. I wasn't throwing my weight around for no cause. I can name film after film where everything went perfectly smoothly when we had the right script and the right cast and the right director. But that didn't happen often.

"Today, a director turns in 'his cut' and checks off the lot and goes somewhere else to make his next picture. A 'director's cut' doesn't mean a damn today. Someone higher up can have the thing chopped up and re-edited. You read about it all the time. So, we get bad pictures that could have been good pictures.

"But, of course, sometimes it works the other way around. Did I tell you that I finally saw the director's cut of *Bunny O'Hare*? Well, it was awful. Bad as the finished picture was, when they added all those new scenes and recut Borgnine's and my scenes—it was better than the original!

"Today I can cry when I see a movie made for television and the star is being misused. Sometimes a performance is ruined by poor direction, or when the star is being badly photographed. Artistry is gone today for making films, even expensive films for theaters."

Bette had never been pleased that her films were remade. She had suffered through both Eleanor Parker's and Kim Novak's Mildred in *Of Human Bondage* ("Eleanor was too healthy looking. At least Kim looked anemic!"); Susan Hayward's *Stolen Hours* treatment of *Dark Victory;* and Elizabeth Montgomery's TV version of *Victory* ("Susie was too strident; Liz didn't have pathos").

When George Cukor came out of retirement to direct the televersion of *The Corn Is Green,* Bette watched the show with disinterest. "Hepburn, as much as I admire her, was miscast," she said. "And can't she do anything without veils? The only good part was the beginning, which showed Miss Moffat touring the coal mines; that should have been in our script. It set the whole tone of the story for the viewer, showing the young boys working under inhuman conditions."

Said Bette of Lee Remick's 1982 televersion of *The Letter:* "She did look cold, too cold." And George Cukor's 1981 treatment of *Old Acquaintance* with Jacqueline Bisset and Candice Bergen, retitled *Rich and Famous,* brought forth this response: "My god, that sex scene in the bathroom of the airplane, I couldn't believe it!"

Bette was sanguine when she heard that there would be a remake of *Dead Ringer,* entitled *Killer in the Mirror* in 1986. "Dammit, why can't they leave my old films alone?" she cried. "They belong to a certain era.

"I felt so sorry for Willie Wyler when they remade his *Wuthering Heights.* I'm not saying that *Ringer* was a great picture, but it had a certain flair, technically. A TV budget can't duplicate all those special split-screen effects!"

I sent Bette flowers on Mother's Day as usual, in memory of *Mother Goddam,* but she sounded depressed when she telephoned to thank me. "It was a tough day, because of B.D."

Fortunately another script, *The Whales of August,* came her way. "What's the part like?" she asked the agent. He told her that she would portray Lillian Gish's blind, older sister.

"Older?" she cried. "Older? My god, Gish has to be in her nineties!"

"Do you play the heroine or the bitch?" I asked when she told me about the role.

There was a long pause. "You can't characterize the parts that way. Let's say that I'm the tough one, and Gish is softer. I'm bitchy, but not a bitch. Gish seems frail, but is strong underneath. Until you read the script, you won't know what I mean. It's all underplayed, how we react."

[It is a matter of record that, once Bette had become a box-office property, she was not enamored of costarring with women. Outside of specialized films like *The Man Who Came to Dinner, The Catered Affair, Pocketful of Miracles, Death on the Nile, Thank Your Lucky Stars,* and *Hollywood Canteen;* or pictures where she received special billing, like *Phone Call from a Stranger, John Paul Jones, The Scientific Cardplayer, Burnt Offerings,* among her ninety-nine feature and television films, she had shared top billing with only nine women. They were: Miriam Hopkins *(The Old Maid, Old Acquaintance);* Olivia De Havilland *(In This Our Life, Hush . . . Hush, Sweet Charlotte);* Anne Baxter and Celeste Holm *(All About Eve);* Joan Crawford *(What Ever Happened to Baby Jane?);* Susan Hayward *(Where Love Has Gone);* Faye Dunaway *(The Disappearance of Aimee);* Gena Rowlands *(Strangers: The Story of a Mother and Daughter);* and Helen Hayes *(Murder with Mirrors).* She always felt that Mary Astor actually played opposite her in *The Great Lie* and was thrilled when she won an Oscar for her supporting role.

[On Broadway, Bette had starred with Margaret Leighton in *The*

Night of the Iguana, and while they had not fought, they had not become friends, either.

[Bette was really fond of only four female costars: De Havilland, Astor, Baxter, and Rowlands, whom she favored above the others. I speculated on how she would fare with Miss Lillian.]

Later, Bette told me, "I'm not going to do it unless I get top billing."

The agents worked out the contracts so that Bette's name was listed first on the left-hand side of the advertisements, but Gish's name, on the right, was slightly higher. (This tactic was much less expensive than the solution Paramount was forced to use for Bette Midler and Shelley Long on *Outrageous Fortune*. They distributed two sets of prints, half of which featured Long's name first and half with Midler's first.)

The Whales of August, a play by David Berry, dealt with the tenuous relationship between two widowed sisters coming to terms with old age. Sarah Louise Webber, the younger, kind and consoling, has become care giver to the self-centered, carping, embittered but affluent Libby May Strong, who lives in a fine old house in Philadelphia. Sarah has inherited a summer cottage located on an island off the coast of Maine, where the action takes place during a two-day period.

Since they were young, Sarah and Libby have always spent the hot summer months on the island together watching the whales. The fact that the whales do not appear this year is symbolic, suggesting that the characters themselves may shortly become extinct.

"The challenge of the role," Bette told me somewhat wearily, "is that I won't be able to use my eyes. In *Dark Victory* I had to go blind, so I know how a sightless person reacts—but that was only the ending scene. I'm blind all the way through this bloody film!"

She laughed hollowly. "Aren't you going to ask how I look, Whitney?"

"You beat me to it!" I exclaimed.

"Well, Libby has long white hair, which is a story point. She compares it to her mother's hair, and it has to be as white as swans' feathers. I've got to find the right wig. She has money, so that means her wardrobe must look like upper-class Philadelphia. Other than that, I'll look as good as I can—with this face!"

It was the first time that Bette had alluded to the slightly pulled-down lip, the final effect of the stroke.

Bette, as usual, turned down the script the first time, but capitulated as the project began to jell, with Gish, ninety-four or thereabouts; Ann Sothern, seventy-six; and Vincent Price, seventy-six.

Bette spoke wistfully. "It's a delicate script, but I wonder if anyone will be interested in these old dames?" Later Vincent Price commented humorously, "It's a very dear story about nothing." When he told his wife, actress Coral Brown, that he was to do the film with an elderly cast for Alive Productions, she quipped, "May I suggest they change the name to 'Just Barely'?"

Bette spent the month of August in New York, where she had another operation on her hip, which had been giving her more problems.

When she took the plane from New York to Boston, friends at the airport were shocked to see Gary Merrill get off the plane first.

"Can you believe that of all the planes in the world, Gary and I would be on the same one?" she said on the phone from her hotel.

"Did you speak?" I asked.

"Of course. We had a nice chat. It was all very cordial. He looked old. The last time I saw him was at Mike's wedding to Chou." She sighed. "I guess he must have been glad that we hadn't stayed together, considering all that's happened over the last twenty-five years!" A nostalgic tone crept into her voice. "Yet, it all might have been different." She laughed wryly. "Oh god, we Aries and our dreams!"

Bette encountered a situation on the movie that had never occurred before. During the last part of her career, she had become accustomed to the generation gap that existed between her and the cast and crew of her films. Bette was always the "old pro." However, in *Whales*, the situation was reversed. Her costar had performed on the stage with such international stars as Sarah Bernhardt when Bette was born, and acted in the great classic *Birth of a Nation* when Bette was starting the first grade in school.

Bette felt rather intimidated. As for Gish, her great film career could be said to have been finished when Bette began to act in Hollywood. Then Bette went on to perform some of the great woman's roles in talkies, a few of which had appealed greatly to Gish, who had especially liked *Dark Victory*.

The Whales of August was not a happy shoot and was soon alluded to as "The Wails of August." The personalities of the ladies were not complementary. They were both shy of each other, and then

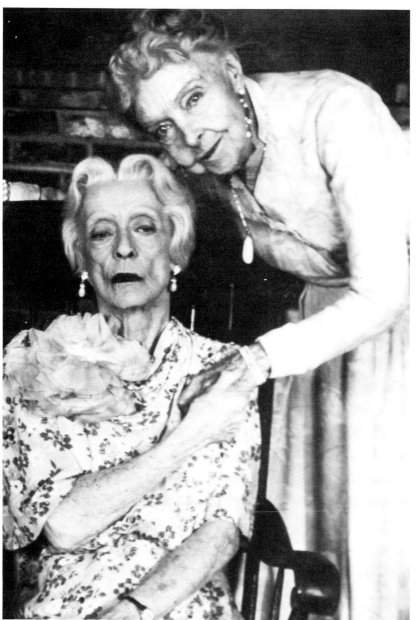

The Whales of August was not a happy shoot and was soon alluded to as "The Wails of August." The personalities of the ladies were not complementary. Bette and Lillian Gish in *The Whales of August*. LESTER GLASSNER COLLECTION

the long hours and cool weather proved difficult for their frail constitutions. Gish said, "I accepted this play five years ago when I was much stronger. I turned it down at first. I guess I was tired, and you have to get up so early!"

In *People* magazine, December 14, 1987, Jill Pearlman, reported by Michael Alexander, wrote about Bette:

> Time and again, when Lindsay Anderson suggested a gesture or a line reading, she snorted, "That's nonsense!" And she cut Lillian cold—seldom spoke to her, rarely even looked at her, except as the script required. Lillian was hurt, yet at the same time she was shocked into sympathy. "That face! Have you ever seen such a tragic face? Poor woman! How she must be suffering! I don't think it's right to judge a person like that. We must bear and forbear."

The crew began to feel that the antagonism between the sisters spilled over in the relationship between Davis and Gish on the set.

"We are too exhausted to talk much," Bette said with her tendency toward exaggeration. "Let's say that we don't particularly like each other personally—and let it go at that. But we respect each other a lot. The location is murder and doesn't help anyone's feelings."

The difference in the temperaments of the ladies might be gathered from embroidered sofa pillows in their respective living rooms. Gish's read: *What you get is a living . . . what you give is a life.*

Bette's read: *NO GUTS. NO GLORY.*

Chapter **18**

ette spent Christmas 1986 in the East, then flew to Hamburg to make another film. However, to her dismay, the finish money never came through. She spent a miserably cold week in a hotel, then flew back to New York only to be confronted with another snowstorm.

"Well," she said, "every time I go abroad, I come back feeling that this is the greatest country on God's green earth. I could kneel down and kiss the ground! I must say this much for Mr. Reagan, he's made us more patriotic. It's so easy to criticize our own country if we're here. But the comments from Americans overseas, you won't believe! Dammit, we should be proud we're a free country!"

Bette had worked for several years on the sequel to *The Lonely Life.* It was extremely hard work, because after B.D.'s book, she had decided to add certain elements of family life that she had not included in the manuscript. She had originally intended to call the book *Bette,* but for a time the property was known in publishing circles as *P.S.,* then *What These Eyes Have Seen: Reminiscences by Bette Davis.*

The book had a long history. The original contract had been signed in 1979 with William Morrow Co., with a writer who later had to leave the job because of other commitments. Next came a new publisher, E. P. Dutton, with a new writer, Michael Herskowitz. Her editor left the company, and Bette then decided to finish the book with

Kath. It was completed in the fall of 1985, with the title *This 'n That*. Problems developed at Dutton, which refused the finished manuscript. Consequently the following advertisement appeared in *Publishers Weekly*, May 9, 1985:

BOOK for SALE

Book written by Bette Davis, her seven-year assistant, Kathryn Sermak, and Michael Herskowitz. This book was turned down, upon completion, by her publishers, because it was not a "kiss 'n tell" book. Title of book is *This 'n That*, a title completely apropos to the contents of this book.

If interested in reading it please contact the Lantz Agency.

Bette Davis

This 'n That was purchased by Putnam's. Bette said it was "like going home again" because the firm had published *The Lonely Life*. During the week of April 19, the book was entrenched in the second position on the *Los Angeles Times* list. The remembrance would remain on *The New York Times* best-seller list for fifteen weeks. Bette was quite touched when many stroke victims wrote, saying that her account of her own recovery had been a source of inspiration to them.

When Bette was scheduled to present the Best Actor award at the fifty-ninth Academy Awards televised on ABC, she had already taped a Barbara Walters special that would be shown directly after the Oscar telecast on the same network.

Over the years, Bette had grudgingly become a Walters admirer. "You've got to hand it to her," she said, "being a woman is tough enough in this business, but for her to get Castro on the show is something else. Plus, she had to outlive all that 'Barbara Wah Wah' stuff, and she did it with dignity."

As it turned out, it was fortunate indeed that Bette did consent to do the Walters interview. Just when it was most important for Bette to show the world that, at age eighty, she was healthy and as sharp as ever, an unfortunate mix-up on the Academy Awards show itself gave the impression that she was over the hill.

Her responsibilities on the program included giving the names of the Best Actor nominees as clips from the films were projected on a large screen onstage. Then she would open the envelope and announce the winner. At rehearsal, director Marty Pasetta suggested that, since the timing was crucial, it would be easier to record her voice over the clips, but she nixed the idea. "I'll be here in person," she proclaimed, "so there's no need to tape my voice now."

The rehearsal went well. But that night, the television audience saw something else. After Bette received applause and a standing ovation, she glanced at the screen, which showed an excerpt of Bob Hoskins in *Mona Lisa*, paused a moment, and gave his name just *after* the image on the screen switched to Paul Newman in *The Color of Money*. The director, not wanting to confuse the audience, cut Bette's mike, so none of the nominees' names was heard after that.

The next view was a long shot, from the rear of the auditorium, showing both the audience and the screen onstage. The tiny, voiceless figure at the podium looked lost. The film clips continued without identification. The fact that much of the audience had not seen her since her illnesses, and was not prepared for her frail appearance, contributed to the impression that she was confused.

Back in medium shot, Bette announced Paul Newman as the winner. To confound matters, when Director Robert Wise appeared to pick up the award for Newman, who was not present, Bette, who had been told to cut her speech in the meantime, was incensed that he would not have an introduction like everyone else. She began to speak about his career, but her mike was cut off again, this time in midsentence. Pasetta then switched the camera to the next presenters, a surprised Chevy Chase and Goldie Hawn.

"Someone kept running on and saying to me, 'Name the winner! Name the winner!'" Bette said. "Then before I could say 'Mr. Paul Newman cannot be here tonight,' they shoved someone onstage to replace me . . ."

The Walters show, following the Oscars, helped revive Bette's image. Although she looked painfully thin, her voice was strong and she was obviously in full charge of all of her faculties.

Bette was furious about the Oscars performance. "It looked like I didn't know what in the hell I was doing! It's true I was late in identifying the first clip, but I was on time after that. I didn't know my mike was dead. And when Bob Wise started his remarks, I interrupted to speak about him."

With all of the furor over her appearance on the Academy Awards show, Bette's eightieth birthday on April 5, 1988, was not a happy occasion.

Still searching for her next film, Bette read *Steel Magnolias*, a play by Robert Harling, and announced that it was the most exciting script she had read in years. Since there were two other major characters, all of whom meet in a beauty shop in Louisiana and go over their lives, she asked Elizabeth Taylor and Katharine Hepburn to see the play.

After a few days' rest in New York, Bette attended the Tuesday, August 25 performance of *Steel Magnolias* at the Lucille Lortel Theatre. Although the play was interesting, Bette, as well as Hepburn and Taylor, found that it read better than it played.

While in Manhattan, she heard good reports about another play and slipped into the John Houseman off-Broadway theater to see *Driving Miss Daisy* by Alfred Uhry, a three-character Pulitzer Prize–winner. The story deals with a Jewish, self-reliant former schoolteacher who totals her automobile. When she's unable to obtain car insurance, her son hires a sixty-year-old black chauffeur. The thrust of the story is the relationship between the two, their growing dependence upon each other, racial overtones, and aging.

The property had been purchased for filming by Richard Zanuck/ David Brown. Bette fell in love with the play. Here, at last, was a character of her age that she felt she could portray to perfection. She wrote young Zanuck, saying that his father had done so much for her career, and she hoped that he would consider her when casting the film. However, it was seventy-nine-year-old Jessica Tandy who was signed for the role.

Bette was weary of waiting for scripts to be submitted to her. "My *real* point is that one really has to become one's own agent in this business," she told Robert Osborne. "It's something I can't point out too emphatically to young people starting out or trying to secure a foothold. I was really my own agent during my Warner Bros. years. I had to fight for *Jezebel, Dark Victory,* and most of the good roles I got, even when the grosses of my own pictures were building new sound-stages for my employers. Jack Warner was going to give *Now, Voyager* to Irene Dunne, *Mr. Skeffington* was going to someone else, so I had to fight for all those, too. I wouldn't have had the career I've had if I wasn't willing to take some of these matters into my own hands. . . . What I really want is one more good part. One great script more . . ."

"Someone kept saying to me, 'Name the winner! Name the winner!' Then before I could say 'Mr. Paul Newman cannot be here tonight,' they shoved someone onstage to replace me." Bette, late 1980s. LESTER GLASSNER COLLECTION

Bette was surprised that she did not get legitimate offers for a follow-up film, once the word was out about the excellence of her performance in *Whales*. She decided not to appear with Gish for the media, preferring a solo role in tub-thumping the film. Besides appearing at the opening in New York, Gish would later make the long trip to the Cannes festival, where the film was to be shown out of competition, but would garner rave reviews. "Look," Bette told the producers, "with Lillian and me going our separate ways, you'll get twice the publicity."

Whales was to be given a gala premiere party on October 16, sponsored by the Women in Film Festival at the Cineplex Odeon Universal City Cinemas. At a party on Soundstage 20, following the screening, Bette was to receive the association's newly established Lillian Gish award.

Bette did not attend. "Really," she said, "having a party on a soundstage. No class at all. And with all of the beautiful hotel ballrooms in town. They bussed everyone over from the theater— imagine, bussed! That kind of catch-as-catch-can party is not for me."

The critical praise for the film was extraordinary; the best reviews for Gish and Davis in many years. While Bette would be the last to admit that she grew weary on long shoots, she was, in truth, more fragile than anyone realized. The stress and strain of filming took a heavy toll, which contributed to her passivity on the set.

Too late she realized that she should have gone after the scheming mother role in *The Two Mrs. Grenvilles*, which brought back Claudette Colbert after decades of screen retirement.

When Bette was notified that she would receive the Kennedy Center Medal of Honor, along with singer/dancer/actor Sammy Davis, Jr., singer Perry Como, choreographer Alwin Nikolais, and violinist Nathan Milstein, she was visibly pleased. "With Republicans in the White House during the last few years, I wasn't optimistic about ever receiving the honor," she said. "And truthfully I've not been very kind to Mr. Reagan on some of the talk shows and in print. But I've wanted this award for years. Once when I received the nomination paper, under the question of whom I thought was worthy—I wrote in me!" She gave her throaty laugh. "What am I going to say to him at the reception at the White House?"

"Well," I answered, "you can always affirm that he's looking very well. That's safe." And I told her about the time that Pat Boone had appeared on the Red Baron radio show in Palm Springs. When the Baron complimented him on his youthful looks, Boone dryly commented, "Dick Clark and I have the same taxidermist!"

Bette laughed. "Well, Mr. Reagan certainly is well preserved." She paused and lighted a cigarette. "Life is so ironic. Back in our Warners days, who would have ever thought that Little Ronnie Reagan would end up as President and would be presenting me with a medal at the White House? Never in a million years!"

While Bette was in the protocol line waiting to greet her hosts, a page, unaware of her identity, whispered, "Please give your name to the next gentleman so you may be introduced to the President."

"My dear," Bette exclaimed, "I don't need to be introduced to the President! I've known him for *years*."

When they met the next night in the Green Room of the White House, Bette told the President, "You are handsome as ever. In fact, you get handsomer every year."

Reagan beamed at her safe remark.

Although Bette sat next to Sammy Davis, Jr., for the official photograph, not *one* newspaper gave the caption, as one wit had predicted: "and Bette and Sammy Davis, Jr."

Bette spent her eightieth birthday with Kath. "What is there to celebrate?" she said. "I'm weary of all the usual fuss. I've had that."

While Bette was hoping for that "one great part," producer-writer-director Larry Cohen decided to create a comedy for her entitled *Wicked Stepmother*.

"I've always felt that we give our great stars too many testimonial dinners and prizes," Cohen told Robert Osborne, "and not enough parts worthy of their talents. I conceived the idea for this script while I was in Hawaii with my family. I told them, 'You all go enjoy yourselves. I'm going to write a script for Bette Davis.'"

Bette turned down Cohen's script, because she thought it was either a fantasy or a horror movie. But the second time around, she found that she liked the property, which dealt with a grown couple who go to Hawaii, and return to the States to discover their elderly father has taken a new wife who has commandeered the family fortunes. The main thrust showed how they planned to dispose of their stepmother, who is in reality a witch.

"I've played plenty of bitches in my day," Bette laughed, "but this is the first witch. The part is different, I must say, and it's modern, and I do get the best of everybody."

Wicked Stepmother started to film under adverse conditions on April 25, 1988. Bette was having pains in her mouth, and five days later left the film. Unhappy with the results of the rushes, she called Harold Schiff to come to her aid, then flew to New York to see her dentist. It was announced that Cohen would shoot around her, and the filming of her scenes would resume at the end of May.

However, upon her return, Bette decided not to finish the film. "I agonized over my appearance," she said. "Terrible. I looked so bad that no producer would want to hire me after the film was released."

Because Bette could not eat with a sore mouth, her weight went down to seventy-seven pounds. When she returned to Los Angeles, it was obvious to Cohen that he could not match the continuity with new scenes yet to be shot, even had she agreed to finish the picture.

MGM executives urged Cohen to replace Bette with Lucille Ball, but he was adamant. But if Bette had hoped that the film would be abandoned, she was in for a surprise. On June 15, 1988, *Wicked Stepmother* resumed shooting. Cohen was not to be bested. He had some twenty minutes of Davis footage, and since she was supposed to be a witch, he came up with a clever solution.

Barbara Carrera, who had much the same type of facial bone structure as the younger Davis, and with makeup that highlighted the resemblance, took over the part. Also a black cat was used as Bette's alter ego during various scenes.

When Carrera was transformed, a shimmering special effect of "gold dust" obliterated Bette's figure, which was replaced by Carrera. During the course of the action, some cast members saw Bette, and others saw Carrera, or Bette, or simply the cat—depending on which scenes had been filmed.

Cutting the film together, Cohen removed the pauses in the dialogue in which Bette's dentures slipped, so that her scenes were edited smoothly together. In the fall of 1988 several screenings were held, and Bette was angered to learn that the scene that received the biggest laugh occurred when the family was talking about how sweet their natural mother was, and the camera panned to the mantle showing a picture of . . . Joan Crawford!

When the MGM brass viewed *Wicked Stepmother,* Cohen was informed that it was the opinion of theater exhibitors that Bette was no longer box-office, and her appeal not only limited, but that she was too old. It was decided to release the film directly to the videocassette market. Cohen was angered. "The piss and vinegar is still there," he told Cindy Adams of the *New York Post* on April 25, 1989, "even if she doesn't look like she did in *Jezebel.*"

When Bette was informed that she would be honored at the annual Tribute of the Film Society of Lincoln Center at New York's Avery Fisher Hall, she was delighted. "I am so thrilled," she said, "and at this point, I'm getting very greedy about awards. Let's face it, I've received most of them in my time."

Bette spent a quiet eighty-first birthday on April 5, 1989, in Santa Barbara with Kath and friends, then flew to New York for television and newspaper interviews prior to the Lincoln Center festivities.

On April 19, Bette appeared on the *Today* show, and then, wearing a red dress decorated with three sparkling question marks, she showed up on the *Late Night with David Letterman* show on April 21. After her ovation, she stood up and remarked that Patrick Kelly had made the dress especially for the show, and since Letterman usually asked his guests three questions, she would ask *him* three questions.

Bette inquired if Letterman was married. He said that he had been, and at that point Bette made a typical, wide gesture and turned over a silver cup filled with water on his desk and trousers. When the crowd laughed, she was apologetic. When asked about *Wicked Stepmother,* she remarked that in Larry Cohen she had "met her Waterloo."

On April 24, 2,700 black-tie patrons who had paid two hundred fifty dollars a seat filed into Avery Fisher Hall. The seventy-minute compilation of film clips, selected by Wendy Keys, were frequently interrupted by cheers. The scenes swept from *Bad Sister* (1931) down fifty-five years to *The Whales of August,* and included de rigueur items: Bette jitterbugging in *Thank Your Lucky Stars;* serving Joan Crawford a cooked rat in *What Ever Happened to Baby Jane?;* Paul Henreid lighting two cigarettes in *Now, Voyager;* shaking Miriam Hopkins in *Old Acquaintance;* and the lines from *All About Eve:* "Fasten your seat belts, it's going to be a bumpy night!" and "Remind me to tell you about the time I looked into the heart of an artichoke!"

Among those paying tribute were Joseph Mankiewicz, director of *All About Eve* ("Everyone predicted a Davis-Mankiewicz head-on collision that could only result in disaster, but Bette was letter perfect, of course. Working with her was an experience as happy and rewarding as I've ever had. Barring grand opera, I can't think of anything beyond her range."); Geraldine Fitzgerald ("She is a true star. Warner Bros. never made Bette Davis a star—Bette was a star from the very beginning."); James Stewart ("I'm glad that, by chance, we finally got to do something together."); Ann-Margret ("Unlike her reputation, she was so kind and caring when we worked together. I think she is not only great, but irreplaceable.").

When Bette came out on the stage dressed in a formfitting black-sequined gown with a pearl necklace and black mink hat, the crowd arose as one and all gave her a one-and-a-quarter-minute standing ovation.

Bette moved forward and, glancing at the elegantly furnished auditorium, exclaimed, "What a dump!"

The crowd went wild with laughter and cheers.

Very graciously, Bette thanked those who had put the program together and her coworkers, who had given her accolades, then she paused and went on carefully, "Looking out on this sea of faces here to honor me, it makes me very proud. *Merci mille fois, muchas gracias,* and a good old American thank you!"

Then, she raised her head slightly, looked into the audience again, and gave her signature last line: "I'd love to kiss you, but I just washed my hair!"

As always, she brought down the house.

The author, Whitney Stine, and Bette, on tour for the publication of *Mother Goddam*. GEORGE HURRELL

Bette in 1989, with her many awards and trophies.
FRANÇOIS LEHR, SIPA

Publisher's Postscript

Bette Davis and Whitney Stine were friends for nearly twenty years. On October 6, 1989, Bette Davis succumbed to cancer. Whitney Stine died of a heart attack five days later.

Awards Presented
to Bette Davis

Academy of Motion Picture Arts and Sciences, Nomination Certificate, *Dangerous*, 1935

Academy Award, *Dangerous*, 1935

Academy of Motion Picture Arts and Sciences, Nomination Certificate, *Jezebel*, 1938

Academy Award, *Jezebel*, 1938

Volpi Cup, *Marked Woman* and *Kid Galahad*, 1938

Academy of Motion Picture Arts and Sciences, Nomination Certificate, *Dark Victory*, 1939

Queen of the Movies, Popularity Crown, presented by Ed Sullivan (Mickey Rooney was King), 1939

Redbook Trophy, for her work in 1939

Academy of Motion Picture Arts and Sciences, Nomination Certificate, *The Letter*, 1940

Academy of Motion Picture Arts and Sciences, Nomination Certificate, *The Little Foxes*, 1941

South American Trophy as Screen's Best Actress, 1941

Golden Apple, Women's Press Club, 1941

Academy of Motion Picture Arts and Sciences, Nomination Certificate, *Now, Voyager,* 1942

Two Gold Medals, combined in a cup, presented by Richard Greene for *Picturegoer* magazine, 1943

Redbook Trophy, shared with cast of *Watch on the Rhine,* 1943

Academy of Motion Picture Arts and Sciences, Nomination Certificate, *Mr. Skeffington,* 1944

Award of Meritorious Service, presented by Brig. Gen. R.M. Cannon for work at the Hollywood Canteen, 1945

Victoire Award, presented by *Cinémonde* magazine, 1946

La Belle France, 1947

Good Egg Award, presented by cast and crew of *Payment on Demand,* 1949

Academy of Motion Picture Arts and Sciences, Nomination Certificate, *All About Eve,* 1950

San Francisco Drama Critics Council Citation as Best Actress of the Year for *All About Eve,* 1950

Liberty Magazine Award (with palm), *All About Eve,* 1950

Photoplay Gold Medal, 1950

Look magazine Movie Award, 1951

New York Critics Circle Award, *All About Eve,* 1951

Academy of Motion Picture Arts and Sciences, Nomination Certificate, *The Star,* 1952

Emmy, West Coast, *Mrs. Lincoln,* 1954

"Bette Davis Day" plaques, presented by L.A. City Council, 1954

Heart Award, Variety Club, 1956

Woman of the Year for Achievement in Drama, *Los Angeles Times,* 1962

Academy of Motion Picture Arts and Sciences, Nomination Certificate, *What Ever Happened to Baby Jane?,* 1964

Photoplay Gold Medal, 1965

Straw Hat Award, presented by Fabergé, 1970

Salute, from Players Club, 1971

Sarah Siddons Award, Chicago Society, 1973

Life Achievement Award, American Film Institute, 1978

Emmy, *Strangers: The Story of a Mother and Daughter,* 1979

Mother of the Year Award (with seven others), presented by *Woman's Day* magazine, 1980

Best Actress Trophy, *A Piano for Mrs. Cimino,* International Television Festival, Monte Carlo, 1981

American Movie Award, 1982

Emmy, Supporting Nomination: *Little Gloria . . . Happy at Last,* 1982

Award of Excellence, Film Advisory Board, 1982

Valentino "Life Achievement in the Cinematic Arts" Rudy Award, 1982

"Bette Davis Day" plaque, presented by the L.A. City Council, 1982

Golden Reel Award, presented by the National Film Society, 1982

Award, presented by the Boston Theatre District Association, 1983

Charles Chaplin Award, UCLA, 1983

Cecil B. De Mille Award (Hollywood Foreign Press Association), 1983

Crystal Award, presented by Women in Film, 1983

Distinguished Civilian Service Medal, from Defense Department for founding Hollywood Canteen, 1983

Louella O. Parsons Award, presented by the Hollywood Women's Press Club, 1983

Lifetime Achievement Award, presented by American Theater Arts, 1983

Kennedy Lifetime Achievement Award, 1987

Legion of Honor, France, 1987

Campione d'Italia Merit of Achievement, Campione, Italy, 1988

Cézar, Cinémathèque Française, Paris, 1988

Film Society of Lincoln Center Award, New York, 1989

Life Achievement Award, San Sebastian Film Festival, 1989

Filmography

Bad Sister—a Universal Picture (March 1931). Produced by Carl Laemmle, Jr. Directed by Hobart Henley.

(*Cast*) Conrad Nagel, Sidney Fox, Bette Davis, Zasu Pitts, Slim Summerville, Charles Winninger, Emma Dunn, Humphrey Bogart, Bert Roach, David Durand.

Seed—a Universal Picture (May 1931). Produced by Carl Laemmle, Jr. Directed by John M. Stahl.

(*Cast*) John Boles, Genevieve Tobin, Lois Wilson, Raymond Hackett, Bette Davis, Frances Dade, Zasu Pitts, Richard Tucker, Jack Willis, Don Cox, Dick Winslow, Kenneth Selling, Terry Cox, Helen Parrish, Dickie Moore.

Waterloo Bridge—a Universal Picture (September 1931). Produced by Carl Laemmle, Jr. Directed by James Whale.

(*Cast*) Mae Clarke, Kent Douglas (Douglass Montgomery), Doris Lloyd, Ethel Griffies, Enid Bennett, Frederick Kerr, Bette Davis, Rita Carlisle.

Way Back Home—an RKO Picture (January 1932). Produced by Pandro S. Berman. Directed by William A. Seiter.

(*Cast*) Phillips Lord, Effie Palmer, Mrs. Phillips Lord, Bennett Kilpack, Raymond Hunter, Frank Albertson, Bette Davis, Oscar Apfel, Stanley Fields, Dorothy Peterson, Frankie Darro.

The Menace—a Columbia Picture (January 1932). Produced by Sam Nelson. Directed by Roy William Neill.
(Cast) H.B. Warner, Bette Davis, Walter Byron, Natalie Moorhead, William B. Davidson, Crauford Kent, Halliwell Hobbes, Charles Gerrard, Murray Kinnell.

Hell's House—a Capital Films Exchange Release (January 1932). Produced by Benjamin F. Zeidman. Directed by Howard Higgins.
(Cast) Junior Durkin, Pat O'Brien, Bette Davis, Junior Couglan, Charley Grapewin, Emma Dunn, James Marcus, Morgan Wallage, Wallis Clark, Hooper Atchley.

The Man Who Played God—a Warner Bros. Vitaphone Picture (February 1932). Produced by D.F. Zanuck. Directed by John Adolfi.
(Cast) George Arliss, Violet Heming, Ivan Simpson, Louise Closser Hale, Bette Davis, Donald Cook, Paul Porcasi, Oscar Apfel, William Janney, Grace Durkin, Dorothy Libaire, Andre Luget, Charles Evans, Murray Kinnell, Wade Boeler, Alexander Ikonikoff.

So Big—a Warners Bros. Vitaphone Picture (April 1932). Production supervisor, Lucien Hubbard. Directed by William A. Wellman.
(Cast) Barbara Stanwyck, George Brent, Dickie Moore, Bette Davis, Guy Kibbee, Mae Madison, Hardie Albright, Robert Warwick, Arthur Stone, Earl Foxe, Alan Hale, Dorothy Peterson, Dawn O'Day (Anne Shirley), Dick Winslow, Elizabeth Patterson, Rita Leroy, Blanche Friderici, Lionel Bellmore.

The Rich Are Always with Us—a First National Picture, released by Warner Bros. (May 1932). D.F. Zanuck in charge of production. Production supervisor, Ray Griffith. Directed by Alfred E. Green.
(Cast) Ruth Chatterton, George Brent, Adrienne Dore, Bette Davis, John Miljan, Mae Madison, John Wray, Robert Warwick, Virginia Hammond, Walter Walker, Eula Gray, Edith Allen, Ethel Kenyon, Ruth Lee, Berton Churchill.

The Dark Horse—a First National Picture, released by Warner Bros. (June 1932). D.F. Zanuck in charge of production. Production supervisor, Ray Griffith. Directed by Alfred E. Green.
(Cast) Warren William, Bette Davis, Guy Kibbee, Frank McHugh, Vivienne Osborne, Sam Hardy, Robert Warwick, Harry Holman, Charles Sellon, Robert Emmett O'Connor, Berton Churchill.

Cabin in the Cotton—a First National Picture, released by Warner Bros. (September 1932). D. F. Zanuck in charge of production. Production supervisor, Hal Wallis. Directed by Michael Curtiz.

(Cast) Richard Barthelmess, Bette Davis, Dorothy Jordan, Henry B. Walthall, Berton Churchill, Walter Percival, William Le Maire, Hardie Albright, Edmund Breese, Tully Marshall, Clarence Muse, Russell Simpson, John Marston, Erville Anderson, Dorothy Peterson, Snow Flake, Harry Cording.

Three on a Match—a First National Picture, released by Warner Bros. (October 1932). D. F. Zanuck in charge of production. Production supervisor, Ray Griffith. Directed by Mervyn LeRoy.

(Cast) Joan Blondell, Warren William, Ann Dvorak, Bette Davis, Grant Mitchell, Lyle Talbot, Sheila Terry, Glenda Farrell, Clara Blandick, Buster Phelps, Humphrey Bogart, John Marston, Patricia Ellis, Hale Hamilton, Frankie Darro, Dawn O'Day (Anne Shirley), Virginia Davis, Dick Brandon, Allen Jenkins, Jack LaRue, Edward Arnold.

20,000 Years in Sing Sing—a First National Picture, released by Warner Bros. (January 1933). D. F. Zanuck in charge of production. Production supervisor, Ray Griffith. Directed by Michael Curtiz.

(Cast) Spencer Tracy, Bette Davis, Lyle Talbot, Arthur Byron, Sheila Terry, Edward McNamara, Warren Hymer, Louis Calhern, Spencer Charters, Sam Godfrey, Grant Mitchell, Nella Walker, Harold Huber, William Le Maire, Arthur Hoyt, George Pat Collins.

Parachute Jumper—a Warner Bros. Picture (January 1933). D.F. Zanuck in charge of production. Production supervisor, Ray Griffith. Directed by Alfred E. Green.

(Cast) Douglas Fairbanks, Jr., Leo Carrillo, Bette Davis, Frank McHugh, Claire Dodd, Sheila Terry, Harold Huber, Thomas E. Jackson, George Pat Collins, Pat O'Malley, Harold Healy, Ferdinand Munley, Walter Miller.

The Working Man—a Warner Bros. Vitaphone Picture (April 1933). D.F. Zanuck in charge of production. Production supervisor, Lucien Hubbard. Directed by John Adolfi.

(Cast) George Arliss, Bette Davis, Hardie Albright, Theodore Newton, Gordon Westcott, J. Farrell MacDonald, Charles Evans, Frederick Burton, Edward Van Sloan, Pat Wing, Claire McDowell, Harold Minjir, Douglas Dumbrille.

Ex-Lady—a Warner Bros. Vitaphone Picture (May 1933). D.F. Zanuck in charge of production. Production supervisor, Lucien Hubbard. Directed by Robert Florey.

(Cast) Bette Davis, Gene Raymond, Frank McHugh, Monroe Owsley, Claire Dodd, Kay Strozzi, Ferdinand Gottschalk, Alphonse Ethier, Bodil Rosing.

Bureau of Missing Persons—a First National Picture, released by Warner Bros. (September 1933). Production supervisor, Henry Blanke. Directed by Roy Del Ruth.

(Cast) Bette Davis, Lewis Stone, Pat O'Brien, Glenda Farrell, Allen Jenkins, Ruth Donnelly, Hugh Herbert, Alan Dinehart, Marjorie Gateson, Tad Alexander, Noel Francis, Wallis Clark, Adrian Morris, Clay Clement, Henry Kolker, Harry Beresford, George Chandler.

Fashion of 1934—a First National Picture, released by Warner Bros. (January 1934). Production supervisor, Henry Blanke. Directed by William Dieterle.

(Cast) William Powell, Bette Davis, Frank McHugh, Verree Teasdale, Reginald Owen, Henry O'Neill, Philip Reed, Hugh Herbert, Gordon Westcott, Nella Walker, Dorothy Burgess, Etienne Giradot, William Burress, Spencer Charters, Jane Darwell, Arthur Treacher, Hobart Cavanaugh, Albert Conti.

The Big Shakedown—a First National Picture, released by Warner Bros. (February 1934). Production supervisor, Samuel Bischoff. Directed by John Francis Dillon.

(Cast) Charles Farrell, Bette Davis, Ricardo Cortez, Glenda Farrell, Allen Jenkins, Henry O'Neill, Philip Faversham, Robert Emmett O'Connor, John Wray, George Pat Collins, Adrian Morris, Dewey Robinson, Samuel S. Hinds, Matt Briggs, William B. Davidson, Earl Foxe, Frederick Burton.

Jimmy the Gent—a Warner Bros. Vitaphone Picture (March 1934). Production supervisor, Robert Lord. Directed by Michael Curtiz.

(Cast) James Cagney, Bette Davis, Alice White, Allen Jenkins, Arthur Hohl, Alan Dinehart, Philip Reed, Hobart Cavanaugh, Mayo Methot, Ralf Harolde, Joseph Sawyer, Philip Faversham, Nora Lane, Howard Hickman, Jane Darwell, Joseph Crehan, Robert Warwick, Harold Entwhistle.

Fog over Frisco—a Warner Bros. Vitaphone Picture (June 1934). Production supervisor, Henry Blanke. Directed by William Dieterle.

(*Cast*) Bette Davis, Donald Woods, Margaret Lindsay, Lyle Talbot, Arthur Byron, Hugh Herbert, Douglas Dumbrille, Robert Barrat, Henry O'Neill, Irving Pichel, Gordon Westcott, Charles C. Wilson, Alan Hale, William B. Davidson, Douglas Cosgrove, George Chandler, Harold Minjir, William Demarest.

Of Human Bondage—an RKO Radio Picture (June 1934). Produced by Pandro S. Berman. Directed by John Cromwell.

(*Cast*) Leslie Howard, Bette Davis, Frances Dee, Kay Johnson, Reginald Denny, Alan Hale, Reginald Owen, Reginald Sheffield, Desmond Roberts.

Housewife—a Warner Bros. Vitaphone Picture (August 1934). Production supervisor, Robert Lord. Directed by Alfred E. Green.

(*Cast*) George Brent, Bette Davis, Ann Dvorak, John Halliday, Ruth Donnelly, Hobart Cavanaugh, Robert Barrat, Joseph Cawthorn, Phil Regan, Willard Robertson, Ronald Cosbey, Leila Bennett, William B. Davidson, John Hale.

Bordertown—a Warner Bros. Vitaphone Picture (January 1935). Production supervisor, Robert Lord. Directed by Archie Mayo.

(*Cast*) Paul Muni, Bette Davis, Margaret Lindsay, Gavin Gordon, Arthur Stone, Robert Barrat, Soledad Jiminez, Eugene Pallette, William B. Davidson, Hobart Cavanaugh, Henry O'Neill, Vivian Tobin, Nella Walker, Oscar Apfel, Samuel S. Hinds, Chris Pin Martin, Frank Puglia, Jack Norton.

The Girl from Tenth Avenue—a First National Picture, released by Warner Bros. (May 1935). Production supervisor, Henry Blanke. Directed by Alfred E. Green.

(*Cast*) Bette Davis, Ian Hunter, Colin Clive, Alison Skipworth, John Eldredge, Philip Reed, Katherine Alexander, Helen Jerome Eddy, Gordon Elliott, Adrian Rosley, Andre Cheron, Edward McWade, Mary Treen, Heinie Conklin.

Front Page Woman—a Warner Bros. Vitaphone Picture (July 1935). Production supervisor, Samuel Bischoff. Directed by Michael Curtiz.

(*Cast*) Bette Davis, George Brent, June Martel, Dorothy Dare, Joseph Crehan, Winifred Shaw, Roscoe Karns, Joseph King, J. Farrell MacDonald, J. Carroll Naish, Walter Walker, DeWitt Jennings, Huntley Gordon, Adrian Rosley, Georges Renevent, Grace Hale, Selmer Jackson, Gordon Westcott.

Special Agent—a Claridge Picture, released by Warner Bros. (September 1935). Produced by Samuel Bischoff in association with Martin Mooney. Directed by William Keighley.
(Cast) Bette Davis, George Brent, Ricardo Cortez, Jack LaRue, Henry O'Neill, Robert Strange, Joseph Crehan, J. Carroll Naish, Joseph Sawyer, William B. Davidson, Robert Barrat, Paul Guilfoyle, Irving Pichel, Douglas Wood, James Flavin, Lee Phelps, Louis Natheaux, Herbert Skinner, John Alexander.

Dangerous—a Warner Bros. Vitaphone Picture (December 1935). Production supervisor, Harry Joe Brown. Directed by Alfred E. Green.
(Cast) Bette Davis, Franchot Tone, Margaret Lindsay, Alison Skipworth, John Eldredge, Dick Foran, Walter Walker, Richard Carle, George Irving, Pierre Watkin, Douglas Wood, William B. Davidson, Frank O'Connor, Edward Keane.

The Petrified Forest—a Warner Bros. Vitaphone Picture (February 1936). Production supervisor, Henry Blanke. Directed by Archie Mayo.
(Cast) Leslie Howard, Bette Davis, Genevieve Tobin, Dick Foran, Humphrey Bogart, Joseph Sawyer, Porter Hall, Charley Grapewin, Paul Harvey, Eddie Acuff, Adrian Morris, Nina Campana, Slim Johnson, John Alexander.

The Golden Arrow—a First National Picture released by Warner Bros. (May 1936). Production supervisor, Samuel Bischoff. Directed by Alfred E. Green.
(Cast) Bette Davis, George Brent, Eugene Pallette, Dick Foran, Carol Hughes, Catherine Doucet, Craig Reynolds, Ivan Lebedeff, G. P. Huntley, Jr., Hobart Cavanaugh, Henry O'Neill, Eddie Acuff, Earl Foxe, E. E. Clive, Rafael Storm, Sara Edwards, Bess Flowers, Mary Treen, Selmer Jackson.

Satan Met a Lady—a Warner Bros. Vitaphone Picture (July 1936). Production supervisor, Henry Blanke. Directed by William Dieterle.
(Cast) Bette Davis, Warren William, Alison Skipworth, Arthur Treacher, Winifred Shaw, Marie Wilson, Porter Hall, Maynard Holmes, Olin

Howard, Charles Wilson, Joseph King, Barbara Blane, William B. Davidson.

Marked Woman—a Warner Bros. First National Picture (April 1937). Produced by Hal Wallis in association with Lou Edelman. Directed by Lloyd Bacon.
(Cast) Bette Davis, Humphrey Bogart, Eduardo Ciannelli, Jane Bryan, Lola Lane, Isabel Jewell, Rosalind Marquis, Mayo Methot, Ben Welden, Henry O'Neill, Allen Jenkins, John Litel, Damian O'Flynn, Robert Strange, Raymond Hatton, William B. Davidson, Frank Faylen, Jack Norton, Kenneth Harlan.

Kid Galahad—a Warner Bros. Picture (May 1937). Executive Producer, Hal B. Wallis, in association with Samuel Bischoff. Directed by Michael Curtiz.
(Cast) Edward G. Robinson, Bette Davis, Humphrey Bogart, Wayne Morris, William Haade, Jane Bryan, Harry Carey, Soledad Jiminez, Veda Ann Borg, Ben Welden, Joseph Crehan, Harlan Tucker, Frank Faylen, Joyce Compton, Horace MacMahon.

That Certain Woman—a Warner Bros. First National Picture (September 1937). Executive Producer, Hal B. Wallis, in association with Robert Lord. Directed by Edmund Goulding.
(Cast) Bette Davis, Henry Fonda, Ian Hunter, Anita Louise, Donald Crisp, Katherine Alexander, Mary Phillips, Minor Watson, Ben Welden, Sidney Toler, Charles Trowbridge, Norman Willis, Herbert Rawlinson, Rosalind Marquis, Frank Faylen, Willard Parker, Dwane Day, Hugh O'Connell.

It's Love I'm After—a Warner Bros. Picture (November 1937). Executive Producer, Hal B. Wallis, in association with Harry Joe Brown. Directed by Archie Mayo.
(Cast) Leslie Howard, Bette Davis, Olivia De Havilland, Patric Knowles, Eric Blore, George Barbier, Spring Byington, Bonita Granville, E. E. Clive, Veda Ann Borg, Valerie Bergere, Georgia Caine, Sarah Edwards, Lionel Bellmore, Irving Bacon.

Jezebel—a Warner Bros. Picture (March 1938). Executive Producer, Hal B. Wallis, in association with Henry Blanke. Directed by William Wyler.
(Cast) Bette Davis, Henry Fonda, George Brent, Donald Crisp, Fay

Bainter, Margaret Lindsay, Henry O'Neill, John Litel, Gordon Oliver, Spring Byington, Margaret Early, Richard Cromwell, Theresa Harris, Janet Shaw, Irving Pichel, Eddie Anderson.

The Sisters—a Warner Bros. Picture. (October 1938). Produced by Hal B. Wallis, in association with David Lewis. Directed by Anatole Litvak.
(Cast) Errol Flynn, Bette Davis, Anita Louise, Ian Hunter, Donald Crisp, Beulah Bondi, Jane Bryan, Alan Hale, Dick Foran, Henry Travers, Patric Knowles, Lee Patrick, Laura Hope Crews, Janet Shaw, Harry Davenport, Ruth Garland, John Warburton, Paul Harvey, Mayo Methot, Irving Bacon, Arthur Hoyt.

Dark Victory—a Warner Bros. First National Picture (April 1939). Produced by Hal B. Wallis, in association with David Lewis. Directed by Edmund Goulding.
(Cast) Bette Davis, George Brent, Geraldine Fitzgerald, Humphrey Bogart, Ronald Reagan, Henry Travers, Cora Witherspoon, Dorothy Peterson, Virginia Brissac, Charles Richman, Leonard Mudie, Fay Helm, Lottie Williams.

Juarez—a Warner Bros. Picture (April 1939). Produced by Hal B. Wallis, in association with Henry Blanke. Directed by William Dieterle.
(Cast) Paul Muni, Bette Davis, Brian Aherne, Claude Rains, John Garfield, Donald Crisp, Joseph Calleia, Gale Sondergaard, Gilbert Roland, Henry O'Neill, Harry Davenport, Louis Calhern, Walter Kingsford, Georgia Caine, Montagu Love, John Miljan, Vladimir Sokoloff, Irving Pichel, Pedro De Cordoba, Gilbert Emory, Monte Blue, Manuel Diaz, Hugh Sothern, Mickey Kuhn.

The Old Maid—a Warner Bros. First National Picture (August 1939). Produced by Hal B. Wallis, in association with Henry Blanke. Directed by Edmund Goulding.
(Cast) Bette Davis, Miriam Hopkins, George Brent, Donald Crisp, Jane Bryan, Louise Fazenda, James Stephenson, Jerome Cowan, William Lundigan, Rand Brooks, Cecelia Loftus, Janet Shaw, DeWolf Hopper.

The Private Lives of Elizabeth and Essex—a Warner Bros. Picture (December 1939). Produced by Hal B. Wallis, in association with Robert Lord. Directed by Michael Curtiz.

(Cast) Bette Davis, Errol Flynn, Olivia De Havilland, Donald Crisp, Vincent Price, Alan Hale, Henry Stephenson, Henry Daniell, James Stephenson, Leo G. Carroll, Nanette Fabares (Fabray), Rosella Towne, Maris Wrixon, Ralph Forbes, Robert Warwick, John Sutton, Guy Bellis, Doris Lloyd, Forrester Harvey.

All This and Heaven Too—a Warner Bros. First National Picture (July 1940). Produced by Jack L. Warner and Hal B. Wallis, in association with David Lewis. Directed by Anatole Litvak.

(Cast) Bette Davis, Charles Boyer, Jeffrey Lynn, Barbara O'Neil, Virginia Weidler, Helen Westley, Walter Hampden, Henry Daniell, Harry Davenport, George Coulouris, Montagu Love, Janet Beecher, June Lockhart, Ann Todd, Richard Nichols, Fritz Leiber, Ian Keith, Sibyl Harris, Mary Anderson, Edward Fielding, Ann Gillis, Peggy Stewart, Victor Kilian, Mrs. Gardner Crane.

The Letter—a Warner Bros. First National Picture (November 1940). Produced by Hal B. Wallis, in association with Robert Lord. Directed by William Wyler.

(Cast) Bette Davis, Herbert Marshall, James Stephenson, Frieda Inescort, Gale Sondergaard, Bruce Lester (David Bruce), Elizabeth Earl, Cecil Kellaway, Doris Lloyd, Sen Yung, Willie Fung, Tetsu Komai, Roland Got, Otto Hahn, Pete Kotehernaro, David Newell, Ottola Nesmith, Lillian Kemble-Cooper.

The Great Lie—a Warner Bros. Picture (April 1941). Produced by Hal B. Wallis, in association with Henry Blanke. Directed by Edmund Goulding.

(Cast) Bette Davis, George Brent, Mary Astor, Lucile Watson, Hattie McDaniel, Grant Mitchell, Jerome Cowan, Sam McDaniel, Thurston Hall, Russell Hicks, Charles Trowbridge, Virginia Brissac, Olin Howland, J. Farrell MacDonald, Doris Lloyd, Addison Richards, Georgia Caine, Alphonse Martell.

The Bride Came C.O.D.—a Warner Bros. Picture (July 1941). Produced by Hal B. Wallis, in association with William Cagney. Directed by William Keighley.

(Cast) James Cagney, Bette Davis, Stuart Erwin, Jack Carson, George Tobias, Eugene Pallette, Harry Davenport, William Frawley, Edward Brophy, Harry Holman, Chick Chandler, Keith Douglas, Herbert

Anderson, Creighton Hale, Frank Mayo, DeWolf Hopper, Jack Mower, William Newell.

The Little Foxes—a Samuel Goldwyn Production, released by RKO Radio Pictures, Inc. (August 1941). Produced by Samuel Goldwyn. Directed by William Wyler.
(Cast) Bette Davis, Herbert Marshall, Teresa Wright, Richard Carlson, Patricia Collinge, Dan Duryea, Charles Dingle, Carl Benton Reid, Jessie Grayson, John Marriott, Russell Hicks, Lucien Littlefield, Virginia Brissac.

The Man Who Came to Dinner—a Warner Bros. Picture (January 1942). Produced by Hal B. Wallis, in association with Jerry Wald, Sam Harris, and Jack Saper. Directed by William Keighley.
(Cast) Bette Davis, Ann Sheridan, Monty Woolley, Richard Travis, Jimmy Durante, Reginald Gardiner, Billie Burke, Elizabeth Fraser, Grant Mitchell, George Barbier, Mary Wickes, Russell Arms, Ruth Vivian, Edwin Stanley, Charles Drake, Nanette Vallon, John Ridgely.

In This Our Life—a Warner Bros. Picture. (May 1942). Produced by Hal B. Wallis, in association with David Lewis. Directed by John Huston.
(Cast) Bette Davis, Olivia De Havilland, George Brent, Dennis Morgan, Charles Coburn, Frank Craven, Billie Burke, Hattie McDaniel, Lee Patrick, Mary Servoss, Ernest Anderson, William B. Davidson, Edward Fielding, John Hamilton, William Forest, Lee Phelps.

Now, Voyager—a Warner Bros. Picture (October 1942). Produced by Hal B. Wallis. Directed by Irving Rapper. Screenplay by Casey Robinson.
(Cast) Bette Davis, Paul Henreid, Claude Rains, Gladys Cooper, Bonita Granville, Ilka Chase, John Loder, Lee Patrick, Franklin Pangborn, Katherine Alexander, James Rennie, Mary Wickes, Janis Wilson, Frank Puglia, Michael Ames, Charles Drake, David Clyde.

Watch on the Rhine—a Warner Bros. Picture (August 1943). Produced by Hal B. Wallis. Directed by Herman Shumlin.
(Cast) Bette Davis, Paul Lukas, Geraldine Fitzgerald, Lucile Watson, Beulah Bondi, George Coulouris, Donald Woods, Henry Daniell, Donald Buka, Eric Roberts, Janis Wilson, Mary Young, Kurt Katch,

Erwin Kalser, Clyde Fillmore, Robert O. Davis, Frank Wilson, Clarence Muse, Anthony Caruso, Howard Hickman, Elvira Curci, Creighton Hale, Alan Hale, Jr.

Thank Your Lucky Stars—a Warner Bros. Picture (October 1943). J. L. Warner in charge of production. Produced by Mark Hellinger. Directed by David Butler.

(Cast) Dennis Morgan, Joan Leslie, Edward Everett Horton, S. Z. Sakall, Richard Lane, Ruth Donnelly, Don Wilson, Henry Armetta, Joyce Reynolds—with guest stars Humphrey Bogart, Eddie Cantor, Bette Davis, Olivia De Havilland, Errol Flynn, John Garfield, Ida Lupino, Ann Sheridan, Dinah Shore, Alexis Smith, Jack Carson, Alan Hale, George Tobias, Hattie McDaniel, Willie Best, Spike Jones and His City Slickers.

Old Acquaintance—a Warner Bros. Picture (November 1943). J. L. Warner in charge of production. Produced by Henry Blanke. Directed by Vincent Sherman.

(Cast) Bette Davis, Miriam Hopkins, Gig Young, John Loder, Dolores Moran, Philip Reed, Roscoe Karns, Anne Revere, Esther Dale, Ann Codee, Joseph Crehan, Pierre Watkin, Marjorie Hoshelle, George Lessey, Ann Doran, Leona Maricle, Francine Rufo.

Mr. Skeffington—a Warner Bros. Picture (May 1944). J. L. Warner in charge of production. Produced by Julius J. and Philip G. Epstein.

(Cast) Bette Davis, Claude Rains, Walter Abel, Richard Waring, George Coulouris, Marjorie Riordan, Robert Shayne, John Alexander, Jerome Cowan, Johnny Mitchell, Dorothy Peterson, Peter Whitney, Bill Kennedy, Tom Stevenson, Halliwell Hobbes, Bunny Sunshine, Gigi Perreau, Dolores Gray, Walter Kingsford, Molly Lamont.

Hollywood Canteen—a Warner Bros. Picture (December 1944). J. L. Warner in charge of production. Produced by Alex Gottlieb. Directed by Delmer Daves.

(Cast) Joan Leslie, Robert Hutton, Janis Paige, Dane Clark, Richard Erdman, James Flavin, Joan Winfield, Jonathan Hale, Rudolf Friml, Jr., Bill Manning, Larry Thompson, Mell Schubert, Walden Boyle, Steve Richards—with guest stars the Andrews Sisters, Jack Benny, Joe E. Brown, Eddie Cantor, Kitty Carlisle, Jack Carson, Joan

Crawford, Helmut Dantine, Bette Davis, Faye Emerson, Victor Francen, John Garfield, Sydney Greenstreet, Alan Hale, Paul Henreid, Andrea King, Peter Lorre, Ida Lupino, Irene Manning, Nora Martin, Joan McCracken, Dolores Moran, Dennis Morgan, Eleanor Parker, William Prince, Joyce Reynolds, John Ridgely, Roy Rogers and Trigger, S. Z. Sakall, Zachary Scott, Alexis Smith, Barbara Stanwyck, Craig Stevens, Joseph Szigeti, Donald Woods, Jane Wyman, Jimmy Dorsey and His Band, Carmen Cavallaro and His Orchestra, Rosario and Antonio, Sons of the Pioneers, Virginia Patton, Lynne Baggett, Betty Alexander, Julie Bishop, Robert Shayne, Johnny Mitchell, John Sheridan, Colleen Townsend, Angela Green, Paul Brooke, Marianne O'Brien, Dorothy Malone, Bill Kennedy.

The Corn Is Green—a Warner Bros. Picture (March 1945). J. L. Warner in charge of production. Produced by Jack Chertok. Directed by Irving Rapper.
(Cast) Bette Davis, John Dall, Joan Lorring, Nigel Bruce, Rhys Williams, Rosalind Ivan, Mildred Dunnock, Gwenyth Hughes, Billy Roy, Thomas Louden, Arthur Shields, Leslie Vincent, Robert Regent, Tony Ellis, Elliot Dare, Robert Cherry, Gene Ross.

A Stolen Life—a Warner Bros. Picture (May 1946). A B.D. Production. Directed by Curtis Bernhardt.
(Cast) Bette Davis, Glenn Ford, Dane Clark, Walter Brennan, Charles Ruggles, Bruce Bennett, Peggy Knudsen, Esther Dale, Clara Blandick, Joan Winfield.

Deception—a Warner Bros. Picture (October 1946). J. L. Warner in charge of production. Produced by Henry Blanke. Directed by Irving Rapper.
(Cast) Bette Davis, Paul Henreid, Claude Rains, John Abbott, Benson Fong, Richard Walsh, Suzi Crandall, Richard Erdman, Ross Ford, Russell Arms, Bess Flowers, Gino Cerrado, Clifton Young, Cyril Delevanti, Jane Harker.

Winter Meeting—a Warner Bros. Picture (April 1948). J. L. Warner in charge of production. Produced by Henry Blanke. Directed by Bretaigne Windust.
(Cast) Bette Davis, Janis Paige, James Davis, John Hoyt, Florence Bates, Walter Baldwin, Ransom Sherman.

June Bride—a Warner Bros. Picture (October 1948). J. L. Warner in charge of production. Produced by Henry Blanke. Directed by Bretaigne Windust.

(Cast) Bette Davis, Robert Montgomery, Fay Bainter, Betty Lynn, Tom Tully, Barbara Bates, Jerome Cowan, Mary Wickes, James Burke, Raymond Roe, Marjorie Bennett, Ray Montgomery, George O'Hanlon, Sandra Gould, Esther Howard, Jessie Adams, Raymond Bond, Alice Kelley, Patricia Northrop.

Beyond the Forest—a Warner Bros. Picture (October 1949). J. L. Warner in charge of production. Produced by Henry Blanke. Directed by King Vidor.

(Cast) Bette Davis, Joseph Cotten, David Brian, Ruth Roman, Minor Watson, Dona Drake, Regis Toomey, Sarah Selby, Mary Servoss, Frances Charles, Harry Tyler, Ralph Littlefield, Creighton Hale, Joel Allen, Ann Doran.

All About Eve—a Twentieth Century-Fox Picture (October 1950). Produced by Darryl F. Zanuck. Written and directed by Joseph L. Mankiewicz.

(Cast) Bette Davis, Anne Baxter, George Sanders, Celeste Holm, Gary Merrill, Hugh Marlowe, Thelma Ritter, Marilyn Monroe, Gregory Ratoff, Barbara Bates, Walter Hampden, Randy Stuart, Craig Hill, Leland Harris, Claude Stroud, Eugene Borden, Steve Geray, Bess Flowers, Stanley Orr, Eddie Fisher.

Payment on Demand—an RKO Radio Picture (February 1951). Produced by Jack H. Skirball and Bruce Manning. Directed by Curtis Bernhardt.

(Cast) Bette Davis, Barry Sullivan, Jane Cowl, Kent Taylor, Betty Lynn, John Sutton, Frances Dee, Peggie Castle, Otto Kruger, Walter Sande, Brett King, Richard Anderson, Natalie Schafer, Katherine Emery, Lisa Golm, Moroni Olsen.

Another Man's Poison—an Eros Production, released by United Artists (January 1952). Produced by Douglas Fairbanks, Jr., and Daniel M. Angel. Directed by Irving Rapper.

(Cast) Bette Davis, Gary Merrill, Emlyn Williams, Anthony Steel, Barbara Murray, Reginald Beckwith, Edna Morris.

Phone Call from a Stranger—a Twentieth Century-Fox Picture (February 1952). Produced by Nunnally Johnson. Directed by Jean Negulesco.
(Cast) Shelley Winters, Gary Merrill, Michael Rennie, Keenan Wynn, Evelyn Varden, Warren Stevens, Beatrice Straight, Ted Donaldson, Craig Stevens, Helen Westcott, Bette Davis.

The Star—a Bert E. Friedlob Production, released by Twentieth Century-Fox (January 1953). Produced by Bert E. Friedlob. Directed by Stuart Heisler.
(Cast) Bette Davis, Sterling Hayden, Natalie Wood, Warner Anderson, Minor Watson, June Travis, Katherine Warren, Kay Riehl, Barbara Woodel, Fay Baker, Barbara Lawrence, David Alpert, Paul Frees.

The Virgin Queen—a Twentieth Century-Fox Picture (July 1955). Produced by Charles Brackett. Directed by Henry Koster.
(Cast) Bette Davis, Richard Todd, Joan Collins, Jay Robinson, Herbert Marshall, Dan O'Herlihy, Robert Douglas, Romney Brent, Marjorie Hellen, Lisa Daniels, Lisa Davis, Barry Bernard, Robert Adler, Noel Drayton, Ian Murray, Margery Weston, Rod Taylor, Davis Thursby, Arthur Gould-Porter.

The Catered Affair—a Metro-Goldwyn-Mayer Picture (April 1956). Produced by Sam Zimbalist. Directed by Richard Brooks.
(Cast) Bette Davis, Debbie Reynolds, Ernest Borgnine, Barry Fitzgerald, Rod Taylor, Robert Simon, Madge Kennedy, Dorothy Stickney, Carol Veazie, Joan Camden, Ray Stricklyn, Jay Adler, Dan Tobin, Paul Denton, Augusta Merighi, Sammy Shack, Jack Kenny, Robert Stephenson, Mae Clarke.

Storm Center—a Phoenix Production, released by Columbia Pictures (July 1956). Produced by Julian Blaustein. Directed by Daniel Taradash.
(Cast) Bette Davis, Brian Keith, Kim Hunter, Paul Kelly, Kevin Coughlin, Joe Mantell, Sallie Brophy, Howard Wierum, Curtis Cooksey, Michael Raffetto, Edward Platt, Kathryn Grant, Howard Wendell, Burt Mustin, Edith Evanson.

John Paul Jones—a Samuel Bronston Production, distributed by Warner Bros. (June 1959). Produced by Samuel Bronston. Directed by John Farrow.

(Cast) Robert Stack, Marisa Pavan, Charles Coburn, Erin O'Brien, Tom Brannum, Bruce Cabot, Basil Sydney, Archie Duncan, Thomas Gomez, Judson Laure, Bob Cunningham, John Charles Farrow, Eric Pohlmann, Pepe Nieto, John Crawford, Patrick Villiers, Frank Latimore, Ford Rainey, Bruce Seaton—and MacDonald Carey, Jean-Pierre Aumont, David Farrar, Peter Cushing, Susana Canales, Jorge Riviere—and Bette Davis as Catherine the Great.

The Scapegoat—a du Maurier-Guinness Production, released by Metro-Goldwyn-Mayer (July 1959). Produced by Michael Balcon. Directed by Robert Hamer.
(Cast) Alec Guinness, Bette Davis, Nicole Maurey, Irene Worth, Pamela Brown, Annabel Bartlett, Geoffrey Keen, Noel Howlett, Peter Bull, Leslie French, Alan Webb, Maria Britneva, Eddie Byrne, Alexander Archdale, Peter Sallis.

Pocketful of Miracles—a Franton Production, released by United Artists (October 1961). Produced by Frank Capra in association with Glenn Ford and Joseph Sistrom. Directed by Frank Capra.
(Cast) Glenn Ford, Bette Davis, Hope Lange, Arthur O'Connell, Peter Falk, Thomas Mitchell, Edward Everett Horton, Mickey Shaughnessy, David Brian, Sheldon Leonard, Ann-Margret, Peter Mann, Barton MacLane, John Litel, Jerome Cowan, Jay Novello, Frank Ferguson, Willis Bouchey, Fritz Feld, Ellen Corby, Gavin Gordon, Benny Rubin, Jack Elam, Mike Mazurki, Hayden Rorke, Doodles Weaver, Paul E. Burns, George E. Stone, Snub Pollard.

What Ever Happened to Baby Jane?—a Seven Arts Associates and Aldrich Production, released by Warner Bros. (November 1962). Executive Producer, Kenneth Hyman. Associate Producer and Director, Robert Aldrich.
(Cast) Bette Davis, Joan Crawford, Victor Buono, Marjorie Bennett, Maidie Norman, Anna Lee, Barbara Merrill, Julie Allred, Gina Gillespie, Dave Willock, Ann Barton.

Dead Ringer—a Warner Bros. Picture (February 1964). Produced by William H. Wright. Directed by Paul Henreid.
(Cast) Bette Davis, Karl Malden, Peter Lawford, Philip Carey, Jean Hagen, George Macready, Estelle Winwood, George Chandler, Mario Alcade, Cyril Delevanti, Monika Henreid, Bert Remsen, Charles Watts, Ken Lynch.

The Empty Canvas—a Joseph E. Levine–Carlo Ponti Production, released by Embassy Pictures (March 1964). Produced by Carlo Ponti. Directed by Damiano Damiani.

(Cast) Bette Davis, Horst Buchholz, Catherine Spaak, Daniela Rocca, Lea Padovani, Isa Miranda, Leonida Repaci, George Wilson, Marcella Rovena, Daniela Calvino, Renato Moretti, Edorado Nevola, Jole Mauro, Mario Lanfranchi.

Where Love Has Gone—a Joseph E. Levine Production, released by Paramount (November 1964). Produced by Joseph E. Levine. Directed by Edward Dmytryk.

(Cast) Susan Hayward, Bette Davis, Michael Connors, Joey Heatherton, Jane Greer, DeForest Kelley, George Macready, Anne Seymour, Willis Bouchey, Walter Reed, Ann Doran, Bartlett Robinson, Whit Bissell, Anthony Caruso, Jack Greening, Olga Sutcliffe, Howard Wendell, Colin Kenny.

Hush . . . Hush, Sweet Charlotte—an Associates and Aldrich Production, released by Twentieth Century-Fox (December 1964). Produced and directed by Robert Aldrich.

(Cast) Bette Davis, Olivia De Havilland, Joseph Cotten, Agnes Moorehead, Cecil Kellaway, Victor Buono, Mary Astor, William Campbell, Wesley Addy, Bruce Dern, George Kennedy, Dave Willock, John Megna, Ellen Corby, Helen Kleeb, Marianne Stewart, Frank Ferguson, Mary Henderson, Lillian Randolph, Geraldine West, William Walker, Idell James, Teddy Buckner and His All-Stars.

The Nanny—a Seven Arts-Hammer Film Production, released by Twentieth Century-Fox (November 1965). Produced by Jimmy Sangster. Directed by Seth Holt.

(Cast) Bette Davis, Wendy Craig, Jill Bennett, James Villiers, William Dix, Pamela Franklin, Jack Watling, Maurice Denham, Alfred Burke, Nora Gordon, Sandra Power, Harry Fowler.

The Anniversary—a Seven Arts-Hammer Production, released by Twentieth Century-Fox (March 1968). Produced by Jimmy Sangster. Directed by Roy Ward Baker.

(Cast) Bette Davis, Sheila Hancock, Jack Hedley, James Cossins, Christian Roberts, Elaine Taylor, Timothy Bateson, Arnold Diamond.

Bunny O'Hare—an American International Pictures release (June 1971). Executive Producers, James H. Nicholson and Samuel Z. Arkoff. Produced and directed by Gerd Oswald. Coproducer, Norman T. Herman.
(Cast) Bette Davis, Ernest Borgnine, Jack Cassidy, Joan Delaney, Jay Robinson, John Astin, Reva Rose.

Madame Sin—a 2 X Production (January 1972). Produced by Julian Wintle and Lou Morheim. Directed by David Greene.
(Cast) Bette Davis, Robert Wagner, Denholm Elliott, Gordon Jackson, Dudley Sutton, Catherine Schell, Paul Maxwell, Piksen Lim.

Connecting Rooms—an L.S.D. Production, released by Hemdale (May 1972). Produced by Harry Field and Arthur Cooper. Directed by Franklin Gollings.
(Cast) Bette Davis, Michael Redgrave, Alexis Kanner, Kay Walsh, Gabrielle Drake, Olga Georges-Picot, Leo Genn, Richard Wyler.

Lo Scopone Scientifico—*(The Scientific Cardplayer* or *The Game)*—C.I.C. Production (October 1972). Produced by Dino de Laurentis. Directed by Luigi Comencini.
(Cast) Alberto Sordi, Silvana Mangano, Joseph Cotten, Bette Davis, Domenico Modugno, Mario Carotenuto.

The Judge and Jake Wyler—Universal T.V. (December 1972). Produced by Richard Levinson and William Link. Directed by David Lowell Rich.
(Cast) Bette Davis, Doug McClure, Eric Braeden, Joan Van Ark, Gary Conway, Lou Jacobi, James McEachin, Lisabeth Hush, Kent Smith, Barbara Rhoades.

Scream, Pretty Peggy—Universal T.V. (November 1973). Produced by Lou Morheim. Directed by Gordon Hessler.
(Cast) Bette Davis, Ted Bessell, Sean Barbara Allen, Charles Drake.

Burnt Offering—United Artists (August 1976). Produced and directed by Dan Curtis.
Starring Bette Davis, Burgess Meredith, Karen Black, and Oliver Reed.

The Disappearance of Aimee—Television film, Hallmark Hall of Fame (November 1976). Directed by Anthony Harvey.
Starring Bette Davis and Faye Dunaway.

The Dark Secret of Harvest Home—Television film (January 1978).

Return from Witch Mountain—Disney Pictures (1978). Directed by John Hough.
Starring Bette Davis, Kim Richards, Christopher Lee, Ike Eisenmann, Jack Soo, and Anthony James.

Death on the Nile—(September 1978). Directed by John Guillermin.
Starring Maggie Smith, Angela Lansbury, David Niven, George Kennedy, Peter Ustinov, Lois Chiles, Jack Warden, and Simon MacCorkindale.

Strangers: The Story of a Mother and Daughter—Television film (May 1979). Directed by Milton Katselas.
Starring Bette Davis and Gena Rowlands.

White Mama—CBS TV (March 1980).
Starring Ernest Harden, Jr., and Bette Davis.

The Watcher in the Woods—Disney Pictures (May 1980). Directed by John Hough.
Starring Carroll Baker, David McCallum, Lynn-Holly Johnson, Kyle Richards, Dan Bannon, and Bette Davis.

Skyward—Television film (November 1980). Directed by Ron Howard.
Starring Bette Davis and Suzy Gilstrap.

Family Reunion—NBC Television film (April 1981).
Starring Ashley Hyman and Bette Davis.

A Piano for Mrs. Cimino—Television film (1982).
Starring Keenan Wynn and Bette Davis.

Little Gloria . . . Happy at Last—NBC Television film (October 1982).
Starring Angela Lansbury, Christopher Plummer, Maureen Stapleton, Glynis Johns, and Bette Davis.

Right of Way—HBO Cable film (Summer 1983). Directed by George Schaefer.
Starring Bette Davis and Jimmy Stewart.

Murder with Mirrors—CBS Television film (1984).
Starring Bette Davis and Helen Hayes.

The Whales of August—Alive Productions (1988).
Starring Bette Davis, Lillian Gish, Ann Sothern, and Vincent Price.

Wicked Stepmother—MGM Videotape (Fall 1988). Directed by Larry Cohen.
Starring Bette Davis and Barbara Carrera.

Index

.